CANADA'S OTHER GAME

CANADA'S OTHER GAME

Basketball from **NAISMITH** *to* **NASH**

BRIAN I. DALY

DUNDURN
TORONTO

Editor: Allison Hirst
Design: Jesse Hooper
Printer: Webcom

Library and Archives Canada Cataloguing in Publication

Daly, Brian I., author
    Canada's other game : basketball from Naismith to Nash / Brian I. Daly.

Includes index.
Issued in print and electronic formats.
ISBN 978-1-4597-0633-0 (pbk.).-- ISBN 978-1-4597-0634-7 (pdf).-- ISBN 978-1-4597-0635-4 (epub)

    1. Basketball--Canada--History. I. Title.

GV885.8.C3 D39 2013   796.3230971   C2013-902975-3
                                              C2013-902976-1

1   2   3   4   5   17   16   15   14   13

We acknowledge the support of the **Canada Council for the Arts** and the **Ontario Arts Council** for our publishing program. We also acknowledge the financial support of the **Government of Canada** through the **Canada Book Fund** and **Livres Canada Books,** and the **Government of Ontario** through the **Ontario Book Publishing Tax Credit** and the **Ontario Media Development Corporation.**

Care has been taken to trace the ownership of copyright material used in this book. The author and the publisher welcome any information enabling them to rectify any references or credits in subsequent editions.

J. Kirk Howard, President

The publisher is not responsible for websites or their content unless they are owned by the publisher.

Printed and bound in Canada.

VISIT US AT
Dundurn.com | *@dundurnpress* | *Facebook.com/dundurnpress* | *Pinterest.com/dundurnpress*

Dundurn   Gazelle Book Services Limited   Dundurn
3 Church Street, Suite 500   White Cross Mills   2250 Military Road
Toronto, Ontario, Canada   High Town, Lancaster, England   Tonawanda, NY
M5E 1M2   L41 4XS   U.S.A. 14150

For my parents, Denis and Victoria
You were my shepherds, who gave me the hope to dream without limits

CONTENTS

PREFACE

Nearly 120 years after a Canadian expatriate and his YMCA students used a soccer ball and peach baskets to make history in Springfield, Massachusetts, Canadian basketball is at a crossroads.

Record numbers of youths are taking up basketball in schools, community centres, and on street courts from St. John's to Yellowknife. College basketball games draw crowds of 5,000 to 10,000 spectators. But the same sport languishes in the seemingly eternal shadow of hockey, with its cannibalization of air time, advertising dollars, and corporate capital.

Faced with limited opportunities here, scores of Canadian teenagers flock to U.S. prep schools and colleges each year to chase their dreams of March Madness and glory in the National Basketball Association.

The bleeding of talent, coupled with scant corporate and media interest, leaves fans of the Canadian game with limited live viewing options. Countless minor pro teams have lived and died over the years, including six squads in Montreal over a 19-year period.

Canada's Olympic basketball team, a permanent poor cousin to the hockey squad, has also produced its share of heartache after a promising run in the 1970s and 1980s.

Even the CIS, the stalwart university association that keeps elite basketball humming in 30 Canadian communities, nearly lost one of its cornerstone programs to the NCAA. The University of British Columbia flirted with joining the U.S. college sports giant before ultimately deciding to stay home following assurances that athletic scholarships would be expanded to stem the growing talent drain.

But the inexorable migration south of the border continues unabated, most notably by Victoria's Steve Nash, who took the NBA by storm in the mid-2000s with a whirling-dervish style and dazzling passing that earned him two MVP awards. Nash vaulted to heights never before reached by a Canadian, but he did it in Dallas, Phoenix, and Los Angeles.

A new generation of Canadian youngsters now stands poised to take Nash's place. But several questions remain — will the skyrocketing legions of young and hungry players continue to flee south to chase lucrative college and pro opportunities? Will darts, mini-putt, poker, and horse racing continue to garner more air time than basketball on the nation's sports networks? Or will a new generation of Canadian basketball entrepreneurs finally succeed in pushing their way into the popular consciousness with a profitable and viable professional league?

Canada's Other Game: Basketball from Naismith to Nash chronicles basketball's struggle to overcome its history as a poor cousin in a hockey-mad nation.

ACKNOWLEDGEMENTS

This book project wouldn't have even happened without the guidance of the Lord Jesus Christ himself. For fifteen years I came up with all sorts of excuses why I couldn't write a book on Canadian basketball — "too many other projects," "not enough free time," and "no chance of a bite from publishers" were some of my preferred excuses. The Lord decided to take matters into his own hands and make it clear to me that I would not only write a book, but that it would be a popular one.

The second part of that prophecy remains out of my hands, but writing this book was suddenly a project that felt realistic. Both the writing process and meeting the dozens of people I interviewed for *Canada's Other Game* have been among my life's great blessings.

I must also thank my wife, Mylene, my live-in coach whose penchant for pertinent advice was surpassed only by her perpetual patience during my late nights at the library.

Thanks are also in order for my children, Jacob, Alyssa, and Matthew, who cheered me on from the sidelines every step of the way.

My agent, Robert Lecker, was indispensable in negotiating my first-ever book deal, thereby insulating me from my Achilles heel — paperwork.

The team at Dundurn, including Allister, Allison, and Margaret, offered all the support I needed to make this a winning project.

A special thank-you goes out to Gino Sovran, Windsor's finest, a member of the Toronto Huskies and a real gentleman. He provided me more information than I could use, not just about the Huskies but also about his boyhood idols from the 1936 Olympic basketball team.

And I must give a shout-out to all the 'ballers, coaches, referees, and administrators who give of their time, usually for free, to keep Canadian basketball afloat. These hoops lovers are mostly anonymous, too numerous to mention, and absolute life-changers for countless boys and girls across Canada. I wouldn't be the man I am today had I not spent my childhood in the gym, chasing my dreams, learning to be part of a team and benefiting from all of the wonderful blessings that basketball has to offer.

Vaudreuil-Dorion, Quebec
November 2012

CHAPTER 1

— Y THE GAME WAS CREATED —

With a thundering crack, the ice gave way under the hooves of two horses that were steps away from the shore of the Mississippi River, which separated Almonte, Ontario, from Ramsay Township south of Canada's capital of Ottawa. Young James Naismith watched in horror as the steeds plunged into the freezing water, thrashing wildly, their sleigh of valuable wheat teetering on the edge of the hole. The boy realized that it was all his fault — he could have taken the long way around the river to lead the horses to a crossing, but instead he decided to take a shortcut across the fragile ice.

He was just a child, but the horses were his responsibility, and now it was up to him to save them. As the two beasts began to sink, Jim grabbed the reins and pulled with everything he had, managing to get one horse back onto the ice. Still yanking on the reins, his knuckles turning white in the winter cold, the hardy young orphan dragged the other massive animal to safety as well. The load of hay also stayed on the ice and was saved — great news for his financially strapped family.

James led the soaking horses to the riverbank. It was only when he sat down to catch his breath that he noticed someone had witnessed the entire drama without intervening. It was his Uncle Peter, who had raised the orphan as his own from the age of nine.

"I saw my uncle standing back in the trees, watching me," Naismith wrote years later. "I never knew how long he had stood there, but I am sure that he was there before I had pulled the horses out."[1]

It was a sign of the times, a common scene in a long-forgotten era when children were expected to pull their weight, and often much more, to make ends meet in a 19th-century Canadian society that was far less affluent than today. But James Naismith saw the near-death incident as a learning experience. "The use of our own initiative was great training for us boys, and prepared us to meet our future problems."[2]

Naismith's independence bred resourcefulness and creativity when life challenges might have otherwise seemed insurmountable. His tough upbringing also taught him to stick to his guns when others tried to railroad him into changing his mind.

It was that strength of resolve that led Naismith to invent the game of basketball as part of a Christian ministry to spread the gospel of Jesus Christ through sports. His unorthodox career choice bucked convention and alienated friends and family members, but now millions of basketball players around the world can thank Dr. Naismith for shaking off his doubters and choosing innovation over tradition.

Toughness was practically bred into Naismith, who came from a long line of Scottish immigrants who settled in Canada at the British government's suggestion in the early part of the 19th century. While earlier Scots immigration waves focused on Prince Edward Island and Nova Scotia, the growing opportunities in Upper Canada (now Ontario) attracted these newer arrivals. They represented a wide cross-section of the lowland and highland Scottish population, and came from a variety of walks of life. Some were poor farmers and craftsmen, while others were businessmen and other professionals. Whereas previous waves of Scottish immigrants spoke Gaelic, the latter group was largely English-speaking.

The stream of Scots became a full-blown wave by the middle of the 19th century. Some 170,000 Scots crossed the Atlantic between 1815 and 1870, and many settled along the Mississippi River south of Ottawa in Lanark County. The Presbyterian Protestant faith was an important part of the lives of these immigrants, and they established a number of churches and schools in Upper Canada and elsewhere.

Naismith's maternal grandparents, Robert and Annie Young, were among a group that settled in the southern part of Lanark County, in a town called Bennie's Corners, in 1852. Robert and Annie had made the transatlantic trip with daughter Margaret, then 19, and the Scottish settler family soon grew with the addition of seven more children.

Just a year after Margaret Young arrived in Canada, 18-year-old John Naismith also made the trip across the pond from Scotland to Canada. But unlike Margaret, John travelled alone while his parents stayed back home. The teenager settled with his Uncle Peter near Almonte to work on a farm for several years.

The Youngs and the Naismiths didn't cross paths right away, but that changed around 1857 when John Naismith started a building contracting business after apprenticing as a carpenter. He partnered up with Robert Young, whose daughter Margaret caught his eye. John and Margaret married in 1858 and settled near the Young family home in Bennie's Corners.[3]

Bennie's Corners had been a small but thriving settlement with its own school, church, and general store. But the town was severely damaged in 1851 when a fire ravaged the village, hampering the community's development and forcing residents to seek work elsewhere. The town of Almonte, directly adjacent to the Mississippi River, became the new regional centre and the Naismiths attended the local Presbyterian church there. Almonte's geography ensured that it would have a bright future as a late-19th-century industrial hub. The Mississippi River drops 65 feet at that spot, creating raging rapids and steep waterfalls. That made it perfect for businessmen looking to set up mills and factories.

Almonte quickly became a busy industrial centre, earning it the nickname "North America's Manchester," after the British city that was the centre of that country's textile industry.

Newlyweds John and Margaret Naismith ran their own farm in Bennie's Corners and Margaret soon gave birth to a daughter, Annie. James Naismith entered the world on November 6, 1861. Another boy, Robbie, followed James.

James, the oldest boy, wasn't much of a student, preferring instead to play sports such as lacrosse and ice hockey. He was also skilled with his hands and resourcefully sharpened old files and attached them to the bottom of his winter boots before hitting the local pond. The Naismiths were too poor to afford ice skates.

In 1867, when James was five, Canada was formed from the British North American provinces of Ontario, Quebec, New Brunswick, and Nova Scotia. The new country was in poor economic shape. The federally funded Grand Trunk Railway snaked westward from Ontario and Quebec in the 1870s at great expense, and the high cost of the new infrastructure weighed on the national treasury amid a global recession. Making matters worse, Canada had trouble selling its natural resources and many people flocked to the United States to find work.

Farm work wasn't bringing in enough money for John and Margaret, so they moved their family up the Ottawa River to the mill town of Grand Calumet in 1869, when James was eight. There John bought a sawmill and planned to ship lumber directly to city clients instead of working through middlemen.

The mill was almost the death of young James, who witnessed first-hand the dangers of a room packed with massive logs. He had tried to roll a log toward a saw, but didn't see a second log had shifted. "My father, hearing something going on above, rushed upstairs just in time to see an immense log rolling towards his son," James Naismith recalled years later. "Fortunately, I had dropped the … hook and it caught the log before it had rolled over me."[4]

Tragedy was avoided on that day, but terrible news was soon to come. In the summer of 1870, John Naismith caught typhoid fever, which is spread through food and water prepared in unsanitary conditions. Margaret sent nine-year-old James and his siblings back to the Almonte area to live with her mother, Annie, and Uncle Peter, where the children soon got the bad news — their father had died. Margaret had tried her best to care for her sick husband, but only managed to catch the disease herself. She died a week later.

Tragedy continued to strike the family in 1873, when James Naismith's grandmother died, leaving him, his older sister, and younger brother in Uncle Peter's care.

The grieving young James poured his energy into farm work, and there was plenty to do. Chopping wood, sawing logs, and driving the horse carriage — the 11-year-old was expected to do it all. James also made the daily five-mile walk to school every weekday morning, which built stamina and made him perhaps the best athlete in the tiny one-room school. Childhood friend Tait McKenzie marvelled at the hardy orphan who was six years older: "Jim was the hero of many boyish exploits: spearing fish on the flooded flats in spring … hunting the dogs that killed the sheep;

riding, rowing, working and fishing in summer, made the round of the life on the farm, with the winters in school at Almonte."[5]

But young Jim's physical prowess didn't translate into success in the classroom. Reading, writing, math, Latin; you name it, Naismith was mediocre at them all, preferring to pour his energy into sports and games with his friends.

Duck on a Rock was an entertaining diversion that the other boys played in the bushes behind the village blacksmith shop near school. The goal of the game was to throw a rock toward the base stone in an attempt to knock away the opponent's rock. Players set up for their shots from a distance of 15 feet, roughly the same distance as the free throw in the game Naismith would create decades later. The boys would line up behind the thrower, with a "guard" standing off to the side. If a thrower missed the guard's stone, a game of tag ensued and the thrower would switch places with the guard if he was tagged before recovering his rock.

Naismith historian John Gossett, an Almonte native, gym teacher, and former secretary of the Naismith Foundation, said Duck on a Rock originated in 19th-century Scotland, where the targets were real ducks. Naismith's father passed the game down to young Jim. The name is derived from the scene on Scottish ponds in which ducks get up on the rocks as the ice and the morning frost melts off. "Boys walking to school see a duck on the rock, they try to throw a pebble towards it and watch it get into the water and are fascinated by that," said Gossett.

As for the fate of the ducks, Gossett preferred to give the Scottish boys the benefit of the doubt. "I doubt their intent was to harm or maim the bird but to get it in the water."

While Duck on a Rock provided a welcome diversion for James and the other kids in and around Almonte, the reality of economic hardship was firmly entrenched in the region, and the entire country.

With money scarce by 1877, James decided to drop out of Almonte High School in his sophomore year to help out full-time on Uncle Peter's farm, where he laboured for four years before he returned to school at age 20. At that time, he started thinking seriously about his future. Now the oldest student in his school, James worked hard on his studies and excelled at math. Grammar was a different story.

However, he worked hard enough his junior and senior years to be admitted to McGill University's General Arts Program in 1883. Leaving home for the first time, Naismith carried all of the hopes of his older sister, Annie, and his Uncle Pete. Both looked forward to James getting a general education and eventually entering the seminary with the aim of ministering the Christian faith so central to the life of the family and the community back home. James packed his bags and headed for Montreal in the fall of 1883, with every intention of turning his back on sports despite a chiselled physique sculpted by years of heavy farm work.

Montreal was a whole new world to 22-year-old Jim Naismith. The city of 200,000 people was the economic and cultural hub of Canada, serving as the crossroads for rail and carriage routes, Great Lakes shipping, and financial services. The hustle and bustle was little more than background noise for a young man eager to dive into the books. Jim focused on philosophy and Hebrew, both essential to a better understanding of the Bible at a level deep enough to eventually teach it to a flock.

And what about sports? Two upperclassmen, Jim McFarland and Donald Dewar, visited him in his room one evening and put him on the

The Dr. James Naismith Basketball Foundation.

Duck on a Rock is a Scottish child's game that young James Naismith used as inspiration to invent the game of basketball. Pictured is the "base rock" that serves as the target in the traditional game.

spot, reminding him that a young man must keep fit through athletics. McFarland and Dewar's appeal was born from a belief in "muscular Christianity," the notion that a God-fearing man must be assertive and fit in order to take his rightful place in society. "McFarland turned to me and said, 'Naismith, we have been watching you for some time, and we see that you never take part in any of the activities,'" he recalled.[6]

Dewar agreed, but Naismith stood firm that education was all that mattered. The classmates left, but when he was done studying that night, Naismith lay down and thought about what they had said. "I began to wonder why those two fellows had seen fit to spend their time in giving advice to a freshman," he wrote. "The more I thought, the more clearly to my mind came the realization that they were doing it purely for my own benefit."[7]

The following afternoon, Naismith joined the athletic program, starting out as a gymnast before he became a stalwart on the rugby team and a forward on the football squad, a game that was particularly close to his heart. James didn't miss a single game in the seven years that he studied in Montreal. He stuck out from his teammates in an 1895 group photo, sporting by far the thickest, best-groomed moustache of the bunch.

Naismith was having a ball, but not everyone agreed with his chosen activity, including classmates who insisted rough sports conflicted with biblical values of love and non-violence. "Football at that time was supposed to be a tool of the devil," he recalled. "And it was much to my amusement that I learned that some of my comrades gathered in one of the rooms one evening to pray for my soul."[8]

Naismith's first year was a success, and he returned home in the summer of 1884 to continue working on the farm and get reacquainted with young brother Robbie. Everything seemed rosy for the Naismith family, but the clan would once again be jolted by tragedy later that summer when Robbie, then 18, was driven to bed by overpowering pain in his stomach. The pain was so excruciating that the teenager asked James to put him out of his misery. James refused, and Robbie Naismith died of a ruptured appendix the same day.[9]

With a heavy heart, James returned to McGill in the fall of 1884 and buried himself in books and sports. His natural leadership abilities began to flourish, and he teamed up with classmates to create the McGill University Athletic Association.

On April 30, 1887, James Naismith graduated with an honours bachelor's degree in philosophy and Hebrew. Much to the delight of Uncle Peter and sister Annie, Jim graduated among the top 10 in his class.

As significant as it was for Naismith to have graduated from one of Canada's finest universities, his studies were far from over. After graduation, Naismith enrolled in the Presbyterian College of Theology, affiliated with McGill. The only problem for this working-class orphan of modest means was how to pay the tuition. Loans and grants weren't forthcoming in those days, so he had to do what he had done his whole life — go to work. The physical education department gave him the perfect opportunity to blend his love for sport with his need for cash. In 1888, he accepted an appointment as phys. ed. instructor at the McGill gymnasium.

The family back in Almonte fully expected Jim to get his theology degree, find a church, and begin to spread the Good News from the pulpit. But Jim didn't believe sports was a distraction from spiritual matters, subscribing instead to the ancient Greek philosophy of Humanics — the balance between body, mind, and spirit, coupled with leadership and selfless service.

He was soon confronted by classmates who had exactly the opposite view. A climactic confrontation is recounted by great-granddaughter Rachel Naismith, a library director at Springfield College, where her great-grandfather invented the game that would make him famous: "They said 'Jim, it is really inappropriate for someone who is going to become a minister, who is studying in the seminary, to be out playing sports the way you are in all kinds of weather,'" said Mrs. Naismith. "'You need to make a choice. Either you will be a minister or you're going to be playing sports.'"

Naismith considered the choice between God and sports to be a false one, reasoning that God created man's body as well as his spirit. Naismith also figured that the maker intended for all of his intricate creation to be fully developed. With that in mind, James joined the rugby and lacrosse teams at seminary while keeping his nose in the books and diving into extracurricular activities such as the Presbyterian College Journal and the Literary and Philosophical Society. He also joined the Missionary Society, learning skills that would serve him well when he left his home country to teach foreigners about athletics and the gospel.

Jim's love for the rough-and-tumble game of rugby also tugged at his heart. He joined the rugby squad in 1889, and circumstances made him even more determined to use sports to help men improve their outlook on life.

A big turning point came his senior year, in 1890, during an on-field encounter with a foul-mouthed teammate. Naismith overheard the young man cursing during a game. The free-swearing player looked up at Naismith and instantly grew contrite, muttering "I forgot you were there."

Naismith wondered why his teammate had become so sheepish about swearing. He quickly realized that his ability to lead by example on the rugby field had rubbed off on others around him. It was at that moment that everything crystallized for the 29-year-old scholar/athlete. He realized that he would be a more effective minister to young men through athletics than by taking a position at the pulpit.

Older sister Annie didn't take too kindly to James's decision, believing he had turned his back on his calling from God. "You put your hand to the plough," Annie told him, "and then turned back."[10] Annie was so upset that she stopped talking to him for a time. She never forgave him for pursuing what she believed to be a demonic diversion, but Naismith stuck to his guns, reasoning that it made more sense to meet young men where they were, rather than preach from churches where many young men would never visit.

Ever determined, James resigned as gym instructor at McGill and began looking around for a place to teach athletics as a full-time job. The Young Men's Christian Association seemed to be the ideal place. Founded in 1844 by department store owner George Williams in London, England, the YMCA began as a bible study for young men trying to escape the hard streets of the Victorian metropolis. Missionaries set up the first North American YMCAs in Boston and Montreal in 1852 and expanded the services to include language instruction, lodging, and athletics.

Run mainly by volunteers, the YMCA catered to immigrants and the less affluent, offering some of the first organized sports programs in North America.

Within a few years, so-called "student YMCAs" were created to teach leadership skills to young men. Education had clearly become one of the cornerstones of the new association, which needed trained leaders to run athletic programs in the growing network. Enter revivalist reverend David Allen Reed, a native of Springfield, Massachusetts, who decided to start up a school in his local Y to train administrators and Sunday school teachers. He named it the School for Christian Workers and offered free classes beginning in January 1885, by which time Rev. Reed and his partners were well on their way to raising the $22,500 needed for a separate building. The school moved into its new campus on April 1, 1886, and it featured a library, dormitories for 75 students, and a gymnasium with its own running track.[11]

A pipeline of Canadians began making the trek from Montreal and other cities almost immediately and by 1890 more than 20 Canadians had begun studying in Springfield. One of the early Canadian supporters of the training school was Donald A. Budge, who as General Secretary of the Montreal Y was perhaps the most powerful Canadian in the organization. James Naismith met Budge at the downtown Y and sought out the older man's advice on where to pursue his love for teaching and sports. Budge, who by then was a trustee at the School for Christian Workers, suggested Naismith beat the well-worn path from Canada to the United States to chase opportunity.

Jim was so enthusiastic about the teaching possibilities in Springfield that he made one of the pivotal decisions of his life — he decided not to seek ordination in the Presbyterian Church after he graduated from the College of Theology in 1890. He instead spent the summer of 1890 travelling to YMCAs across the United States, including a surprise visit to Springfield.

The first physical education superintendent at Springfield College was Dr. Luther Halsey Gulick, who later became known as a giant in the field. It was Gulick who developed the upside-down triangle that became his school's logo as well as the internationally recognized symbol of the YMCA. The triangle was inspired by the scriptural view that humans should serve God with body, mind, and spirit.

Gulick, the Hawaiian-born son of missionaries, was just 25 years old, but already possessed a medical doctorate from New York University when James Naismith, four years older, arranged a meeting during his brief visit. The redheaded Gulick was not what Naismith expected of such a distinguished faculty member. "I had been brought up in a

British university, where all the professors with whom I was acquainted were elderly men, sedate and dignified," Naismith wrote later. "After I had waited a few minutes, a man about my own age entered the office. He was tall and angular, his eyes were a bright piercing blue, and his hair and whiskers were a peculiar shade of carroty red. This man crossed the room with a rapid, jerky stride, fingered the mail on his desk, and then crossed to where I sat. With a winning smile on his face and a freckled hand extended, he welcomed me to the school."[12]

The two men hit it off immediately and Naismith, certain that he had found his school, returned to Canada to finish up a summer teaching job in Lachute, northwest of Montreal, while readying his application to Springfield.

The registration form included a question about why applicants were seeking work as a YMCA Physical Director, a question James had already given much thought. "My life work is to do good to men and serve God wherever I can," was his reply. Jim added that his work would allow him to teach "the future fathers of the country" and to "keep some, at least, from vice and sin."

Administrators in Springfield were impressed by Jim's varied experience as a Sunday school teacher, athlete, and gym instructor, and the 29-year-old gained entrance for the 1890–91 school year. He would spend two semesters in class while playing centre for the football team, an activity that not only allowed him to keep in shape but which also tested the resourcefulness he had learned as a horse-team driver back in Almonte.

Naismith's ears took a heavy beating during those football games, which were played bare-headed in those days. Naismith would collide with opponents so often while protecting the quarterback that he began to develop a cauliflower ear, and also once suffered a concussion. He enlisted the help of Maude Sherman, a young woman he had recently begun dating, to sew him a cloth head covering that he could pull over his ears as an early version of the modern football helmet.

Studies, and football, went well during the spring of 1891 and Naismith completed his courses before accepting a full-time faculty position under Gulick. The new job was much to Naismith's liking. He would teach Bible study and psychology as well as boxing, wrestling, swimming, and canoeing. But Gulick had a much more challenging assignment for Jim, one the young instructor initially balked at.

Gulick asked James to handle a class of hard-to-please administration students nicknamed the "incorrigibles." These rugby and football players, several of whom were Canadian, were restless and entirely unimpressed with the gym activities suggested by two previous teachers, who had quit in frustration.

"Naismith, I want you to take that class and see what you can do with it," Gulick said to his charge, who didn't greet the assignment with much enthusiasm. "If I ever tried to back out of anything, I did then," Naismith wrote later. "I did not want to do it."[13]

The young teacher's reluctance was understandable. Gym teachers in the late 19th century had far fewer curriculum options than they do today, especially in the winter. You were pretty much limited to calisthenics, gymnastics, and drills. Volleyball and indoor hockey hadn't yet been invented, leaving a big gap between the end of football season in November and the start of baseball in the spring.

Gulick had been one of Naismith's instructors during his first year in Springfield, and had mentioned this void one day in a sports psychology class. Gulick said someone needed to invent a new indoor game "that would be interesting, easy to learn, and easy to play in the winter."

As the leaves tumbled from the trees in the fall of 1891, Naismith gazed at the line of glum young men before him and assessed the challenge that lay ahead.

These men were not at all interested in spinning on parallel bars and doing other repetitive workouts all winter long. As he wrote in his 1892 book *Rules for Basket Ball*, the system — not the students — was to blame.

"A number of gymnasiums have running tracks, but even then it is more or less uninteresting to run around a gallery so many times per day," he wrote, before laying out the must-haves for this new game, including:

1. The ability to be played "on any kind of ground" ranging from a gymnasium to a large room or a small lot.
2. A game that provides an all-around workout.
3. Easy to learn and fun to play multiple times.
4. Less rough than rugby or football.

He tried having his students play indoor rugby, soccer, and lacrosse, but the solid walls, posts, and aggressive young men combined to keep the campus nurses very busy. Naismith recalls the hazards of indoor lacrosse: "No bones were broken in the game, but faces were scarred and hands were hacked. The beginners were injured and the experts were disgusted; another game went into the discard."[14]

The carnage convinced Naismith that a totally new non-contact game was needed that would combine elements of the existing sports without all of the rough stuff. As with soccer, hockey, and football, scoring would require two goals, set on opposite sides of the playing surface, to space out the competitors. Baseball elements would be of no help because a bat and a small ball could cause problems with windows. A larger ball that could be held and thrown with bare hands would be needed. He decided on a regulation soccer ball, which was small enough to be handled easily but large enough that it didn't require special equipment to trap.

Naismith historian John Gossett said there had to be more freedom of movement than in football or rugby. Naismith decided that his sport should have forward passing to facilitate the flow of the game. "He eliminated the offside rule [because] he didn't want you to run with the ball," said Gossett, a long-time gym teacher who, like Naismith, is from Almonte. "Running created the means to have contact. You have to slow that person down. If you don't allow the contact then you'd better not allow the running."

But even if contact was avoided in the middle of the floor, how could you discourage pileups in the goal area? Naismith decided that the goal would be suspended in the air, out of the reach of the players (at least the ones of his era). Solving that problem created yet another one — how to teach the players to score.

The Scottish game of Naismith's youth held the answer. Childhood Duck on a Rock games in Bennie's Corners had planted a seed in James's mind about the importance of creating arc for a more accurate throw. If the rock was tossed straight to the target, there was more chance of a long bounce, and a better chance at getting tagged out. But if the rock was lobbed high in the air, it could settle gently on the base stone.

He jotted down a set of thirteen rules and had his stenographer, Mrs. Lyons, type them up. Now it was time to set up the first match of the game that had no name. Naismith went to the gym and pondered different goal designs.

He figured foot-and-a-half-wide goals would do the trick, so he asked the school's janitor, "Pop" Stebbins, for a pair of boxes. The janitor didn't have them, so he suggested an alternative. "I have a couple of old peach baskets about that size if they will do any good."[15]

Naismith grabbed a ladder and hammer and nailed the baskets to the balcony on each end of the gym. It just so happened that the goals were ten feet above the floor, and that became the height standard the world over.

The final test would come when Naismith called in the incorrigibles. The 18-man class that gathered in the gym on December 21, 1891, included four Canadians: T. Duncan Patton from Montreal, and three players from Nova Scotia — John G. Thompson from New Glasgow, F.G. Macdonald of Pictou, and Lyman W. Archibald of Truro.

Gossett says Naismith was eager for his men to take to the new game by the Christmas break, or else the second semester would be the longest of his short career. "They were the test pilots for it," said Gossett. "He was not sure at all."

Naismith named Patton, the Montrealer, as one of the captains, and picked Californian Eugene Libby as the other leader, asking them to pick eight players each. Naismith served as referee, tossed the soccer ball up, and the game was on.

American William Chase is believed to be the only one who scored, converting a 25-foot shot for the only point in what must have been one of the lowest-scoring organized games the sport has ever seen.

That first game included three officials — Naismith plus two other men who were parked up in the balcony to throw the ball back down to the court after each basket. As per Naismith's rule, there was a jump ball at centre court after each goal was scored. It would be a few years before someone suggested cutting the bottoms out of the peach baskets to let the ball drop through after each score.

The young instructor was thrilled. The game was a hit, and he could breathe easier about the remainder of the semester. "It was the start of the first ... game and the finish of trouble with that class," he later recalled.

The game still didn't have a name by the time students returned from Christmas break in January 1892. One of Naismith's students, Frank Mahan, suggested "Naismith Ball," which prompted a chuckle from his teacher, who retorted "that name would kill any game."[16] Mahan, thinking about the peach baskets hanging in the gym, suggested "basket ball" and the name stuck.

Soon YMCAs across Massachusetts began nailing boxes or baskets to their gym balconies and setting up their own matches. Women were among the first wave of players as the sport took off across the United States and Canada, popularized by Naismith's article and 13 original rules that were published in the January 15, 1892, edition of *The Triangle*, the YMCA periodical that was published at the training school and distributed throughout the network.

Naismith believed the new game would become "popular among the associations" and that it could be played in a gym or "in the open air, at a picnic, etc." The Canadian took great pains to caution phys. ed. teachers to keep the competition clean by taking care to "make every man conform

James Naismith persuaded an unruly class of "incorrigibles" to take up his new game in 1891, and the rest is history. The first "basket ball" team: back row (l–r) John G. Thompson, Eugene S. Libby, Ed P. Ruggles, William R. Chase, T. Duncan Patton; centre row (l–r) Frank Mahan, James Naismith; front row (l–r) Finlay G. MacDonald, William H. Davis, Lyman W. Archibald.

to the rules strictly at first" so that players "would soon get accustomed to playing ball instead of trying to injure his neighbour."[17]

The flurry of games in the Springfield gym frayed the baskets and the wear and tear was soon noted in gymnasiums across the Northeast. In late 1892 an inventor in Hartford, Connecticut, created sturdier rims by weaving wire into a cylindrical shape. It would be two more years before backboards were introduced.

Naismith continued to control the development of the game and its rules for five years, expanding to 21 rules in 1893. He expanded use of the centre jump, throwing the ball up after tie-ups, time outs, and fouls, with one point awarded for three opponent fouls and three points for any field goal.

He stipulated that courts smaller than 1,200 square feet have five players per side — "right and left backs, right and left forwards, and center."[18] Backs later became known as guards. The nine-man game had a goalkeeper to help the two backs, and right and left centres in the mid-court with a "home man" at the other team's goal, along with the two forwards.

There was one notable mainstay of modern basketball that was absent from Naismith's first two rule books — dribbling. While it wasn't explicitly banned, Naismith expected players to elude their defenders by passing and cutting, and their general reluctance to do so continues to cause headaches for coaches the world over.

Naismith noticed in those first few years that players would instinctively throw or roll the ball a short distance away to get better passing position. It was only a matter of time before players realized that bouncing the ball in a controlled fashion allowed them greater movement on the court.

Shortly before his death in 1939, Naismith reflected on the development of the dribble, calling it "one of the most spectacular and exciting manoeuvres in basketball."[19]

James Naismith's years of involvement as a gym teacher stoked his curiosity about the human body, and he decided that he would enter medical school. He started looking around for a city that had both a med school and a YMCA where he could offer his leadership abilities, and he and Maude soon settled on Denver, Colorado.

He left Springfield for Denver in 1895 to become the physical education director for the YMCA in that city and to study for his medical doctorate. That left a huge responsibility for his old boss, Luther Gulick, who found himself fielding scores of questions about Naismith's original 13 rules from across America. Dr. Gulick mailed out questionnaires to other schools that solicited suggestions for rule changes, but Gulick and his staff soon became overwhelmed. The Amateur Athletic Union eventually relieved Gulick of the workload, taking charge of basketball rules in 1896, and the Basketball Co-Operating Committee followed soon after.[20]

Naismith and Maude spent three years in Denver, with Naismith obtaining his medical degree from Gross Medical College while Maude gave birth to their second child.

Opportunity reared its head just two years after Naismith settled in Denver. In 1897, the University of Kansas was seeking an athletic coach and a director for their 650-seat chapel, which students attended each morning. Naismith was ideally prepared for the post, and friend Amos Alonzo Stagg recommended him as a "medical doctor, Presbyterian minister, teetotaler, all-round athlete, non-smoker, and owner of a vocabulary without cuss words."

Naismith was hired as Associate Professor of Physical Culture and Chapel Director at the University of Kansas, where he would spend the rest of his life. It was there that a young student and basketball aficionado named Forrest "Phog" Allen learned the game from the master. Their relationship would sow the seeds for the largest elite basketball phenomenon of the 20th century — college basketball. Allen would later build the college game's first great dynasty right there in Lawrence, setting the stage for the game's explosion onto the sporting landscape.

Naismith's phys. ed. class in Springfield was ground zero in the development of a game that was quickly spreading westward, thanks to the Spalding guides and YMCA *Triangle* magazines that popularized the rules.

But in 1891, basket ball was also about to make its big debut in the home country of the man who invented it. Two of Naismith's incorrigibles, T. Duncan Patton and Lyman Archibald, graduated and decided to start their careers in Canada, eager to introduce a sport that Phog Allen called "the only international game that is the product of one man's brain."

The Dr. James Naismith Basketball Foundation.

James Naismith parlayed two simple peach baskets and a heavy ball into a sport played the world over.

CHAPTER 2

– TAKING ROOT –

Phys. ed. instructor Lyman Archibald made history twice over as one of James Naismith's original basketball guinea pigs. Not only was the native of Truro, Nova Scotia, part of the first basketball game ever played, he also introduced the sport to Canada at a tiny New Brunswick town on the province's southwestern border with Maine.

Archibald, a fine athlete who competed in football and track in Springfield, left the YMCA Training School in the spring of 1892 after that historic first game and headed home to the Maritimes. His route led him from Massachusetts through Maine and up to St. Stephen, New Brunswick.

The St. Croix River divides St. Stephen from its sister town of Calais, Maine, narrowing to less than the width of a Canadian football field at some spots. The relationship between the two communities is even closer. Firemen from St. Stephen rush across the U.S. border to fight fires on the other side of the river, with border guards waving them through. An annual festival, jointly organized by residents of both towns, celebrates their shared geography, culture, and history. Part of that history is a tramway that linked St. Stephen and Calais from 1894 to 1929, perhaps the only local, cross-border transit link ever seen in North America.

Locals in Calais recall the hospitality that St. Stephenites showed them during the War of 1812 when the New Brunswickers received a shipment of gunpowder to be used to fire cannons and guns at any pesky Americans who might have tried to make aggressive moves across the St. Croix. But hostilities were forgotten on the eve of the Fourth of July when Calais officials contacted St. Stephen to inform them of a shortage of fireworks for their national celebration. The polite Canadians couldn't let the big party be ruined, and they loaned Calais a portion of gunpowder, making sure to sit back and enjoy the pyrotechnic show from across the water that evening.

When Lyman Archibald brought "basket ball" to the region in 1892, it was only a matter of time before St. Stephen and Calais found a way to share the new game as well.

Archibald had been appointed as General Secretary and physical director at the St. Stephen YMCA in the fall and he immediately set out to replace the calisthenics program, which was just as uninspiring to young sports-minded members as it had been down at the YMCA Training School. Archibald saw a perfect opportunity to introduce the activity he had just learned from his old teacher James Naismith. A couple of goals were set up in the upstairs gym, and the city's first basketball game took place on those hardwood floors.

Darren McCabe, a St. Stephen historian, points out that the game pitted YMCA members from both sides of the St. Croix. "It wasn't just the first game of basketball in Canada. It was actually the first international basketball game ever played, right here in this little gym."

Just like down in Massachusetts, basketball was an immediate hit.

An international rivalry developed during pickup games that followed, pitting players from St. Stephen, neighbouring Milltown, New Brunswick, and athletes from Calais. Archibald kept himself busy in those early days overseeing physical activities in both towns. He also found time to run the YMCA's summer camp farther to the south, in Lubec, Maine.

St. Stephen became one of Canada's early basketball hotbeds. The *Saint Croix Courier* of November 20, 1902, reported that both men and women were playing the new game. Aficionados had set up basketball clubs and published members' lists.

By this time Archibald had moved on to take an executive position outside the province and he was succeeded by a young local scholar named J. Howard Crocker, a recent graduate of Dalhousie University in Halifax who had returned to his St. Stephen hometown to work as a teacher.

Crocker, like Archibald, had also lettered at the training school in Springfield, obtaining his master's from the acclaimed institution, and he was eager to make his mark in international sport. He maintained the basketball program at the St. Stephen YMCA before taking it across the Bay of Fundy to Amherst, Nova Scotia, when he was appointed as director of the YMCA in that town near New Brunswick's eastern border.

Crocker and Archibald were among the dozens of Training School graduates from that era who shared the new game they had learned. Naismith noted that of the five Canadians on his first basketball team, "all of these men, with the exception of myself, returned to Canada and took basketball with them."[1]

Another Canadian Training School graduate who wound up back home was William H. Ball (Class of '91), who took a job as director of the Montreal YMCA and oversaw the first game of basketball played in that city. Though he wasn't one of Naismith's incorrigibles, Ball had worked closely with the game's inventor in Springfield, co-founding *The Triangle* student newsletter with Naismith in February 1891. Some have suggested the inaugural game at Ball's Montreal YMCA took place even earlier than the first match in St. Stephen, and in the absence of a precise date, both communities might justifiably lay claim to being the birthplaces of Canadian basketball. Montreal, like St. Stephen, could also boast of being the first Canadian club to play an organized international basketball game, a November 21, 1893, match against a team from Vermont, which Montreal won 14 to 10.[2]

By the late 18th century, the YMCA Training School was providing a steady stream of phys. ed. leaders to staff the exploding number of centres that were fanning east and west from Montreal, where the first Canadian YMCA opened in 1851. More than a third of the 70 YMCA secretaries in Canada by 1900 had come from Springfield, and many were also leaving the organization to bring their expertise to municipal governments as outdoor courts and indoor gyms were sprouting up in Halifax, Montreal, Toronto, Vancouver, and elsewhere.

Intercity games between YMCAs were common as the turn of the 20th century approached, with the Toronto Central YMCA beating Hamilton 7 to 1 on December 19, 1895.[3] Hamilton bounced back dramatically, however, with one researcher concluding that the boys' team was "probably the best team in Canada until the turn of the century." The Steeltown 'ballers earned the praise by virtue of their undefeated record against American opponents on an 1898 tour of western New York.[4]

Though basketball was slower to spread to Western Canada, where populations were smaller and economies less developed, YMCAs were crucial to the development of the game there, with well-established leagues in Vancouver and Victoria taking root by 1904. The Edmonton YMCA Basketball League followed suit in 1908, and by the start of the First World War in 1914, basketball had become one of the most popular winter sports after hockey.

Basketball games in the late 19th and early 20th century would have seemed strange to today's eye. Many courts had no backboards, which explained the prevalence of 1–0 and 2–1 final scores, since anything other than a perfect heave was likely to bounce away. The shot clock wouldn't be invented for decades, meaning that teams were tempted to hold the ball for several minutes once they got a lead. There wouldn't have been much, if any, dribbling, since early players were accustomed to passing and cutting to get out of defensive traps. One element of 1890s basketball would definitely be familiar to any modern basketball lover who has coached young players — the near-constant shouting of "pass it here!" and "give me the ball!" that would have been the norm prior to the advent of complex offensive schemes.

Uniforms would certainly have been a little jarring to some modern observers. Shorts were usually cut-off trouser style, secured with belts instead of strings, and thick, knee-high rugby socks protected shins from abuse in a young sport where spills and collisions were par for the court.

The Toronto-based Harold Wilson Co. helped to popularize basketball by distributing the rules while also producing basketballs and uniforms.[5]

Protestant churches were the big drivers of the game in the late 19th and early 20th century as Methodists and other parishes erected hoops in their basements for pickup games that soon became wildly popular among church leaders because of the emphasis on teamwork and fair play. The industrial New Brunswick town of Saint John, known for its plentiful churches, soon became one of the early adopters of the new game.

The first basketball game in Saint John was actually played in the YMCA on Charlotte Street, which was one of the few places that had a full-sized gym. In fact, the organization had been among the first to house a gym back in 1873. The game spread to Young Men's Associations (Y.M.As) in southern New Brunswick, and by 1907 the pickup games had evolved into a five-team league that featured intense rivalries in Canadian basketball.

The Algonquin club and the Portland Y.M.A. quic top two teams in the city league, and players couldn't resis as they chased wins, as noted in the book *Saint John: A Sporti 1785–1985*.

"Despite the fact that they were young Christian men, there wa tainly no love lost between the two rivals," the authors noted, singling o the Algonquins, who "played a rough style of basketball and were inclined towards intimidating their opponents."[6]

The bad blood continued off the court and by 1908 the Saint John league had dissolved because Portland and Algonquin couldn't even agree on a playing schedule.[7] Despite the absence of a league, the Algonquins challenged Portland to a one-game playoff to decide the city champion, but Portland refused and Algonquin declared themselves champs by default. Portland Y.M.A. quietly simmered, vowing revenge, and they would get their chance the very next year when the Y.M.As got together and formed a nine-team church league.

The Y.M.A. league was one of the first intercity leagues in Canadian history and included teams from St. Stephen, nearby St. Andrews, and the faraway Moncton YMCA.

As fate would have it, Algonquin and Portland made it to the 1909 city finals, which would be decided in a three-game series that the Portlands took two games to one.

In 1901, to the north in Sackville, New Brunswick, students at the Ladies' College at Mount Allison University got permission to use Beethoven Hall, normally the site of music concerts, for entertainment of a different kind. Women, dressed neck to toe in their flowing dresses, had started pickup basketball runs every chance they got and in no time they challenged the women from Mount Allison's general student body to matches. The Ladies' College players became so good that they formed A and B teams and organized one of Canada's first intercollegiate basketball squads in 1904.

On February 6, a half-dozen Ladies' College players, their coach, ten fans, and a piano teacher boarded a CPR train for a late-evening match against a club team at the YMCA in Saint John.

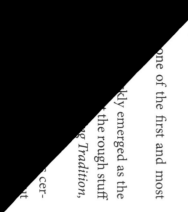

ent paper, *The Allisonia*, captain
)f the points for Mount Allison,"
al loss didn't dampen spirits for
)egan a campus rivalry with the
llege Trophy by 1910, the same
sium.[8]

seminal year for intercollegiate
a mater of McGill began its first
:tually began in 1901 when stu-
iying pickup games and decided
Club, approaching the Athletic
Association, the same one Naismith had co-founded nearly two decades
earlier. The association agreed to budget $25 in annual expenses for the
club, and the group quickly caught the attention of McGill's director
of physical training, Dr. R. Tait McKenzie, who just happened to be
Naismith's childhood friend from Almonte. Intrigued by the students'
interest in his old friend's new game, Dr. McKenzie donated trophy cups
to the winning intramural team. The *Old McGill Yearbook* noted that by
1903, students were showing up to catch the "swift and exciting game
from a spectators' point of view."[9] The budget doubled to $50 and the
club organized its first-ever exhibition game against an opponent from
Malone, New York, which travelled to McGill for the contest on January
29, 1904. McGill lost a tight game, 12 to 11.

Courtesy of Mt. Allison University Archives.
Ref. 2007.07/002.

University basketball was born in 1901 at the Ladies' College at Mount Allison University in Sackville, New Brunswick. Players wore full-length dresses in those early games. Pictured here, the Mount Allison Ladies' College women's basketball team, 1902: (l-r) Nell Pickup, Ethel MacArthur[?], Henrietta Burchell, Lillian Redmayne, Greta Pratt, Florence Porter.

There weren't many other teams for McGill to play, since few universities were serious about the game at the time. Queen's University was an exception, and McGill decided to head up to Kingston to take on their rivals in what's now considered Canada's first interuniversity basketball game.

It was played at the Kingston YMCA on a Saturday, and McGill jumped out to a 4–3 lead at the half, before Queen's bounced back in the second to tie it up at seven apiece at the end of regulation. Sudden-death overtime would decide things, much to the delight of the students and faculty in attendance. But to the consternation of the home crowd, McGill scored the winning basket to take the game 9–7. The local student paper reported later in the week that "(visitor) A. Ross was the most conspicuous on the McGill team."[10]

Now that coach C.B. Powter had bragging rights over his Upper Canada rivals, he could turn his attention to the remainder of the season, such as it was. The team completed their home-and-home season with Malone, triumphing 23–11 at their own aging gymnasium, and finished their first intercollegiate season with a 2–1 record.

"The Basketball Club has, during the last season, shown itself worthy of being placed in the front ranks of college athletics," the editors of the *Old McGill Yearbook* wrote in 1905. "The student body, as a whole, now recognize the importance of the game."

The absence of Canadian competition presented the team with an opportunity to increase their travel schedule for 1904–05, leading to some colourful road stories when the guys made their second trip to upstate New York, as documented in the 1906 yearbook.

The school agreed to pick up the travel costs and the guys organized matches against college and club teams in upstate New York, earning them the nickname "McGill International Club Team."

Captain P.H. Higgins joined team manager E.E. Locke at Montreal's Windsor Station on January 16, 1905, for a trip to northwestern New York to take on the University of Rochester. The rest of the roster was J.A. Rowell, C.E. Holbrooke, O.B. Keddy, and George Trenholme. They were representing their school in a foreign country and dressed accordingly; long coats, pressed buttoned-down and collared shirts and shined derby shoes were worn with pride as they boarded the train. Higgins, the lone holdover from the previous season, was the only player with road trip experience.

He told his players to catch some sleep in the coach, but the car was "heated to a degree that few thermometers would record," so instead they took in the sights during the 12-hour trip. The farms and flatlands of southern Quebec gave way to the mountainous ranges of northern New York State before the terrain levelled out again as the train pulled into the red-brick NY Central Station in Rochester.

Instead of getting some rest, the McGill boys took in the sights of picturesque Rochester, America's unofficial "flower capital" with lovely nurseries that dotted the industrial town along the Erie Canal. But the lack of rest caught up with Higgins and his teammates when they arrived at the University of Rochester and took to the court before 300 fans.

Down just 10–7 at the half, McGill ran out of gas and Rochester ran away with the match, winning 38–13. McGill bid Rochester goodbye, grabbed four hours' sleep, and on the 17th they boarded a 6:30 train and doubled back east to Potsdam, New York, where they took on Potsdam Normal School, a teaching college now known as the State University College at Potsdam. Different town, same result, as they again gave up 38 points while this time scoring 18 of their own.

The disappointment of their 0–2 record was quickly forgotten, however. As recounted in the yearbook: "After the game somebody mentioned 'food' and there was an immediate stampede to the nearest restaurant, where an assortment of pies, etc., was sampled." Player George Trenholme was said to have wolfed down five or six mincemeat pies in one sitting.

The road trip continued to Fort Covington, on the Canadian border across from southern Quebec, where people were just mad for basketball, showing up in huge numbers to cheer on their local club team. "It was here of the five places visited that we had the largest number of spectators," players noted in the *Yearbook* report, recalling how hoops lovers came "in two's and three's [sic] and sledge loads from all the country round." Though a number of Canadians crossed the border to cheer on their countrymen, Fort Covington came away victorious, aided in part by a slippery floor that caused problems for McGill all game long.

McGill's 0–3 record and days of travel called for some down time, and the American hosts had just the thing — a dance and a chance to meet some girls. The McGill students made the most of the opportunity, so much so that Locke, the manager, had to drag them back to their hotel and assess the damage. "Suffice to say that the Captain confessed to six or seven dances with the same girl, and [a teammate] made known his desire to remain in Fort Covington."

Somehow, Locke persuaded them to pack their bags the next day, and the boys were surprised when some of the Fort Covington fans offered to drive them to their next stop in Malone, 25 kilometres away.

Little did the travellers know that there was an ulterior motive behind the hospitality. Malone and Fort Covington had developed an intense hatred for each other in the few years since the sport was introduced to the region, and Malone's fans wanted nothing more than to see the Canadians whip the tails off of their dreaded neighbours.

McGill did its part, managing to win a rough 25–17 match "in spite of the referee," a win that "made … lasting enemies of the respective supporters of Fort Covington and Malone."

But the bad blood cooled enough for more partying after the game at the local dance before the 'ballers made their last stop in Burlington, Vermont, to take on Vermont University.

The road trip ended with a loss as players admitted they were a little "dopy" after five days with little sleep and plenty of socializing.

As the players boarded a train back to Montreal, their minds were reeling with memories, not only of the hospitable Americans, but also the large and modern gyms at all of the colleges, facilities that only served to highlight the inadequacy of their own tiny gym.

Higgins and the players used the annual *Yearbook* to lobby for an upgrade to their "ancient" facility: "Little wonder is it that with such gym's [*sic*] to play in basketball has become a popular sport in the United States," they wrote. "Let us hope, then, that McGill will in the near future build a gym that will enable her students to compete on an equal footing with those of other universities."

Unfortunately, McGill's first intercollegiate team wouldn't be around to see the upgrade, which didn't come until 35 years later, in 1939, when the Currie Gymnasium opened on Pine Avenue.

Canadian university teams had no choice but to cobble together exhibition schedules in the early days, as there was no coast-to-coast organization to arrange games and championships.

Not only was enthusiasm rampant for basketball on college campuses, the sport was also a hit in high schools. Toronto high schools began offering basketball for boys and girls in 1900, with an 18-school league forming across the city. The city's church league offered ample opportunities for both genders, creating 31 girls' teams. Any girls looking for role models on the court had only to read news articles about the Edmonton Grads, a club team based out of McDougall Commercial High School in Edmonton, Alberta. Their record of 502 wins and 20 losses from 1915 to 1940 was a testament to their greatness, and their .933 winning percentage remains a North American record.

Records were also being broken across Canada in terms of basketball participation. The *Manitoba Free Press* reported in 1921 that Winnipeg's city championship had more teams signing up than ever before.[11] Back east, Spalding's *Official Basketball Guide for 1921–22* reported that basketball "thrived in the city of Montreal as it never thrived before. More leagues, more players, better officiating and larger attendance all combined to make the season the greatest ever experienced in this city."[12]

Farther east in the Maritimes, where the spread of basketball had slowed after its breakthrough 30 years earlier, Spalding noted that hoops had become "second only to hockey as the favourite winter sport."[13]

But with popularity came the possibility of abuses in an era when amateurism was a treasured principle among sporting organizations. While a pro career is a dream for modern 'ballers, such aspirations were frowned upon by Canada's sports administrators, who even viewed professional hockey with suspicion up until the 1920s.

The Amateur Athletic Union of Canada, looking to regulate club basketball and prevent professionalism from creeping in, adopted a code that would "maintain ... a high amateur standard" while establishing a Canadian basketball championship. Initially, only Ontario and Quebec teams took part, while Atlantic and western Canadian teams continued to play each other, filling out their schedule with exhibitions against American squads.

By 1923, the Canadian AAU had spun off the Canadian Amateur Basketball Association (CABA) to run national championships and administer many aspects of the growing sport. The highest level of 'ball in the country was the men's Senior "A" division, with teams often run by businessmen interested in creating their own travelling teams to gain visibility for their brand names, and the prestige that came with fielding a winning club. The Saint Johns (from Saint John, New Brunswick) and Montreal powers such as the YMHA and Yvon Coutu did battle against the Toronto Dow Kings and London 5B Sports for Eastern Canadian titles.

The top western powers included the Victoria Blue Ribbons, later known as the Dominoes, as well as the Winnipeg Toilers.

The Toilers were the top team of the first decade of Senior A ball, winning national titles in 1926, 1927, and 1932 during a magnificent run of 14 Manitoba championships in 15 seasons. The key to their dynasty was longevity. The Toilers Basketball Club was founded in 1910 at the Winnipeg YMCA and over the next 20-plus years grew into a juggernaut and fan favourite.

The Toilers hosted the 1927 national championship and tried to book the Amphitheatre Rink, Winnipeg's main hockey facility. Rink owner Bill Holmes wasn't too enthusiastic about renting out his building to practitioners of this strange American fringe sport played in shorts. He certainly didn't think anyone would ever pay to watch the two-game total-points series between the Toilers and the Windsor Alumni, but Toilers president A.C. Samson knew better. He realized that the skeptical rink owner needed to hear from a respected voice to help him realize Winnipeggers were eager to see the showdown, so he enlisted help from Bruce Borreham, editor of the *Winnipeg Tribune* newspaper, to lobby Holmes on his team's behalf. The businessman relented, and he wasn't disappointed as fans packed the stands and the home team beat Windsor to defend their Senior Men's championship. The Toiler dynasty was cut short the following season when, returning by plane from Oklahoma, their turboprop crashed in a Kansas rainstorm on March 31, 1933, killing players Mike Shea and Joe Dodds. The tragedy marked the end of the Toilers' reign as the top team in the West, as they were overtaken by the Victoria Blue Ribbons/Dominoes dynasty, which won its first title in 1935.

By the outbreak of the Second World War in 1939, basketball was still largely an amateur pursuit in Canada. For fans of the game, the Senior A championships became the holy grail of hoops and the titleholder had the added prestige of representing Canada at the Olympics, as there was no centralized national team at the time.

A Windsor-Victoria axis of excellence emerged during the wartime period, with the Blue Ribbons winning three more Canadian titles in 1939,

1942, and 1946. Windsor emerged as Canada's other basketball capital, vying with the Dominoes for national titles every step of the way.

The same year as the Dominoes launched their basketball dynasty in 1933, 10-year-old Norman Henry Baker first picked up a basketball in the B.C. capital, and a love affair was born. Though the young athlete also excelled at lacrosse, he quickly rose up the ranks to become one of the greatest Canadian basketball players of the 20th century. He joined his hometown Dominoes in 1939, when he was just 16 years old, becoming the youngest player to compete in a Senior A championship when the Dominoes won their third Canadian title.

A natural scorer, the six-foot, 180-pound guard wowed crowds with his exploits and led the Dominoes to two more Canadian championships in 1942 and 1946 before turning pro. He had a brief stint with the Chicago Stags of the Basketball Association of America (BAA) before heading back to B.C. to star with the Vancouver Hornets of the Pacific Coast Professional Basketball League (PCPBL).

The Victoria Blue Ribbons, later known as the Dominoes, were stocked with the best players from the B.C. capital. They won Canadian championships in 1933, 1935, 1939, 1942, and 1946. The 1942 champs are pictured here.

Baker was sensational, placing second in the league in scoring and winning the scoring title in his second season before the league folded. He remains the top scorer in PCPBL annals by a wide margin, and his skills caught the attention of Abe Saperstein of the world-famous Harlem Globetrotters, who called the Canadian "one of the greatest natural players I have ever seen."

Baker travelled with the Globetrotters for two years as a member of the Boston Whirlwinds, a regular foil for the Globies, who featured legendary talents including dribbling wizard Marques Haynes. This was back in the day when the top black players, barred from American professional leagues, were hand-picked by Saperstein, making the Globetrotters one of the best squads in the world at the time. "We had some great times traveling with the Globetrotters," Baker recalled in 1982. "In fact we beat them a couple of times when we went to Europe."[14]

In 1950, Baker was voted the top Canadian basketball player of the first half of the century, and for good reason, though a jumping-jack talent from Canada's other basketball centre gave him a run for his money.

Windsor's Freddie Thomas actually one-upped Baker by becoming the first Canadian ever to suit up for the Globetrotters. Saperstein was so

Greater Victoria Sports Hall of Fame Collection.

Victoria native Norm "The Swede" Baker was one of the first Canadians to play in the NBA, suiting up for the Chicago Stags in the 1946–47 season. He later played for the Harlem Globetrotters' foil, the Boston Whirlwinds. Baker was voted the top Canadian basketball player of the first half of the 20th century.

impressed by Thomas's performance in two Assumption College wins over the Trotters that he added the Canadian to his team for two years.

It bears mentioning that the Harlem Globetrotters of the 1940s and 1950s weren't the same modern comedy act that draws laughs but whose players wouldn't survive a day of NBA training camp. The colour line governing American pro sports in the early 20th century allowed the New York–based outfit to secure America's best black players in those early days. Most college teams would have only dreamed of taking them on, but Windsor's Assumption College, already accustomed to beating the best American colleges, scored two landmark victories over the world-famous barnstorming team as the Second World War drew to a close.

The Trotters fell to Windsor's finest by the score of 55–51 in over-time in 1944 before a raucous home crowd. Assumption repeated the feat in 1945, winning 49–45 on the strength of two-sport star Hank Biasatti, who scored 11 points including two decisive free throws. Assumption also defeated four Division I college teams during that special season.

Assumption's success over the Globetrotters wasn't even unique as basketball reached an all-time zenith in Canada. Across the country in Vancouver, 1936 Olympian Bob Osborne had big plans for his alma mater, the University of British Columbia Thunderbirds. The former team captain had been lured back to campus in 1945 to run the physical education program and coach his old unit, which played annual games against the Trotters. On January 11, 1946, the Thunderbirds welcomed the all-black touring showmen to Varsity Gym and people from far and wide packed the building. The Globetrotters at the time featured Reece "Goose" Tatum, whose hook shot was the stuff of legend but who would find UBC to be a rare challenge. The *Ubyssey* student newspaper said the home team "out-ran, out-shot, and out-played" the Globetrotters on their way to a 42–38 win. The Thunderbirds kept the score low with a measured offence led by 18-year-old scoring whiz Pat McGeer, who poured in 14 points.

Freddie Thomas and Norm Baker were among the few Canadians who had a chance to make money in the early days of basketball. Most domestic players, even once they reached the senior level, weren't paid, but were compensated in other ways by the entrepreneurs who ran the team.

Such was the case for Paul Thomas, a star basketball player from Niagara Falls who played semi-pro baseball in the summer. In 1951, looking to continue post-graduate studies, he received a call from Gerry Livingston, owner of Livingston Wood manufacturing in Tillsonburg, Ontario, just north of the shores of Lake Erie southeast of London. Tillsonburg had just 5,000 residents, but that didn't dash Livingston's dream of creating a team that would win the Senior championship and send a team to Helsinki, Finland, to represent Canada at the 1952 Olympics.

Thomas was just the man Livingston needed, since he was highly educated and also a dangerous scorer. Thomas was a graduate of the University of Western Ontario, and prior to that he had set the Niagara Region high school scoring record with a 59-point outing at Niagara Collegiate.

Thomas began building a juggernaut, enlisting the services of players such as Bobby Simpson, an American who was one of the all-time great football players of the era and also an athletic force on the basketball court.

Though Livingston wasn't offering Thomas a salary, he was happy to offer him the equivalent of an athletic scholarship. Livingston did the same for Windsorites Harry Wade, a bullish six-foot-five centre, and Bill Coulthard, a pioneer of the one-handed shot and a former All-Michigan player at the Detroit Institute of Technology. Thomas recalls that both stars had top positions on the court and in Livingston's company. "Harry Wade became president of the company," he said. "Bill Coulthard became comptroller of the company. They had tremendous lives." Thomas and his Livvies achieved their goal, taking the 1952 Senior A championship and placing ninth at the Summer Games.

When Thomas returned to Canada, he made the most of Gerry Livingston's educational offers, driving three and a half hours to Ann Arbor, Michigan, to earn a degree at the University of Michigan. He rode the Senior A gravy train as far as he could, moving on to the Toronto Tri-Balls, where he was player-coach and was given money to earn a graduate degree. His teams even paid for him to fly to Los Angeles every summer, where he earned a doctorate. Thomas later became a distinguished coach at the University of Windsor.

Though he hadn't lived in Canada for decades, James Naismith continued to watch Canadian hoops with keen interest from his home in Lawrence, Kansas. In his book *Basketball: Its Origins and Development*, released two years after his 1939 death, the campus chaplain was bullish on the sport's future in his birthplace: "Although basketball is not so far advanced in Canada as it is in the United States, I feel sure that in a few years, Canadian teams will be playing on an equal basis with other teams in the world."[15]

But Naismith's rosy forecast came with a caveat. The game's inventor took note of his country's sparse population and the dominance of outdoor winter sports. Both factors would prove to be roadblocks that threatened to stall the growth of basketball in Naismith's home and native land just as it was taking off in the star-spangled nation that he had adopted as his permanent, and final, resting place.

CHAPTER 3

— GRADS SCHOOL THE WORLD —

Shouting and the sound of squeaking shoes wafted out the balcony door at the YMCA Training School gym in the winter of 1892. The curious sounds of grunts, whistles, and cheering could be heard clearly from the street outside just as a group of teachers from nearby Buckingham Grade School were walking by.

When they came in to check out the commotion, they were treated to quite the sight — one hundred fans packed the balconies for the nine-on-nine games, refereed by a tall, strapping young instructor with close-cropped brown hair and a well-kept moustache. His name was James Naismith.

It didn't take long for the teachers to get hooked on the spectacle, but it wasn't immediately clear if there was a place for them on the court. Women in those days were essentially barred from the rougher sports such as rugby and football, steered instead toward non-contact pursuits such as badminton and tennis.

The women from Buckingham Grade School approached Naismith on that day in 1892 and asked for court time. "About two weeks after they had first come, a group of them asked me why girls could not play," he wrote years later.[1]

He said he saw no reason why they couldn't and the Buckingham teachers went on to form the world's first women's basketball team. Dozens of eager athletes showed up for that first women's game at Springfield gym. Some of the twenty-somethings were dressed in tennis shoes, most were in street shoes, and all were clad in street clothes.

"I shall never forget the sight that they presented in their long trailing dresses with leg-of-mutton sleeves," Naismith wrote. "None of the other fundamentals was observed; often some girl got the ball and ran halfway across the floor to shoot at the basket."[2]

But the women soon got much better, one team grew into two, and within no time the college stenographers and professors' wives got into the act. One of the first members of the women's team was Miss Maude Sherman, the one who had caught James's eye when he first arrived in Springfield, and whose hand he would ask for in marriage, a request she accepted in 1894.

Naismith was asked to referee, or "umpire" the first women's games, and he noticed that the so called "gentler sex" was anything but on the court. "We got along nicely until I called a foul on one of the girls," he recalled in a 1932 speech at Springfield College. "She asked 'Did you call a foul on me?' and then she told me where I came from, where I was going to, and what my character was!"

Perhaps not wanting to suggest that women were uncouth, he reminded the audience that those pioneering players displayed "some of the finest sportsmanship" he had seen in those early days. But Naismith's open mind notwithstanding, most of his Canadian compatriots in the early 20th century didn't share his egalitarian view of women in sports.

Sports in those days were almost exclusively a celebration of manliness, a cultural expression of the strong masculine image publicized in the sports pages as local and regional football, hockey, and lacrosse leagues gained popularity.

Even as the Amateur Athletic Union (AAU) exploded on the scene at the start of the 20th century, Canadian women were shut out despite their obvious physical hardiness in agriculture and textiles. Even on university campuses, where sports were thriving, women who tried to run on the track or lace on skates to play hockey found themselves mocked and jeered for delving into male bastions. The University of Toronto in the 1920s refused to officially acknowledge women athletes, claiming that they "could not display the same prowess as men."

Although there's evidence of woman playing organized sports as far back as the 1880s, the practice was not widely encouraged until the early 20th century.[3] Women's sports were mostly played in universities prior to the First World War.

High school and club basketball games were relatively hard to come by and women who were not in school and who wanted to play settled for pickup games on outdoor courts, church basements, or YWCAs.

Basketball nonetheless quickly became very popular among girls, offering them a good workout and the chance to be part of a team. But parochial attitudes stubbornly refused to die up to the time of the First World War; the AAU refused an application for female membership in 1914, at a time when women still did not have the right to vote in Canada.

Another sign of the times was the fact that girls were forced to play by different rules than boys in the early days of basketball. Instead of five-a-side, girls played six per team with two guards, two forwards, and two centres. Rule-makers, concerned about the effects of strenuous exercise on developing women's bodies, severely restricted their on-court movements.

The court was divided into three sections for women's games and only the forwards were allowed to shoot, but they were also forbidden from running back to the other team's goal to play defence. Guards could only bring the ball to half court under girls' rules; then they passed ahead to the forwards and waited to play defence when the opponent secured possession.

Physical contact between players was forbidden and the rule was enforced by limiting players to three fouls before they were disqualified. Early-20th-century girls were further limited by a two-dribble rule.

But in the budding oil town of Edmonton, Alberta, on the eve of the Great War, one visionary educator and a few dozen young athletes would forever change Canadians' ideas of what women could achieve in sports and in society.

Twenty-five-year-old John "Percy" Page arrived in the Alberta capital from New Brunswick in 1912 to help the education ministry introduce commercial training to high school–aged youth.

Alberta was gradually moving away from the one-room schoolhouses typical in most regions to large, diverse facilities that were beginning to teach youngsters a variety of marketable skills. The oil and gas industry, though small at the dawn of the First World War, was growing and in need of skilled labour. Page's bachelor of commercial science degree from the American Institute of Business would serve him well when newly built McDougall Commercial High School hired him as principal and teacher.

Aside from academics, someone had to teach physical education, and there were separate classes for boys and girls. Page and colleague Ernest F. Hyde had to decide who would coach the girls, though neither was terribly enthusiastic about the prospect. After all, the prevailing view at the time was that girls should be offered a watered-down gym program to account for their physical differences, with some even speculating that excessive strain could hurt a woman's fertility!

According to some accounts, Page and Hyde flipped a coin to decide on the assignments.[4] Page lost the toss and Hyde took the boys' team. Page then got to work preparing a program for the girls at Commercial.

Drills and calisthenics were still commonplace in high school gyms across Canada during the time of the Great War as most instructors taught Physical Training, or PT, to ready young students for eventual conscription into the fighting forces. But Page had another idea to keep their attention: basketball, which Naismith student Lyman Archibald had helped to introduce to Western Canada in the late 1890s when he took a post at the Winnipeg Y.

Page's first problem was obvious — Commercial High School didn't have a gym, meaning they had to practise and play their six-on-six games on an outdoor cinderblock court. Given Edmonton's notoriously cold winters, the outdoor practices certainly helped develop toughness and endurance.

Page had a second problem: he didn't know much about basketball, having played the sport "rather ordinarily" during his youth in southern Ontario, though he had taught hoops during earlier stints at Rothesay Collegiate and St. Thomas Collegiate in New Brunswick.

He beefed up his knowledge with some instructional books and employed a methodological approach to practice with an emphasis on shooting, as guard Kay MacRitchie (later MacBeth) recalled: "We did lots of shooting, [the Grads] were always good shots."

Coach Page held practices twice a week and the girls were also encouraged to play other sports, decades before cross-training became the norm. "We were all great skaters and we did a lot of roller skating in those days," said MacBeth. "We did a lot of ice skating in the winter."

Coach Page's first team wasn't called the Grads, because none of the players had yet graduated. They were still made up primarily of 12th-graders, taking on local teams in a 1914 season in which they made an immediate impression. Commercial blitzed through the competition by impressive margins to set up a showdown against Camrose Normal School.

Camrose, about 100 kilometres to the south, had more seniors on their team, but Commercial's discipline won out and the final score of 12–7 earned them the first of what would be a motherlode of hardware. The haul included a shield donated by the Toronto-based Harold A. Wilson Company, maker of sporting equipment, to mark the Alberta girls' high school champion.

Commercial dominated the competition in 1915, as well, setting up a rematch against Camrose that the Grads won 13–2.

Several of Page's players were graduating in the spring of 1915, but they didn't want to give up the sport just yet and their coach was all too happy to oblige. On the players' urging he created a post-secondary club team built around captain Winnie Martin, who would go on to play with the team for another decade.

On June 15, 1915, Page formed the Commercial Graduates Basketball Club, later shortened to the Grads. The elite team honed their offensive and defensive plays during 90-minute practices that stressed quick ball movement and precise shooting.[5] The girls weren't especially tall, but their marksmanship and low turnover rate made them an impossible matchup for most teams in the fledgling sport.

Page's mantra of "play basketball, think basketball and dream basketball" perhaps explains why his teams so easily handled other squads that were still treating the game as a recreational pursuit. But Page, far from the modern stereotype of the hard-driving taskmaster obsessed with winning at all costs, was described by his players as a "nice man and a wonderful gentleman." He insisted the young women carry themselves with class and dignity at all times. "You are ladies first and basketball players second," he was once quoted as telling his protégés. "If you can't win playing a clean game, you don't deserve to win."[6]

Grads were also expected to keep it clean off the court, as Page imposed a curfew on road trips even though most of the players were in their twenties. "Nobody ever drank or smoked. You wouldn't dare," MacBeth recalled. "If you smoked, you wouldn't be on the team. I don't even know that anybody ever had a drink, or even a glass of wine."

Coach Page restricted spending money on road trips, in part because he didn't want to compromise their amateur status, but it also had the added effect of limiting social options during their lengthy voyages. Dating was also a no-no, and Coach Page even informed his players that they'd have to wait until they left the team before marrying or having children.

Once he had laid down the ground rules for his new elite team, Percy Page turned his attention to finding opponents.

The Grads were immediately barred from the Edmonton high school league since they were made up of older women, and they instead set up games against other club teams. They also kept sharp in a manner unheard of in women's team sports at the time — by scrimmaging against men.

As Kay MacBeth recalled, the guys often got the tougher end of the matchup against the finely tuned Grads machine. "We beat them," she said matter-of-factly, referring to the team's 7–2 record in battles of the sexes.

Page also laid the groundwork for his budding dynasty by setting up a farm system that consisted of the Commercial junior and senior girls' teams as well as the Gradettes, a feeder club team of budding prospects. Page would promote promising high-schoolers to the Gradettes before the best among them got the call-up.

The results were immediate, as the Grads reeled off five consecutive provincial titles from 1915 to 1920. They were so dominant that in 1917 they were allowed to hold on to their 1916 championship without defending it.

The 1919 season was noteworthy for being the first of three consecutive provincial championships that pitted the Grads against top university teams. The first two of those games were close affairs, given that universities had a longer history of playing organized basketball than any of the high schools.

The Grads entered the 1921 Provincial Championship with a gaudy undefeated record after six seasons of play, and their 17–13 win against the University of Alberta appeared to be the perfect capper to yet another perfect campaign.

But the university protested the win for an unusual reason — the Grads won with McDougall Commercial student Connie Smith on their roster. Most protests of the kind are lodged because of the presence of older, not younger, players, but the Grads nonetheless agreed to a rematch.

The game was replayed and U of A won 29–23. It was the only Provincial Championship the Grads failed to win in their 25-year history.

At the same time, women across Canada were taking to basketball and other sports in huge numbers, leading some observers to refer to the 1920s as the "Golden Age of Women's Sport."

Athletic activity had been largely an upper-class male pursuit in the 19th century but was soon embraced by Canadians of all genders and classes, particularly as high school sports began to flourish.

The Grads had firmly established themselves as the prime force in basketball by the start of the 1920s, but in those early days the juggernaut was strictly a regional phenomenon. They cobbled together a schedule against club teams but still had no gym to call their own.

That all changed in 1922 when the Shamrocks of London, Ontario, declared themselves to be Canadian champions without playing a team west of Ontario.[7] The Grads, insulted by the claim, demanded a playoff and were granted their request — provided they could find the money to make the 3,200-kilometre trek east. That wouldn't be easy since none of the players was paid to play, all had full-time jobs, and their team had no sponsors.

Paying the women to play was out of the question. They wanted to maintain amateur status in case basketball ever became a sport in the Olympics, which forbade professional participation. Even with the Shamrocks putting up $600 for the showdown, each of the Grads had to pay $25 out of their own pockets.

Team Captain Winnie Martin helped to fund the trip by capitalizing on her greatest skill, which was not basketball but typing. She had recently been crowned the Canadian typing champion using an Underwood machine,[8] and rightly guessed that her newfound fame would be a great promotional opportunity for the Toronto manufacturer. Martin contacted Underwood head office and asked if the firm would be willing to sponsor the Grads. Company president J.J. Seitz donated $250 out of his own pocket to help cover Grads' expenses in London, and he even showed up to cheer the team on.

Page brought the core of his dominant unit. Martin was joined in the backcourt by Connie Smith. Daisy Johnson, a teacher at Edmonton's Irma High School, was a forward along with her younger sister, Dorothy, a centre. Stenographer and sharpshooter Nellie Perry was a dangerous offensive force and Eleanor Mountifield was a bookkeeper by day and a post by night. Page didn't bring along any alternates, to keep costs down. Everyone made sure to pack lunches to avoid dining-car charges.

The Grads boarded the train at Edmonton's CNR station lacking in finances but not in confidence. Little known outside Alberta, they were underdogs for that first-ever East vs. West showdown for the Dominion of Canada women's basketball championship. The two-game series would be decided on total points at London Armouries, a 17-year-old facility that had been used to train Canadian Corps soldiers bound for the Great War.

The Grads would be playing unfamiliar boy's rules for the first of the two games. Boys played five-on-five, meaning the Grads would have to alter their six-woman offence and play everyone all over the court. Making matters even worse was the fact that the Shamrocks had a full roster while the Grads had only one substitute.

About 1,000 hostile fans (Underwood's president excepted) packed the Armouries for Game 1 as the visiting Grads, still accustomed to playing outdoors, took the court in their black and gold dresses and heavy wool stockings complete with knee pads and bloomers.

Not exactly sleek athletic wear, and their game was as ungainly as their attire in that first match.

The Shamrocks trounced the Grads 21–8 in Game 1, putting the pressure on the visitors, who needed to win the second game by more than 13 points to avoid heading home as losers.

Percy Page was forced to referee the second game, since none of the local officials understood the complexities of 6-on-6 basketball.

With the Grads back in their comfort zone, they dominated the Shamrocks by a score of 41–8, silencing the crowd of 1,500 and putting to rest any notion that a Canadian basketball championship could be decided from among eastern squads.[9]

Why quit when you're ahead? The visitors scheduled two more games against Ontario teams and won them both, setting up a homecoming that even most modern Canadian teams, amateur or pro, will never see.

CNR station was packed to capacity for the triumphant welcome. A band blared rousing tunes as the train pulled into the station, a sign of just how much Edmonton had rallied around the hardworking young amateur giants. The district school board treated the Super Six to a banquet and medals. The capper came when they had breakfast with Mayor David Duggan.

But the euphoria died out quickly; just 200 fans showed up for a hastily arranged exhibition game meant to capitalize on the Grads' status as Canadian champions.

As the 1923 season loomed, it quickly became clear to Percy Page that he would have to find new opportunities, and revenue streams, if his elite team was to survive. Achieving success outside Alberta would require the first major adjustment under his reign — abandoning six-on-six basketball.

Most teams in North America played men's five-on-five rules, under which the Grads had struggled in the previous year's Canadian championship. Coach Page decided that the only way to make the change was to step up the intensity of practices to a fever pitch. Five-on-five basketball was a faster, more free-flowing game. A team hoping to thrive under the boys' rules needed endurance and the ability to run their offence at a quick pace without turning the ball over excessively.

Coach Page put his athletes through mile runs on top of twice-weekly practices that ended with scrimmages against men's teams.[10] The Grads' experience with girls' rules actually gave them one advantage — the dribble limit had led to a focus on passing and ball movement. "We never practiced dribbling," centre Edith Stone Sutton recalled in a 2001 interview. "Dribbling slows the game. It's an individual, look-at-me kind of playing — hogging the ball while there is someone over there screaming for a pass. Team play means passing."[11]

The revamped Grads steamrolled through the 1923 season with an undefeated record, including a 22–2 drubbing of Barons High, a school from outside Lethbridge. They also defended their Dominion of Canada championship against the London Shamrocks for the second straight year, this time at home. The 51–28 two-game victory was achieved entirely under the boys' rules, a testament to the Grads' ability to adjust to changing times and styles. They had only lost one game in nine years, and people outside the sport began to take notice.

Back east, J.J. Seitz had become an enthusiastic supporter of women's basketball, and came up with the idea of an "Underwood Trophy" to crown the North American champion and publicize his brand before anyone even knew what branding meant. Seitz went a step further by setting up a board of directors for the championship, which selected the American title-holders, the Cleveland Favorite-Knits, as the Grads' opponent.

But Cleveland was in no better position to travel than the Grads had been the previous season. The Ohio club let it be known that it would need $1,800 to make the trip — well beyond the Grads' means.

Enter local promoter and Edmonton Eskimos football coach Deacon Whyte. Not only did he foot the entire travel bill, he even told the Grads that they could keep two-thirds of the profits from the championship.[12]

The inaugural Underwood Challenge was to be played at Edmonton Arena, and with Whyte promoting the game, a hefty crowd was assured.

On June 12, 1923, Edmonton Arena was packed with nearly 5,000 fans — a good crowd in any era of Canadian basketball. What's more, thousands more listened to the game on local radio.

The commemorative booklet "Edmonton Grads: 25 years of Basketball Champions" describes the wildly divergent styles of the two teams:

> That first game presented Edmontonians for a moment with an almost comical spectacle. The Favorite-Knits came onto the court in their short-shorts and jerseys boldly emblazoned, 'World Champs'. Then the Grads came out in the uniforms they had become accustomed to — loose-fitting sailors' middies, pleated bloomers made of three yards of British serge, long wool stockings and black-and-gold headbands.[13]

Style points didn't count in this series and the hometown girls won Game 1 19–13 and took Game Two 34–20 a night later to become the toast of Edmonton. Not only was the landmark win good for bragging rights, it was good for the Grads' bank account. They earned $2,400 for the two-game series after Deacon Whyte made good on his promise to give the club a majority share of the profits.

As usual the players were not paid in order to retain their amateur status, though the women and their coach did receive medals and gifts. Coach Page received the biggest gift of all — a Chevrolet coupe donated by local businessmen.

Page quickly capitalized on his team's newfound popularity by scheduling three defences of the Underwood Trophy in 1923. The Grads swept through the competition once again, earning a whopping $11,000 and a chance at their dream trip — the 1924 Olympics in Paris.

Basketball was only a demonstration sport in Paris, but that didn't take away from the joy that the ladies felt at getting the chance to show off their superior skills on the world stage. The eight-woman roster included the same six who had dominated North America for nearly a decade. Only Abbie Scott and Mary Dunn were new additions.

Edmontonians turned out in droves on June 18, 1924, to see off their treasured sports heroines, whose employers had agreed to give them time off of work for the historic trip.

The headline in the following day's *Edmonton Journal* read, "Popularity of Grads is shown by send off: Thousands Congregate at Depot to Say Farewell to City's Idols."

The Edmonton Grads won titles the world over in the early 20th century. Their record of 502 wins and 20 losses from 1915 to 1940 was a testament to their greatness. They were the first Canadian team to travel by plane, the first to secure national corporate sponsorship, and the first to draw 8,500 fans to a game. The 1923 team: (l–r) Eleanor Mountifield (captain), Connie Smith, Abbie Scott, Dorothy Johnson, Nellie Perry, Winnie Martin, Elizabeth Elrich, and Mary Dunn.

Provincial Archives of Alberta.

The first leg of the trip was a train ride to Montreal. Then it was on to an ocean liner bound for Europe in the days when transatlantic passenger flights were but a dream.

Both men's and women's basketball were still demonstration sports at the 1924 Olympics, but while the men were playing for medals by 1936, attitudes toward women players weren't as welcoming.

Leading the charge against female Olympians was none other than the father of the modern Olympic movement, Baron Pierre de Coubertin. Under his leadership, women were banned from competing in any Olympic sports until 1900. All women's sports were for demonstration purposes only until 1912 with de Coubertin believing women weren't worthy of official standings or medals. "Olympics with women would be incorrect, unpractical, uninteresting and unaesthetic," de Coubertin said following the 1896 Olympics in Athens. "We feel that the Olympic Games must be reserved for the solemn and periodic exaltation of male athleticism with internationalism as a base, loyalty as a means, arts for its setting and female applause as its reward."

But the eight well-conditioned athletes from Edmonton weren't in Paris to be spectators. They were in businesslike mode as they prepared for the six-game series organized by the Fédération Sportive Féminine Internationale (FSFI).

The FSFI was formed by de Coubertin's nemesis and fellow native of France, feminist Alice Milliat. Upset about the International Olympic Committee's banishment of women from the Olympics, the prominent feminist convened a group of women's sports enthusiasts in March 1921 and formed FSFI later that year.

The federation's crowning achievement was the establishment of the Women's World Games which were held in 1922, 1926, 1930, and 1934. But Milliat ran up against the cold, hard reality of chauvinism when she tried to petition the IOC for full women's participation in the Olympics. The IOC's ally, the International Amateur Athletic Federation, told the French feminist that it was prepared to impose absolute power over the governance of women's track and field in key countries, a move that would cripple the women's games. Milliat backed down when the IOC offered her a watered-down proposal of nine women's events at the 1936 Games in Berlin, in exchange for her agreement to cancel the Women's World Games forever.

The women's exhibition basketball tournament at the 1924 Olympics pitted the Grads against teams from Paris, Strasbourg, Roubaix, and Lille. The women from Paris were the first ones on the chopping block. The Grads took Game One by a score of 64–16 and the rout was on. When it was over, the Canadian court queens had won by average scores of 60–10, including 65–4 and 61–1 blowouts in their final two games.[14]

The Grads returned home as full-fledged celebrities and Page now had sponsor support and financing to organize more road trips. The women found themselves in hot demand for social functions, and local sponsors were eager to attach their names to the winning Grads brand in newspaper ads. Coach Page secured Edmonton Arena as a full-time home venue and he had a hardwood floor installed for the popular contests. A regular ticket sold for 75 cents and a single ticket in the box section was $1.00. The income began pouring in.

But if Page planned to continue his team's winning ways, he would have to do it without his hardy veteran captain. Winnie Martin, who had offered leadership through nearly 200 games dating back to the team's inception, retired in the summer of 1924. The captain's title was handed to Connie Smith, the four-year veteran whose presence as a high-schooler had caused such a ruckus back at the 1921 Alberta final.

The 1925 season saw the Grads pick up right where they left off, rolling through one opponent after another and embarking on a series of lengthy road trips. One of their marathon voyages included a sojourn to British Columbia, where they easily handled opponents in Victoria and Kamloops before eking out their toughest win of the year against the Kamloops Boys team, who they defeated 23–20.

The season's big shocker came on February 28 when they took on the Varsconas club team for the provincial championship at the University of Alberta's Varsity Gym. The Varsconas were made up of former university players, and the Grads took the first game of the three-game series. But the second game was a different story, with the Varsconas winning 22–18. It was only the third loss in team history up to that point and was such big news that the *Edmonton Journal* headline later in the week read "Basketball History Was Made Saturday When Grads Suffered Defeat."

The Grads bounced back for the rubber match of the series, taking their 11th provincial title in 12 seasons. They also picked up one of their nemeses from the series, signing Varsconas star Gladys Fry, who went on to become of the greatest players in Grads history, placing fourth on the team's career scoring list with 1,679 points.[15]

The Grads finished 1925 in style, sporting a perfect 8–0 record in the Underwood Challenge. They had travelled to Oklahoma, where they swept the Guthrie Redbirds before a crowd that included one proud Canadian who had made the trek from Kansas to see the fruits of the game that he had invented nearly 35 years earlier.

James Naismith was by then a chaplain and basketball coach at the University of Kansas who had just taken American citizenship after serving with the U.S. military. He had spent much of his life living out his dream of teaching and preaching to young men. He had also found time to obtain a medical doctorate.

Naismith, despite his pioneering work in introducing the game to women, still had reservations later in life about the long-term effects of elite sports on women's health. It was a prevailing view at the time, as centre Edith Stone Sutton remembered: "It was said that playing would make us sterile," she told reporters at her 100th birthday party in Edmonton in 2010. "If we were lucky enough to have a baby, it would only be a girl. We'd have cancer and all be dead before we were 40." She added slyly, "As you can see, that's hardly the case."[16]

Any concerns Naismith had about female hoopsters were quickly forgotten once the 64-year-old saw the Grads run roughshod over the Redbirds at the 1925 Underwood Challenge. The ball whipped around the perimeter in a flash and shots went up fast and furiously. The Grads pulled away from Oklahoma at the end, and Naismith was enthralled, particularly because his fellow Canadians had won without relying on the dribble, just as he had envisioned when he had drafted his original 13 rules for that first game with the incorrigibles.

Naismith addressed the crowd in Oklahoma, gushing that he "never expected the day when girls play basketball as these Canadian girls play it." He went on to call the Grads "the finest basketball team that ever stepped on the floor," and lauded them for their "grace and poise" while taking pains to commend the American competitors as well.

A decade later he admitted that his expectations for the women were lower than they should have been. "The girls' playing was a revelation to me," he wrote. "They handled the ball as the boys do, and their floor work was far superior to what I believed possible for girls." He also took note of the class and femininity of these fine young athletes, noting that "they were typical young ladies, not the tom-boy type at all."[17]

As the 1920s drew to a close, Edmonton's finest went about living up to Naismith's lofty words, capturing every Underwood Trophy up for grabs while sweeping the provincial finals, Canadian championships, and the 1928 Olympic exhibitions in Amsterdam.

Crowds began to pack arenas and stadiums to catch a glimpse of a team whose legend had begun to draw national interest. The *Edmonton Journal* even sent reporter George MacIntosh to travel with the team to Cleveland in 1926.

The grads went east to Toronto for the Canadian championships that same year to take on the Lakesides in what would be a nail-biting two-game series. The games were held in the Arena Gardens, then the largest indoor sports facility in Canada.

To the delight of the home crowd, the Lakesides beat the Grads 24–19 in Game 1, led by Nora Gordon's game-high nine points. The Grads bounced back with a 26–6 win the following day to take the championship on total points, scoring a victory not only for themselves but also for the profile of basketball in Canada.

While it's not clear exactly how many fans turned out for the Grads-Lakesides series, local media billed the crowds as the largest ever to see a basketball game in the Queen City. The wire reporter who attended Game 1 on April 14, 1926, said fans applauded the smart play by both teams throughout the game, adding that "never before in this city has such excitement been packed into forty minutes of basketball."

But while the historic nature of the game might have been obvious at the time, the ensuing years have dulled the collective memory.

The Arena Gardens building was demolished in 1989 and a plaque sits at the site, now taken up by an apartment building on Mutual Street in Toronto. The Toronto Historical Board mentions that the building was home ice for the Toronto Arenas, later known as the Maple Leafs. The plaque also mentions that "other sports, including bicycle racing, curling, boxing, wrestling and tennis used the space." It even notes an appearance by the Glenn Miller Band in 1942 and Frank Sinatra in 1948. The Grads-Lakeside thriller is nowhere to be seen.

As the Edmonton Grads closed their second decade of play in 1929, there had been very little roster turnover. Only 22 players had suited up for Page's squad since 1920, forging a sense of familiarity that no other team of the day had achieved.

Their popularity was at an all-time high; they had drawn a home crowd of 6,500 for the 1929 Underwood Trophy final,[18] a total that they surpassed that season in a game against the Torrid Zones in Regina. A whopping 8,500 fans showed up to watch the Grads trounce the home team 50–12. It was the biggest crowd ever seen in that province for a sport other than hockey.[19]

With the Grads feeder system working at full bore, the highest-scoring players in program history took the court in the early 1930s. The lineup included Margaret McBurney, Gladys Fry, Babe Belanger, and Mildred McCormack, who all finished among the top five scorers ever to play for the Grads.

The team racked up the miles, including a trip to Los Angeles for an exhibition tournament to coincide with the 1932 Olympics. The demonstration was noteworthy in part because three of the four teams in the draw were Canadian. The Grads swept to a 3–0 record against teams from San Francisco, Prince Rupert, and Victoria.

They made several cross-country voyages by train in that era, the easy luxury of rail travel being the primary means of transport across much of the world in 1932. But the Grads, already pioneers for their on-court exploits, were about to try something new.

In mid-May 1932, Coach Page was running the athletes through their final practice as they prepared to chase their 10th consecutive Underwood Trophy. Their opponent would be the Chicago Red Devils, who they were scheduled to play at home on a Saturday evening and again the following Monday. Coach Page also agreed to a third game in

Calgary to raise money for the Benevolent and Protective Order of Elks charity fund.

But due to scheduling restrictions, the Calgary game could only be played on the Tuesday — just 24 hours after their home game. Getting time off from work on such short notice was simply out of the question. Captain Margaret McBurnie informed the team that there was only one option, as Edith Sutton recalled later that month with great unease:

> In order to make the date, we would be flying. We looked at our captain in disbelief and complete misunderstanding. Nobody flew! The only people who flew were the bush pilots ... they flew in wealthy entrepreneurs who owned mining interests or transportation businesses in the far North Country and had stratospheric amounts of money. They could own their own planes or at least hire daring young flyers to take them up there. No passenger flights, of course. No need, nobody flew! And here we were told we were about to fly![20]

Two Fokker 14 aircraft were waiting for them at the airport, known as Blatchford Field. As usual, the Grads were on the cutting edge, though it probably didn't feel that way as menacing storm clouds gathered over Edmonton on the morning of May 16, 1932. The clouds had the team briefly considering a cancellation, but the Red Devils had already arrived in Calgary and would have been left high and dry, 2,500 kilometres from home. What's more, the Shriners had sold tickets and brought in a special floor and lighting for Edmonton's finest.

As soon as the players finished their shifts on Tuesday afternoon, they were picked up at work, hustled to Blatchford Field, and six players and staff were loaded onto the two planes. The turboprops weren't built for luxury — the Fokkers were air mail carriers with no permanent passenger seats. Sets of wicker chairs had to be fastened to the floor to accommodate the players, and there were no flight attendants to calm their nerves with food and drink.

Edith Sutton and her twin sister, Helen, boarded one of the planes together, against their mother's wishes, recalls Edith's son Phil. "My grandmother wanted them each to go on a different plane just in case," he said. "And they said 'no, we're not doing that, we're going together.'"

Edith Sutton remembers a rough two-hour flight to Calgary in time to squeeze in a pre-game supper, "for those who could manage it." Then they took care of Chicago by a score of 27–18. Not bad considering Chicago had arrived hours earlier and had all afternoon to relax prior to the game.

Thankfully for Percy Page and the players, the trip back home would be made by train. They took the midnight run, arriving home just in time to wash up in the restroom, change clothes, grab a quick breakfast, and get to work for their office shifts. It was clear there would be no rest for the weary winners.

Road stories abounded during the Grads' 25-year, 200,000-kilometre travelogue, including a love story that would have drawn Coach Page's ire — had he known about it.

Holding down the centre position in the 1930s were twins Edith and Helen Stone, whose five-foot-seven frames were no hindrance in an era in which ultra-tall players were relatively scarce. The twins were stalwarts on the 1932 Olympic team, which was the highlight of careers that lasted about four years each. Edith is also remembered as the only Grads player ever to break *omertà* on Coach Page's reputedly iron-clad curfew.

While most of the Grads have stuck to the story about the team's squeaky-clean image, Edith Stone revealed a little-known story of a 1934 exhibition in Winnipeg in which the 64–4 blowout over the Eagles was just the beginning of her fun.

The Eagles-Grads matchup was organized by William Sutton, secretary of Winnipeg's local basketball association and a former player with the Winnipeg Toilers senior men's team.

Sutton quickly became smitten with Edith, a dark-haired beauty with porcelain features, and started to think up ways to get a closer look at her. He decided to contact her and arrange a meeting at a local roadhouse, unbeknownst to Coach Page.

"You weren't supposed to do that — go out with boys," she said in a magazine interview in 2001. "I did something I wasn't supposed to."[21]

The two clearly hit it off, because William Sutton immediately found a way to see her again — he got work on a grain elevator in Edmonton to be closer to the apple of his eye. Edith quit the Grads in 1934 and married William soon afterward. Percy Page apparently never found out that his precious team curfew had been violated in the name of love, and the three Sutton children can thank their parents' mischievous streak for helping to bring them into the world.

The winds of war began to blow when Adolph Hitler established his fearsome Third Reich in 1933, and it quickly became clear that the Fuehrer would use the 1936 Olympics in Berlin as a chance to demonstrate white superiority and the efficiency of the "master race."

While some labour groups pushed for a boycott, Nazi appeasement was the order of the day on Parliament Hill. The Canadian Olympic Committee (COC) fell into line, as did media commentators, who were often harshly critical of any talk of a boycott.

The Grads entered the 1936 Olympic exhibition tournament unaware of the effect that Hitler would have on the future of their program just a few years later. They rolled through the competition as they had at three previous Games, their 9–0 record matching the dominance of 1928 in Amsterdam. The opening game set the tone for the tour as they dismantled a hapless team from London 100–2.

Kay MacRitchie was a 15-year-old freshman at McDougall Commercial High School when the Grads made their triumphant return to Edmonton. Like many other young girls in town, the Grads held a near-mythical status in her heart, though most would only ever watch from the stands at Edmonton Arena. MacRitchie, however, was hard-wired for sports from a young age, an admitted tomboy who preferred the baseball diamond and the football field to make-believe tea parties as a youth in Saskatchewan. Every summer her parents, both Scottish immigrants, would treat the family to summer vacations in White Rock, British Columbia, where, in a harbinger of her future basketball prowess, Kay and her siblings would play Duck on a Rock, that old Scottish favourite, on the beach.

The MacRitchies lived in Saskatoon and Moose Jaw before settling in Edmonton, where Kay's coach, Arnold Henderson, taught her to do a layup during her freshman year. Kay was hooked on hoops, improving to such a point that by the age of 17 she caught the attention of Coach Page.

Dazzled by her quickness and passing ability, Page called young Kay into his office at McDougall to tell her that he'd like for her to join the Grads at practice. He was no doubt aware that in selecting MacRitchie he would be breaking with his own tradition. Under the feeder system he had set up in 1915, no one was allowed to join the Grads until they had first cut their teeth on the McDougall High School team and then on the Gradettes farm club; but little Kay's dynamic skills convinced Coach Page to make an exception.

Kay MacRitchie joined the Grads in the fall of 1938 as it prepared to defend its Canadian, Underwood, and North American titles. She stood out in those early sessions as a quick player and tremendous ball handler, who deferred to high-scoring teammates Noel McDonald, Helen Northrup, and Etta Dann.

The youngest on the team by five years, Kay was all too happy to pass off to the veterans as the Grads piled up the wins, though she made an exception when it came to rookie initiation traditions such as carrying bags and ordering food for the vets. "I was the rookie, but I didn't co-operate," she said, before adding, "I'm a Scotsman! On the train they were trying to make me clean the runners and I said no."

The 1938–39 and 1939–40 seasons ended in typical fashion, with the Grads defending their Canadian championship in 1940 against the Vancouver Westerns in a two-game series. The previous year, the Underwood Trophy had been retired from competition and given permanently to the Grads, which no one could have credibly challenged. The Grads had won all 17 Underwood titles, amassing a record of 114–6.

The team's legacy was already secure, what with 13 consecutive Canadian championships, three straight North American championships, and a spotless 27–0 record in Olympic exhibition play.

In a country in which basketball teams still fail to earn a national following or coast-to-coast media coverage, Grads team captain Noel MacDonald was named by The Canadian Press as the country's top woman athlete for 1938. She's the only woman basketball player ever to receive the honour. In a show of solidarity, MacDonald refused to accept the award as an individual and insisted that her entire team be recognized.

The Grads were clearly one of Canada's greatest franchises in any sport and with a stellar feeder system, stable leadership, and strong fan and corporate support, were in position to become the centre of women's basketball for decades to come.

But in 1939–40, it all came crashing down, and Adolf Hitler was to blame.

The story of the Edmonton Grads' juggernaut was overrun by much more serious matters as the team began play in the 1939–40 season.

Hitler's quick and surprising invasion of Poland on September 1, 1939, led Britain and France to declare war. It had become clear to Prime Minister Mackenzie King that his policy of appeasing the Nazis was no longer viable, and Canada declared war on Germany on September 10. The mobilization of troops and resources led to severe restrictions on non-essential travel, forcing the Grads to play close to home while American opponents travelled north to meet them for cross-border battles.

The increased number of home games exposed a new problem — the love affair between Edmontonians and the Grads was fading. For the first time since those fledgling days 25 years earlier, the Grads played to small crowds as the novelty of Grads' blowouts lost appeal. The fact is that in the entire history of the team, no one had emerged as a clear rival. The only team that ever won a series against the Grads was a team from Cleveland that took three out of four in a 1926 exhibition series that didn't count for any title.

The sparse crowds were about to get a whole lot smaller when Canada, the UK, Australia, and New Zealand signed the British Commonwealth Air Training Plan. It was part of Canada's contribution to the air attack against Hitler. Britain's airstrips were vulnerable to attack and Mackenzie King decided to provide air training and support facilities to mother England. Edmonton Arena was one of the buildings co-opted as part of the plan, leaving the Grads without their home court and main source of revenue.

No official announcement was made at the time, but as they prepared to welcome the Chicago Aces for a two-game exhibition series, the players had a feeling their team's days were numbered. "I think we just knew it (was over) as the war started," said Kay MacRitchie. "I guess they were just told they had to get out of (the arena)."

Some 6,200 fans packed into the building on June 5, 1940, to watch Chicago put up a tough fight before bowing to the Grads 62–52, in a game that was as much a reunion as a swan song. All but three of the team's alumni were in the stands.

In the space of just a few months the Grads had lost their arena and their fan support, and even their stalwart coach was ready to move on. Fifty-three-year-old Percy Page, a career educator and the team's loyal leader for a quarter century, made the jump into provincial politics as an independent MLA. Once again he was a winner, splitting the Edmonton riding with four other candidates in the general election of March 21, 1940.

Continuing on as coach would have been out of the question given his new duties in the legislature, coupled with the fact that he had decided to keep his job as principal at McDougall High School. But, ever dutiful to his beloved players, Page couldn't allow the Grads' era to die out with a whimper. He found a way around the wartime travel limits and organized one final, epic road trip with his players, but this time they would be leaving their basketballs, jerseys, knee pads, and sneakers at home.

Coach Page took the team on the vacation of a lifetime, a trip that began with a jaunt to the Rocky Mountain town of Jasper, Alberta, where the women went horseback riding and enjoyed dips in the lake. Page even relaxed his usually tight social restrictions. "We had lovely dinners and we danced, if we could find someone to dance with," said Kay MacBeth, who recalled spotting young American acting star Mickey Rooney in town.

The team continued on to Lake Louise before ending their train voyage in Vancouver, where they hopped on a ship for Alaska, which at that time was just a territory of the United States.

Then it was down to the northern British Columbia town of Prince George, where the team visited a pulp-and-paper mill and played fastball against local schoolboys, against whom they suffered an uncharacteristic loss.

Then it was back to Edmonton, where everyone said their goodbyes and went on to get married, have children, and move on to middle age as the memory of the Grads began to grow fainter.

The team is unique in Canadian basketball history, and likely the only women's team outside of hockey that managed to captivate sports fans in multiple regions of the country.

Their list of firsts is difficult to fully quantify. They were the first Canadian basketball team to travel by plane, the first to secure national corporate sponsorship, and the first to draw 8,500 fans to a game. From 1915 until 1940, the Grads played 522 official games in Canada, the United States, and in Europe, winning 502 and losing only 20.

But mere dominance on the court doesn't explain the huge crowds the team drew as they ran opponents ragged on both sides of the Atlantic. Phil Sutton, whose mother Edith was still going strong at the age of 101, said the Grads played in a simpler age, when entertainment options were fewer, cynicism was scarcer, and captivating the popular imagination was easier. "There's too much for young people to do (now)," he said. "Hockey, and the Internet. Back then, there weren't even that many movie theatres, and basketball, that was there to entertain."

Compare that to the halcyon days of Percy Page's classy outfit that held a generation of Edmontonians in a frenzy while rewriting records with every crisp pass and back-door cut. They were respected on the road but beloved at home, and their spell moved an *Edmonton Journal* columnist to verse in a 1935 column that captured the mood of the town on game nights:

> Nations may totter and politicians rave
> Great issues may hang in the balance
> And even the end of the world may be in sight
> But what does it matter?
> The Grads are playing tonight!

CHAPTER 4

— OPENING NIGHT —

The wild success of hockey in Canada sometimes leaves basketball aficionados feeling left out of the party, but the truth is that professional basketball has piggybacked off of hockey at key points in its history.

Professional basketball was a sporting afterthought, in the United States as well as Canada, prior to the First World War. Fans and athletic associations alike viewed pro athletes with suspicion, seeing them as mercenaries who tainted the purity of sport. In early-20th-century Canada, sports organizations saw university and Olympic sport as the pinnacle of athletic competition, with pro sports ranked somewhere near prostitution in the minds of the elites.

Some of the athletes did their best to live up to that reputation, taking bribes to fix outcomes, associating with gambling rings, and agreeing to circus-style exhibitions that fell far short of the lofty sporting ideals of the day.

Any athletes who took money to play did so at their own peril, given that their eligibility for national amateur championships, and even the Olympics, could be quashed by the Amateur Athletic Union and other governing bodies.

But by the 1920s, entrepreneurs on both sides of the border realized that the average fan felt differently. Canadians were increasingly eager to watch pro hockey, prompting a group of hockey club owners to meet at Montreal's Windsor Hotel in November 1917 to form the National Hockey League (NHL) out of the ashes of the old National Hockey Association.[1] By that time, upwards of 7,000 fans were turning out for each Stanley Cup final game. Canadians even came out in large numbers to watch games in the NHL's farm system, the American Hockey League.

Pro basketball was far less popular, making its American debut back in 1896 when the YMCA-based Trenton Basket Ball team made the rounds in New Jersey, playing exhibitions against all comers. The National League became the first professional basketball league in 1898, and Dr. James Naismith took a keen interest in the nascent organization. "As the game grew in popularity they were able to equip the teams and it was not long until they had a surplus," he wrote in a letter reflecting on the game's growth. "This surplus was divided among the members of the team, thus making them professionals."[2]

The National League had six or seven teams in New Jersey and Pennsylvania by the turn of the 20th century and an array of other leagues followed, but all were plagued by roster turnover, a lack of funding, and franchises that would sometimes pack up and move mid-season. What's more, pro hoops failed to move the meter in the press, with baseball firmly entrenched as the national pastime.

In his 1892 book *Rules for Basket Ball*, Naismith wrote that his new sport should have "little or none of the reputed roughness of Rugby or Association foot ball," but early pro 'ballers obviously hadn't read that book, based on their tendency to beat each other up as much as play the game.

Making matters worse were the wire cages that organizers set up around the court to protect players from fans, and sometimes vice versa. The result was a mix of bodychecking and brutality that failed to gain a wide following.

But while pro basketball remained a marginal affair through to the 1940s, NHL and AHL owners continued to float the idea of starting up a hoops league to fill empty dates between hockey matches.

The success of one-off exhibitions at Madison Square Garden and other major arenas piqued the interest of the owners, who operated under the umbrella of the Arena Managers Association of American (AMAA), of which Maple Leaf Gardens was a member.

The plan hinged on setting up strong franchises in North America's biggest markets, to take the wind out of the sails of the rival National Basketball League (NBL). The NBL operated basketball teams in places like Fort Wayne, Indiana, and Oshkosh, Wisconsin, and had attracted many of the top college players.

Arthur Wirtz, co-owner of the Chicago Black Hawks and Chicago Stadium, rallied support around the NBL rival, to be named the Basketball Association of America (BAA). Wirtz and Al Sutphin, owner of the AHL team in Cleveland, decided in the spring of 1946 to hire AHL president Maurice Podoloff as the first BAA president, a decision that would be made official at a summer meeting in New York.[3]

The Toronto ownership group stood out from the start because it had many more partners than most of the American franchises. Maple Leaf Gardens' manager Frank Selke had conscripted former basketball coach Ben Newman as one of the team's co-owners. Eric Cradock, co-owner of the Montreal Alouettes football team, joined Newman on the ownership team, and they added a third member, Harold Shannon.

Lawyer and senator Salter Hayden also became involved in those early stages and Grey Cup–winning football player Annis Stukus was a consultant. They designated Charles Watson as their spokesman, and Alouettes coach and general manager Lew Hayman, a co-founder of the football team with Craddock, was the Huskies' first general manager.

On June 6, 1946, Shannon joined 12 other BAA representatives at the Hotel Commodore on East 42nd Street in Manhattan to hammer out the final details for the fledgling league. It would be based out of the largest NHL and AHL sports arenas in major centres such as New York, Philadelphia, Chicago, and Detroit. The salary cap would be set at $40,000 per team and the season would begin play on Saturday, November 2, 1946.[4]

The dominance of hockey in Toronto immediately became an obstacle. The league had to move opening night ahead to Friday, November 1 because the Leafs were playing on the Saturday.

The Huskies' owners then set out to sell basketball to hockey fans. Sporting the catch phrase "Here Come the Huskies," they took out a full-page ad in the *Globe and Mail* that made the bold prediction that the Huskies would eventually draw crowds as large as the Leafs and the Argonauts.

The owners predicted 12,000 fans would pack the Gardens and ticket prices started at 75 cents and topped out at $2.50. Another sign of the team's ambition was the decision to market basketball in that first ad blitz as the "World's Most Popular Sport" — perhaps a tad premature given the place that baseball, hockey, and football held in the North American consciousness.

Hayman hired hulking 29-year-old centre Ed Sadowski as his player-coach, which was a common hybrid position in the mid 20th century. Sadowski, at six foot five and 270 pounds, was known as a space-eater who had bounced around several fly-by-night leagues in the 1940s. His claim to fame was a right-handed hook shot that no one could block since it was nearly impossible to get past his bulky torso to deflect it.

One of his first orders of business was to stock the Huskies with as many fellow New Yorkers as possible, conscripting players such as Dick Fitzgerald and younger brother Bob.

Training camp was held at St. Jerome College in Kitchener, and the players stayed in a hotel in nearby Galt.[5] The front office decided it would be a good idea to try out some Canadians, but they decided to hedge their bets by petitioning the league to exclude the local picks from the league-maximum 12-man roster — all of whom would likely be American. The minutes of a league board meeting held a month before opening night read that "allowing these [Canadian] players to enter the lineup in Toronto would serve to increase interest in the game."

The minutes also note that Detroit was the only team to vote against Toronto's motion, so the Huskies set out to look for homegrown athletes known as much for familiarity among Toronto fans as their on-court prowess. One call went out to two-sport star Hank Biasatti, who had just finished two stints of AAA baseball for the Toronto Maple Leafs of the International League, including time as a starting first baseman. Of the six Canucks at Huskies camp the 24-year-old seemed best-placed to crack Sadowski's roster. If things didn't work out, Biasatti planned to return to his true love of baseball, having shown promise just one notch below the Major Leagues.

As great an athlete as Biasatti was, he had nothing on another Canadian camp invitee, fellow Windsorite Joe Krol. The Toronto Argonaut was on the verge of being awarded the Lou Marsh Trophy as Canada's top athlete, but in football, not basketball. The man known as "King Krol" was a jack-of-all-trades who could punt, pass, and kick like no one in the history of the Canadian Football League. Krol played both sides of the line of scrimmage with equal aplomb, excelling at quarterback, halfback, defensive back, and punter. Krol acquitted himself quite well at Huskies camp, surviving until the final cut. Biasatti made the team and was one of two Canadians to crack an opening-day BAA roster along with B.C.'s Norm Baker, who made the lineup for the Chicago Stags. It was only fitting that the BAA's sole Canadians were a Windsorite and a Victorian, given that the two cities had been battling it out for senior championships and the title of Canada's basketball capital for more than a decade. Not long after Biasatti was selected, he and the Huskies agreed to a $650-a-month contract.

Toronto's first opponent would be the New York Knickerbockers, who travelled to Canada through Niagara Falls on the Wednesday before the game and were met with a less-than-enthusiastic reception, at least from one skeptical border agent. The guard noticed that several members of the group stood over six foot one — tall for those days — but he had no idea what coach Neil Cohalan was talking about when he identified the party as members of the Knicks. "I don't imagine you'll find many people up this way who understand your game — or have an interest in it either," the guard quipped dismissively.

Welcome to Canada.

The Knicks kept up their spirits enough to continue on to Toronto for practices as the Huskies made last-minute preparations for the first regular-season pro basketball game in Canadian history. Workers laid down a wooden court right on top of the ice at the Gardens — leading to a condensation problem that would plague Huskies games all season.

Fans began filing into Maple Leaf Gardens at 8:00 p.m. on Friday, November 1, 1946, as BAA president Maurice Podoloff and Toronto mayor Robert Saunders took part in opening ceremonies. The 48th Highlanders pipe and drum band played for the crowd, officially announced at 7,090. The team had earlier announced that any fan taller than six-foot-eight Toronto centre George Nostrand would get in for free. No one met the height standard, but reports say the team ended up giving away a number of free tickets anyway.

The Huskies walked on to the court wearing blue and white uniforms that would have been familiar colours to Leafs fans. The home team began its inaugural game on a positive note, winning the opening tip, but their first shot misfired and Knicks guard Ossie Schectman got the ball, passed to veteran backcourt mate Leo "Ace" Gottlieb, and got the ball right back for an open layup.

The Knicks scored the first three baskets of the game before the Huskies dropped in their first hoop. The fans were enthusiastic about the unfamiliar spectacle, so much so that they cheered no matter who scored, prompting *Toronto Star* sportswriter Joe Perlove to remark, "these people aren't basketball conscious."

Huskies forward Harry "Moose" Miller remembered that hockey was never far from the minds of the crowd. "Canadians didn't know a lot of the basketball terms. We'd be playing defence, the other team would be coming down the court, and the fans would be yelling 'Check him, check him.'"[6]

The visitors led 37–29 at the half, with the Huskies' offence consisting mainly of coach Ed Sadowski instructing his players to feed the ball to centre Ed Sadowski as often as possible.

The one-dimensional attack appeared ready to sink the Huskies, except that Big Ed was whistled for his fifth and disqualifying foul early in the second half. He was forced to replace himself with Nostrand, who made the most of his opportunity and led a furious charge capped by a layup that gave the home squad its first lead, 44–43. The Huskies led 48–44 heading into the fourth quarter.[7]

Biasatti hadn't been much of a factor in the game to that point (and wouldn't be for much of the season) but the crowd wanted that to change, chanting "Bi-a-sa-tti! Bi-a-sa-tti!" in a show of solidarity with their country-man. Though the game was tight down the stretch, Sadowski decided to put his untested Canadian reserve guard into the game, which didn't work out the way he had planned.

The *Toronto Telegram* reporter noted that Biasatti's "anxiousness ruined the play and one almost sure chance was blown."[8] The Knicks held on to a slim lead until the final buzzer, edging out the Huskies 68–66.

As Lew Hayman and his colleagues tallied their opening night take, they had no idea if they had a winner on their hands. The Leafs and the Argos were playing to sold-out crowds every night, but the projection of 12,000 fans a night for basketball seemed ambitious, to say the least.

The fact is that aside from the occasional barnstorming exhibition, Torontonians weren't acquainted with big-time basketball. On November 15, in their third home game, the Huskies rolled over the Providence

Steamrollers 85–68 to improve to 2–3, but crowds were already dwindling down to the 5,000 mark. Searching for a hook, team executive Vern DeGeer figured fans might show up to cheer on another Canadian.

DeGeer had been a sportswriter with the *Windsor Star* before joining the Huskies front office, and he remembered a talented scorer who had recently starred at Assumption College around the same time as Biasatti. Gino Sovran, like Biasatti, was of Italian descent and part of a golden generation of Windsor players who dominated high school, college, and club basketball in the first half of the 20th century. A national team made up mostly of players from the Windsor Ford V8s club team had won the silver medal for Canada at the 1936 Olympics, and 12-year-old Gino idolized the local heroes and dreamed of one day following in their footsteps.

Eventually growing to six foot three, above-average for a player in those days, Sovran scored exactly 1,000 points at Assumption from 1942 to 1945 and moved across the border to Detroit Mercy, where he studied engineering and was leading scorer on the basketball team in 1945–46.

Sovran had used up his four years of eligibility prior to the 1946–47 season and focused on his studies, which alternated one semester of class work with another semester of field work. The fall of 1946 was an engineering semester and Sovran was working on the Detroit campus one day when he received a cold call from DeGeer inviting him to try out for the Huskies, a team Sovran had never heard of.

Engineering was a far surer thing than pro basketball in those days, but Sovran decided to give it a shot, hopping on a train and showing up for a practice at the Toronto YMHA. The director of the Y was another Windsorite, 1930s Assumption star Bill Rogin, who knew Sovran and noticed the young student didn't even have shorts or a shirt. Rogin found a uniform so that Sovran would at least look the part and might even stand a chance at making a good showing for Sadowski.

Sovran was a very quiet young man, but his game was impressive enough that Sadowski asked him to hang around in Toronto while the team did some paperwork. A few days soon became a week, and still no news from the Huskies. Just when Sovran was wondering what he'd gotten himself into, he received word 10 days after the tryout that the Huskies were offering him a contract worth $550 a month.

The young student moved into a rooming house on King Street and took the streetcar to Maple Leaf Gardens for what he hoped would be a big debut. But with Big Ed calling the shots, and taking most of them on the court, there wasn't much room for anyone else, and certainly not much playing time for the soft-spoken Canadian.

His one moment in the sun came early in his Huskies stint when Sadowski put him into an overtime game. "That's the game where I scored almost all the points I made," he recalled. "I scored I think seven or eight points in that game. So an article in the Toronto paper said 'oh, boy, Sadowski's going to use him a lot more from now on.'"

But Sadowski had bigger fish to fry — Sovran recalls a "very dysfunctional" team that turned against their coach quite early on, because of the New Yorker's insistence on ordering players to feed him the ball constantly — not that the 21-year-old Sovran was about to complain. "I wasn't in a position to make many comments. I was one of the youngest guys on the team," said the Canadian, who added that there weren't many practices, or much in-game strategy. The Huskies would either dump it into Sadowski or bomb away from long range with their two-handed set shots, the latter option drawing ire from the coach. While the Canadian student kept his mouth shut, the same wasn't true for Sadowski's fellow New Yorkers, some of whom were said to have approached management to ask for a coaching change.

Sadowski also seemed to realize the ship was sinking in Toronto, since he failed to show up for a November 30 road game in Providence, Rhode Island. Forward Dick Fitzgerald was forced to take over, but the Huskies couldn't stop the Providence Steamrollers from charging to a 79–65 win.

Sportswriters back home had a field day with the headless Huskies. "The Toronto papers said 'how can you lose a guy who's six foot five and weighs 250 pounds?'" Sovran recalled reading in one paper.

It turns out that Sadowski had gone all the way to the top, approaching league president Maurice Podoloff to demand a trade to a contender. Even today's most entitled NBA superstars would never dare to attempt such a move.

Hayman suspended his petulant post player and soon traded him to Cleveland, installing Robert "Red" Rolfe as coach following a one-game stint by Hayman and three by Fitzgerald. Rolfe had coached the men's basketball team at Yale, but he was much better known as a steady third baseman for the New York Yankees back when Babe Ruth and Lou Gehrig ruled The Bronx. Sovran remembered Rolfe as "a very, very nice guy" who for the first time all season implemented offensive and defensive schemes, gently guiding his squires at practice in his distinctive New Hampshire accent.

The plan seemed to pay off initially as Toronto reeled off consecutive wins and finished December with a 6–4 record, though it came at the price of one Canadian player. Hank Biasatti was granted his release that month to focus on his budding baseball career, a gamble that paid off — his appearance with the Philadelphia Athletics in 1949 made him the only Canadian ever to play at the top pro level in both baseball and basketball.

The Huskies' other Canadian, meanwhile, wasn't exactly making an impression on Rolfe, who gave Sovran scant few minutes and usually in garbage time. But things were looking up just after Christmas as the team prepared to travel to Sovran's stomping grounds for a December 29 game against the Detroit Falcons.

He stayed in Windsor where he enjoyed an abbreviated holiday with his family. But much to the chagrin of his loved ones, Sovran remained nailed to the bench.

Back in Toronto after the game, he got more bad news from his coach. "That's when I was told that I was being cut by Red Rolfe," he said. "It was a disappointment, but I just got back to school in time for the next academic term, so I essentially didn't miss any school."

Sovran had been little more than a modestly paid benchwarmer, recording five field goals in six games and earning $1,100 for two months of work. Though casual fans might assume pro reserves can't play, Sovran knew differently. "I like to think I was a pretty good basketball player," he says, "but I think I can also recognize that they wanted another Canadian on the team. But I never felt I was overmatched when I was with that bunch."

When the Huskies returned to Toronto for a three-game homestand against Chicago, Boston, and Detroit, fans quickly realized that Sovran wasn't in his usual place on the bench, which didn't exactly stoke their enthusiasm for the team. Little did they know that behind the scenes things were unraveling as the Huskies had already hemorrhaged thousands of dollars. Hayman ramped up his sales pitch, looking for all sorts of promotions to draw fans to Maple Leaf Gardens. A January 23, 1947 ad in the *Toronto Star* touted a high school game between York Memorial and Etobicoke — perhaps not a bad idea since amateur teams had a longer history than the pros in the Queen City.

By January the pro product looked downright unfamiliar, with seven players traded away or released and several new faces added, including Leo Mogus and Dick Schultz, a pair acquired from Cleveland in December for Sadowski, Ray Wertis, and cash. Mogus ended up as the second-leading scorer on the team after Mike McCarron, but that didn't excite fans, who began to stay away in droves. By this time word of Toronto's troubles had filtered back to the league office amid rumours that the franchise might be relocated to Montreal, where co-owners Eric Craddock and Lew Hayman could piggyback off of their beloved Alouettes as well as the powerhouse Canadiens.[9]

But Hayman convinced the league office that he could at least finish out the season in Toronto before reassessing the team's future. He launched into even more aggressive publicity, offering free nylon stockings to the 100 fans who came closest to guessing the attendance at the following game. Unfortunately for Hayman, the promotion fell flat when the Ontario government ruled that the Huskies couldn't hand out nylons because of war-rationing rules that were still in effect.[10]

The Huskies' acquisition in February of seven-foot-one Ralph Siewert, the league's tallest player, might have presented brief potential as a publicity campaign, at least until team brass saw him play. Siewert ended up averaging just 1.1 points per game and was the team's worst shooter.

By the final month of the season it was obvious that the Huskies were running on fumes. Only 500 souls showed up for a game against Providence and the team limped to the finish line, winning just seven of its final 20 games to finish with a 22–38 record, tied for last with the Boston Celtics (in their pre–Auerbach and Cousy days when the team wasn't scaring anyone).

Toronto did get a measure of revenge against their Opening Night conquerors, beating the Knicks 71–61 in their final home game of the season. The Huskies then hit the road for Detroit where they were edged out 66–63 to finish out of the playoff race.

As winter turned to spring and the Philadelphia Warriors were crowned BAA champs, there was no official announcement about the future of the Huskies. In a straw poll of league clubs to decide which teams planned to participate in the 1947–48 season, the Huskies were listed as "not decided" at the May 21, 1947 Board of Governors meeting.

The Toronto owners were still officially undecided as the BAA began its second season of play in the fall of 1947 without Toronto on the schedule. The obvious was only made official following that second season, when at the May 10, 1948 Board of Governors meeting the Huskies were "cancelled" along with other "non-operating franchises" — Pittsburgh, Cleveland, Detroit, Buffalo, and Indianapolis.

Estimates of Huskies' financial losses during its only season of operation ranged from $100,000 to $215,000, and the size of the payroll might have been a factor. There were rumours that Ed Sadowski was paid a coach's salary on top of his league-high $10,000 player's contract, and Henry "Moose" Miller recalled that he and some of his teammates earned more than some of the Maple Leafs hockey players.

He said the Huskies and Leafs would occasionally travel on the same train and that the athletes would inevitably discuss money matters. "I was making $3,500 and I used to bitch and moan about that until I found out what some of the hockey players were making," Miller said in a 1996 interview to coincide with the 50th anniversary of Opening Night. "[The Leafs] were in the $2,400–$2,600–$2,800 range. They would say, 'What makes you so special?'"

Though Miller kept it a secret from his bosses at the time, he later admitted that he could have been had at a much cheaper price. "We were just so happy to be out of the service and [to] get the hell back home, we really would have played for nothing."

Also playing a role in the demise of the Huskies were the dynamics of a city whose fans clung much more tightly to hockey than some other North American markets where support for the sport was soft enough to leave room for other products. While Toronto had a core of basketball fans, the diehards were a tiny minority in the days before the metro population ballooned past five million and immigration diversified the city with an influx of Asian and West Indian newcomers.

Biasatti, who died just after the Toronto Raptors and Vancouver Grizzlies concluded their first season of play in 1996, said timing was not on the Huskies' side. "The fans just weren't ready for basketball," he once told the *Toronto Sun*. "But there's a big difference between then and now."

Big-time pro basketball wouldn't return to Toronto for 50 years, but at least the status of that opening game would be forever entrenched in history.

The BAA had been meeting with the rival National Basketball League (NBL) since May 1947 to discuss a merger, which was finalized in 1949 to create the National Basketball Association (NBA). Results, records, and statistics carried over from both older leagues, meaning that the November 1946 Huskies-Knicks showdown was officially considered to be the first game in NBA history.

But though the Huskies were one of the NBA's founding franchises, the experiment had died almost as soon as it began and big-time pro basketball in Canada would remain a distant dream for decades.

CHAPTER 5

– OLYMPIAN EFFORT –

A bespectacled, greying Dr. James Naismith held back tears as he placed Olympic medals around the necks of the two dozen basketball players at Berlin's Empire Sports Field as steady evening rain beat down on 900 athletes, officials, and spectators on August 14, 1936.

The 74-year-old inventor of the game had every right to be choked up with emotion — the winter diversion he had created nearly 50 years earlier was now an Olympic sport for the very first time, and his adopted United States and native Canada had made the final.

There was a mix of feelings in this gentlemanly, elderly eastern Ontarian orphan as he reflected on his life and legacy. Back in 1891 he resented the assignment from Dr. Luther Gulick, his boss in Springfield, to invent a new game at the YMCA Training School. But once he saw the wild enthusiasm that his game had generated, he became a tireless promoter of "Basket Ball."

The game had grown so quickly around the world that he found it impossible to keep track. "I have received numerous pictures of contests and courts from Australia to Alaska. In spite of the fact that I have also written many letters trying to determine just when basketball was introduced into other countries, I have been unable to gather complete and accurate data."

The photos from Japan, where basketball made its debut in 1900, must have been particularly curious to Dr. Naismith. Dressed in long, dark kimonos, two groups of men could be seen squaring off at centre court as a referee, dressed in dark trousers and a vest, prepared to toss up the ball. Dozens of spectators crowded around the court to get a glimpse of the new sport, which the Japanese called *basukettobo-ru.*

The Japanese and the Chinese took to the sport quickly, with both countries sending teams to the inaugural Olympic basketball tournament in 1936. Also representing Asia in Berlin was the Philippines, where some of the world's most passionate basketball fans can be found. The Filipinos went on to earn bragging rights over their larger Asian rivals with a fifth-place showing in Berlin that was the best of any Asian team in the 20th century.

But the United States and Canada were head and shoulders above the fray in 1936 with corporate support and a hoops tradition that far outstripped that of the 21 other nations gathered for the week-long elimination tournament.

The '36 Canadian team was an amalgam of the best of Canada's dual basketball hubs at the time — Windsor, Ontario, and Victoria, British Columbia. The Victoria Blue Ribbons, later known as the Dominoes, were stocked with the generation's best players, winning Canadian championships in 1933, 1935, 1939, 1942, and 1946. Collegiate and Senior A Windsor teams, meanwhile, competed with Victoria every step of the way and dominated the national club circuit in the 1940s. The western Ontario border town seemed destined for hoops dominance, what with its strategic location next to Detroit, where players could get a run against strong American teams or even cross the border to join them. It didn't hurt that Windsor was a smorgasbord of the very same Irish, Italian, Jewish, and Eastern European immigrants who were kings of the court across North America.

The added advantage for elite Windsor basketball was the support provided by its economic engine — the automotive industry — which spurred nearly unprecedented population growth between the two world wars.

American industrialist Henry Ford's pioneering assembly-line process revolutionized automotive production in 1904 and the Ford Motor Company of Canada began manufacturing cars in Windsor that very year. The industry ramped up to a new level in 1908 when the landmark Model T became the world's best and fastest-selling car. Windsor began to develop around the various tool and plant factories that popped up in town, with Ford City serving as the industrial nexus for the rapidly growing urban area.

Home to just under 18,000 people in 1911, Windsor's population had ballooned to 100,000 by the early 1930s with the amalgamation of four neighbouring municipalities. Ford had sold 20 million vehicles by the mid-1930s and the world's largest automaker was eager to outspend its rivals in peddling cars to every corner of every market.

Ford's hottest product in 1936 was the powerful, 90-horsepower V8 engine. First introduced in 1932, the flathead V8 was one of a kind, and with Ford's mass-production lines in high gear, millions of the cheap, efficient power plants soon hummed under the hoods of sedans, coupes, tractors, and army vehicles from Georgia to Guam.

Ford Canada was seeking sponsorship opportunities for its V8 at just the same time as legendary local basketball coach Gordon H. Fuller wanted financial support for his new team of local stars. Fuller had attractive credentials, as he had formed the first senior men's basketball team in the region a decade earlier, a squad that virtually owned the Ontario Senior Championship. Fuller-coached men's and women's teams won a total of 11 provincial titles and two national titles between 1926 and 1936. The Ford/Fuller partnership paired up two proven winners, and there was a formidable pool of players from which to build a team. They would be named the Windsor Ford V8s.

Obvious picks included the "Five Fighting Freshmen" from Windsor's Assumption College, a young core of talented 'ballers who had bested American competition in 1935 as winners of the cross-border Michigan-Ontario Collegiate Conference.

Assumption mainstays Irving "Toots" Meretsky and Stanley "Red" Nantais teamed up with local stars such as Scotsman Ian "Al" Allison and Jimmy Stewart to power up the V8 hoops machine. Detroit Tech engineering student Julius "Goldie" Goldman, an American, came across the river to serve as captain.[1]

The 1935–36 Ford V8s became a dominant force in senior basketball, putting them on a collision course with Canada's other hoops juggernaut — the Victoria Blue Ribbons.

Victoria had developed into a basketball centre largely on the strength of the YMCA and the Protestant Church. Introduced to the B.C. capital by educator Carey Pope in 1896, basketball quickly grew into a six-team league that included school and church teams as well as the 5th Regiment.[2]

One name loomed large over sports in the B.C. capital in the early 20th century — the Pedens. Scottish by descent just like Naismith, the Peden boys did it all, from rowing, to boxing, football, and basketball. William Peden was part of the first Victoria team to win the B.C. title in 1898, brother Johnny Peden was a member of the 1909 YMCA International League Basketball Champions and both teamed up with brothers Tommy, Bob, and Alex to play benefit games and exhibitions. They sharpened their shooting skills on iron rims with no backboards — a setup that left little margin for error but rewarded them with a knack for pinpoint accuracy that passed down to the next generation of the sporting clan.[3] Even as middle-aged men, the Peden brothers were a fixture on YMCA teams that won several Vancouver Island elimination tournaments.

The construction of a new YMCA building in 1913, coupled with the creation of the Sunday School Basketball League, allowed the Pedens and other players to develop their skills against top city competition and soon led to a golden age of hoops talent.

The first great Victoria team to make an impact outside of the city was the First Presbyterians. While earlier Victoria teams were unable to beat their Vancouver nemeses, the Presbyterians, known locally as the "First Pres" team, broke through and won the 1924 B.C. championship against steep odds.

They had received a last-minute telegram telling them to report to Vancouver within 24 hours to take on the YMCA team in that city. With regional air travel nonexistent, the players boarded a steamship to the mainland, got to the Y that same evening, and promptly beat the home team 30–23.[4]

By the early 1930s, Victoria's Sunday School League had given way to the Victoria City Basketball League, which included a powerhouse founded by local cager Ross "Bud" Hocking, who had gathered together other top players including recently graduated high school standout Chuck Chapman. Together the team, called the Pedens and later the Commercials, fought their way up the ranks of B.C. basketball but couldn't quite break through until a food maker gave them the opportunity of a lifetime.

The Blue Ribbon Tea Company of Canada had a basketball aficionado, J.A. "Barney" Barnwell, as a representative in Victoria, and in 1932 he came up with the idea of financing the team on the condition that they be rechristened the Blue Ribbons.

Bud Hocking voiced no objection, and with Barnwell scheduling games and managing the business side of the operation the players were finally free to begin carving up opponents. Their bench boss was Victoria High School Head Coach Ernie Cook, a teacher and former hockey player who also had a passion for hoops.

Success came right away as they grabbed the city, provincial, and Western Canada titles to set up a matchup against Gord Fuller's Windsor/Walkerville Alumni for the 1933 Dominion of Canada championship. Victoria prevailed, beginning an east-west rivalry that would be the greatest and most enduring in Canadian senior men's basketball history.

The Blue Ribbons won their second national title in 1935 with a victory over Assumption College and its Five Fighting Freshmen. The Blue Ribbons changed their name to the Dominoes the following year and they sported spectacular talent, with Art Chapman joining brother Chuck and boy wonder Doug Peden, the second generation of the Victoria sporting dynasty and one of the greatest athletes Canada has ever known. The 20-year-old Peden was a multisport star who excelled in soccer, basketball, cricket, tennis, and other sports.

With the Ford V8s having beaten Ottawa to take the Eastern Canada title, the stage was set for a final in April 1936 with the highest possible stakes. Both teams knew that the winner would represent Canada at the first Olympic basketball tournament that counted for medals.

Basketball had been an exhibition sport as far back as the 1904 Games in St. Louis but the tournament consisted only of American teams. The winning side that year was the Kansas City AC Blue Diamonds, one of the top AAU basketball teams of the era featuring sharpshooter Forrest Clare "Phog" Allen, who also played for the University of Kansas under one James Naismith. Allen was an innovator and a dreamer as well as a player, and he envisioned not only national college basketball championships but also Olympic competitions that would pit the best teams in the world against each other. He tried and failed to have basketball upgraded to a demonstration sport for the 1932 Games in Los Angeles, as officials chose American football instead.

Forty years had passed since Naismith invented the game and in private letters the Canadian expat expressed exasperation at the fact that basketball still flew under the IOC's radar. "Basket ball, I think, comes the most nearly being [*sic*] an International game of any of the sports," Naismith wrote in the early 1930s. "Yet it has been impossible to get it included among the Olympic sports, perhaps because the United States is so far ahead in their technique and skill in playing the game."[5]

But Coach Phog Allen was persistent, and at his urging the IOC finally agreed in 1934 to include basketball as a medal sport at the upcoming Games in Germany,[6] giving new urgency to the 1936 Canadian Basketball Championship between Victoria and Windsor. The three-game series drew throngs of fans to Kennedy Collegiate high school, the sprawling new gothic-style institution that was the pride of Windsor. Despite Victoria's size advantage, Windsor's well-drilled rotation stormed to a clean sweep and a berth in Berlin. All wasn't lost for the B.C. 'ballers, however, as Coach Fuller added three Dominoes to his Olympics-bound team — Chuck and Art Chapman and Doug Peden.

But now a new problem emerged — a lack of funds. The Canadian economy was still recovering from the Great Depression, and the public purse was so stretched that the COC wouldn't provide the athletes with any financing. Even canoer Frank Amyot, Canada's only gold medalist at the 1936 Games, got to Berlin only by paying his own way.

Enter Gordon Fuller, who got back in touch with his sponsors at Ford[7] and tapped them for enough cash to send not only 14 basketball players but also five officials and five wives.[8]

Fuller gathered his squad in Windsor for summer training camp and couldn't help but be pleased with what he saw. Young, strapping, and athletic, the guys knew their plays and were excited at their prospects for a medal. Doug Peden was the youngest player on the squad at 20 years of age, and Ian Allison from the V8s was the oldest at 29. The two Fighting Freshmen, Merestky, 24, and Nantais, 25, were in their primes.

Canada had more top-level experience than the Europeans, who had only begun competing for continental championships the previous year, with Latvia taking the title over Spain. The Asian teams, while enthusiastic about basketball, were at a severe height disadvantage. The South Americans, particularly Uruguay and Argentina, could pose more of a problem given that they had played in continental championships beginning in 1930.

The big stumbling block would certainly be the Americans, and the game's inventor had a lot to do with their favoured status. U.S. college and AAU basketball had taken off like nowhere else, thanks largely to Naismith and his student Phog Allen, who in 1907 succeeded his mentor as head basketball coach at the University of Kansas in Lawrence. Intensely competitive, Allen was the first college coach to spearhead a basketball dynasty in the days before March Madness, leading the Jayhawks to 24 conference titles and three national championships.

His dominance from Lawrence triggered an arms race among collegiate athletic departments that sought out coaches and players who could compete with Allen's Jayhawks. The momentum has yet to abate, as college basketball has become one of the most valuable sports properties in the world today, commanding multi-billion-dollar TV contracts and a rabid international following.

Five college teams were among the eight squads that converged on Madison Square Garden in early April 1936 for the qualifying tournament to decide America's Olympic representative. Naismith, who travelled to New York to witness the spectacle, was certainly happy about the presence of the AAU champion McPherson Globe Oilers, based in McPherson, Kansas, just three hours from Lawrence. He was even more thrilled when the Oilers advanced to the finals where they squared off against Hollywood's Universal Pictures team, which McPherson had just beaten for the AAU title two weeks earlier in Denver.[9] The Universals gained a measure of revenge in New York, edging out the Oilers 44–43.

As the winners, the Universals had the right to pick seven players while McPherson contributed five. University of Washington centre Ralph Bishop was the sole collegian on the roster. Universal's mammoth forward duo of six-foot-nine Willard Schmidt and six-eight Joe Fortenberry were the tallest players in the entire Olympic tournament, with two-time AAU all-star Fortenberry possessing skill to boot. Referred to as "athletic freaks" by *Time* magazine, the two American giants stunned observers and media alike at the New York City trials when they eschewed the usual layup shots and took their game above the rim.

"The McPherson version of a layup shot left observers simply flabbergasted," Arthur J. Daley wrote in the *New York Times*. "Joe Fortenberry, 6-foot-8-inch center, and Willard Schmidt, 6-foot-9-inch forward, did not use an ordinary curling toss. Not those giants. They left the floor, reached up, and pitched the ball downward into the hoop, much like a cafeteria customer dunking a roll in coffee."[10]

Daley's turn of phrase might have been the first reference to a dunk in the history of basketball, but Schmidt and Fortenberry's height advantage was good for far more than style points at the Olympics because of one of Naismith's original rules stipulating that there be a jump ball after every basket. The rule would naturally favour a team with a tall player who was in a great position to give his side one possession after another. The United States had two such trump cards while Canada found itself down a man from the start.

Goldie Goldman, the most dominant player on the V8s during the 1935–36 season, could only make the trip to Germany as an assistant coach since his U.S. citizenship disqualified him from wearing the red and white. Fuller nonetheless seemed confident about his team's chances in an interview with the *Toronto Daily Star* on the eve of the transatlantic voyage. "There seems to be an opinion among some people that we wouldn't stand a chance against the United States teams," Fuller told the paper. "We wouldn't want to go over unless we had a chance."[11]

One great equalizer in Berlin was going to be the weather, since all of the games were to be played outdoors. To prepare his team for the elements, Fuller gathered the men on an outdoor schoolyard court in Windsor and put them through their paces in the summer heat.

The national teams would also have to contend with quirky Olympic rules, including a stipulation that coaches were not allowed to communicate with their players during the game. In addition, any player who was removed from a game could not return to the court during the same half.

Canada, however, was prepared for the challenge, with assistant coach Julius Goldman noting that the rules framework had been in place in international competition for some time.[12]

Rule books packed away, the Canadian contingent boarded the *Duchess of Bedford* ocean liner in Montreal and set off for the first leg of their trip on July 20, 1936.[13]

Five days earlier, the U.S basketball team had steamed out of New York City for Germany aboard the SS *Manhattan* with more than 320 other athletes, including track star Jesse Owens.[14] Also along for the ride was a Canadian guest — Dr. James Naismith. He made the trip after a heartwarming show of love and respect for his near half-century of devotion to mind, body, and spirit through basketball. The National Association of Basketball Coaches, at Phog Allen's request, began a nation-wide fundraising campaign to gather enough travel money for Naismith to be honoured at the Games for his role as inventor of the sport. All over the United States at high school games, AAU senior matches, and college showdowns, pennies were collected in huge numbers to form the Naismith Fund. It swelled to $5,000 through contributions culled from nearly every basketball game played in the United States between February 9 and February 15. Money was even raised in Naismith's home-town of Almonte.[15]

As the SS *Manhattan* neared Europe, the *Duchess* steamed up the St. Lawrence for open water as Coach Fuller tried to set up practices on the ship's deck. But things didn't work out as planned aboard the vessel known as the "Drunken Duchess" for its tendency to bob forcefully atop Atlantic waves. The Canadians suddenly found themselves short of equipment as two balls bounced off the deck and right into the ocean.[16]

Staying fit was all the more challenging due to the luxury service aboard the *Duchess*, with reams of food so irresistible that two Canadian boxers "ate themselves right out of their weight division."[17]

Fortunately, the basketball players managed to make weight despite the eight-day voyage, and they had ten days to practise on dry, and solid, land before the tournament got underway on August 7.

Everyone knew that the Olympic tournament would be played out-doors, but no one was prepared for what they saw when they arrived at Berlin's Imperial Sports Field. Organizers, apparently unfamiliar with the sport of basketball, had erected the goals on clay and dirt tennis courts. That might not have posed much of a problem under clear skies, but while Hitler's fascist regime tried to control most everything in Germany, the weather was beyond their grasp. In an ominous sign of things to come, light rain wafted down on the moustachioed Fuehrer and 110,000 others who gathered at the sprawling Olympiastadion for the opening ceremonies on August 1.

Sam Balter, a Jewish member of the U.S. basketball team, mocked the Germans as he remembered the court conditions years later. "The Nazi men-tality, which was supposed to be the apotheosis of detail and organization, had certainly misfired," Balter told *Sports Illustrated* in 1996. "Why hadn't the Master Organizers bothered to find out basketball was an indoor game?"[18]

Field conditions were temporarily forgotten as the Canadians, proudly sporting white Maple Leaf emblems on their red blazers, marched into Olympiastadion with nearly 4,000 other athletes from 49 countries. Toots Meretsky, the only Jewish athlete on the basketball team, remembered gazing up at Hitler's platform and feeling none of the fear and dread that one might expect given the hatred Hitler felt for Meretsky's people. Instead, the prevailing thought in the head of the 24-year-old was how comical the dictator looked with his short moustache, beady eyes, and high boots. *He looks like Charlie Chaplin!* Meretsky thought as the fascist leader and his cronies raised their hands in Nazi salutes to the teams parading past their stand.

War was still three years away and Canada still favoured appeasement of the Nazis, but Meretsky was well aware that his fellow Jews were already suffering under Hitler's rule. The Nuremberg Laws had stripped German Jews of their citizenship the previous year, and Jews, blacks, and others were barred from marrying ethnic Germans. The IOC had awarded the Games to Germany prior to the Nazi rise to power in 1933 and considered moving the event over concerns that Hitler would use the Games as a platform for his racist ideology.

The IOC decided to keep the games in Germany following a meeting between the organization's president, Henri de Baillet-Latour, and Hitler in late 1935. But left-leaning and Jewish organizations in Canada pushed hard for a boycott and the president of the Canadian Jewish Congress, S.W. Jacobs, wrote to Prime Minister R.B. Bennett to push the matter. Meanwhile, boycott supporters in Europe announced the People's Olympiad, an alternate sporting event that was scheduled to be held in Barcelona just prior to the Berlin event. But the plan was derailed on the eve of the event after Spanish army general Emilio Mola attempted a coup that plunged Spain into civil war.

The Canadian Olympic Committee held off on making its own boycott decision until it saw what the Americans and the British would do. Both countries decided to send their athletes to Germany once they received assurances from Hitler that Jews would be permitted to compete and would not be mistreated.

Much to the consternation of boycott supporters, the COC quickly passed a motion to compete in Berlin. The most prominent Canadian Jewish athlete to stay home was lightweight boxing champion Sammy Luftspring of Toronto, who boycotted the Olympics after pressure from family and members of the local Jewish community.

Toots Meretsky had no such plans, figuring that a good showing by a basketball team with a Jewish player would send a stronger message than a boycott.[19] "A lot of people will ask, 'Being Jewish, why did you go to Berlin in the first place?'" he said in a 1991 interview. Listen, we won the [Canadian] championship, and I looked forward to it."[20]

Meretsky wanted to see for himself what Jews were experiencing under Hitler's hostile rule, travelling to Jewish areas of Berlin where he was met with an eerie quiet. "No one was on the streets, and the shades were drawn," he said. "I knocked at a few doors and was finally let in. It was obvious they were all scared."[21]

Canada's first game of the tournament was against Brazil on August 7. It turned out to be a tough matchup, with Fuller's men jumping out to a 14–7 halftime lead before Brazil played them even in the second half and fell short 24–17.

Among the many idiosyncrasies the Canadians faced was the soccer-style German-made ball, which was quite a bit smaller than a regulation basketball and "wobbled when it was passed and took odd bounces when it was dribbled."[22]

With Brazil behind them, Canada became progressively more dominant, dispatching of the European champs from Latvia by 11, Switzerland by 18, and Uruguay by 22 before recording their biggest blowout of the Games, a 42–15 drubbing of Poland in which young Doug Peden scored a tournament-high 18 points.

On the other side of the draw, the Americans ran into an unexpected adversary — FIBA itself. In what must have seemed a blatant bid to curb their dominance, the Americans were told there would be a height limit of six foot three, which would have kept half of their giant team on the sidelines. The Americans protested, and FIBA backed off, but the team still had to contend with a seven-player limit for each game. Head coach James

Needles shrugged off the latter restriction, splitting his 14-man squad into two and having them alternate games while the other side rested.

They didn't even need to dress for their first game against Spain since that team had been called home for the civil war.

The U.S. road to the final was even easier than it had been for the Canadians, as a 52–28 steamrolling of Estonia was followed by a 56–23 shellacking of the Philippines and a relatively low-scoring 25–10 triumph over Mexico, the eventual bronze medalists. Fortenberry and his AAU teammate, five-eleven guard Francis Johnson, had emerged as the best players on the team along with high-scoring Universals guard Sam Balter and six-foot-seven forward Frank Lubin. The big U.S. centres were particularly effective at stopping opponents' shots above the rim, as there were no rules against goaltending at the time.

James Naismith had split allegiances in Berlin. Although he had arrived in the German capital with the American team on July 31 and spent time with them for his first couple of days, he was also eager to catch up with the Canadians. He got his wish after the opening ceremony when the Windsor players held a special reception for him.[23] Naismith also spent time watching practices during that week leading up to the start of the tournament. He was astonished at the progress that he saw — the players were bigger and the game was faster, with much more dribbling than he had envisioned when he dreamt up the sport.

He was nonetheless wary of excessive innovations and actually opposed rule changes in American ball such as the elimination of the centre jump and the 10-second limit to advance the ball from the backcourt.

But he was certainly not opposed to the fact that the game had spread to dozens of countries and had attained Olympic status within his lifetime. "There is little doubt that this did much to increase the interest in basketball over the entire world," he wrote not long after the Games.[24]

The Can-Am showdown was ready to go on August 14 and Naismith was in attendance, but the weather did not co-operate. Steady rain had turned the court into a muddy mess, delaying tipoff for 25 minutes, and the Canadian wives and other officials couldn't even seek refuge as the absence of grandstands forced them to sit or stand around the court. But if anyone was so much as thinking about postponing the match, they could forget about it. The Canadians had already booked their return ocean liner trip.[25]

Mary Stewart, wife of team captain Jimmy Stewart, covered herself with a Hudson's Bay blanket to keep warm in temperatures that hovered around 12 degrees Celsius as the Chinese referee finally got things under-way at around 6:30 p.m.

Coach Fuller sent out Stewart along with leading scorer Doug Peden, Dominoes teammate Art Chapman, British-born passing and defensive ace Malcolm "Red" Wiseman, and Ian Allison, who had provided steady scoring in the previous five games.

The jump ball against big Texan Fortenberry was a moot point and Canada focussed on defence. But the Americans were quick as well as tall, and their shooting coupled with Fortenberry's inside dominance on both ends had the Canadians against the ropes at halftime, 15–4, which was about the best score one could have expected given the near-unplayable conditions.

There was hardly any dribbling because of the muddy court, and wind blew the ball around wildly before it had a chance to drop into the basket. "We couldn't execute any plays," said Canadian guard Ed Dawson. "When the ball hit the water it didn't move, so we simply passed the ball around. Michael Jordan could have slid from foul line to foul line and scored a basket without taking steps."[26]

American forward Frank Lubin, who didn't dress for the game and watched from the sideline, later recalled that "it was almost like watching a water-polo match."[27]

At the halftime break, Fuller and his muddy, drenched players needed to come up with a plan to get back into the game, and that's when Julius Goldman spoke up, suggesting the team switch to a zone defence to stop penetration by U.S. guards Francis Johnson, Carl Wheatley, and Carl Shy.

The strategy worked in the second half as the Canadians bottled up their rivals, but the slippery ball hindered their own offence, as well. A *Toronto Star* reporter observed that "the North American neighbours battled the conditions as well as each other."[28]

Though Canada tied the Americans 4–4 in the second half, they couldn't make a dent in the big first-half lead and the Americans cele-brated the historic victory at the final whistle. Fortenberry led all scor-ers with eight points to match the entire Canadian total, completing a tournament-leading 14.5 points-per-game average. Four of the top eight tournament scorers were American, with Doug Peden placing ninth at 8.4 points per game.

Team captain Stewart made sure that the Americans didn't make off with that dreaded greasy ball, so he grabbed it and walked over to his wife, Mary, who stood at the sideline. He put the ball under her blanket and it's been a family heirloom ever since.

As players lined up to receive their medals from Naismith, coaches Fuller and Goldman knew they would only be able to watch the proud moment from a distance, since the IOC has never awarded medals to coaches in any sport. Nor would there be any medals for the six players who didn't appear in any games — Norman Dawson, Alphonse Freer, Donald Gray, Robert Osborne, Stanley "Red" Nantais, and Thomas Pendlebury. And there was another odd man out — Toots Meretsky, who had appeared in games against Latvia and Brazil, scoring a total of four points. The Nazis had only prepared eight silver medals, though nine Canadians had made a game appearance, meaning that Meretsky and the six reserves only received commemorative medals.

Meretsky still had much for which to be thankful — after all, his experience in Berlin had proven that Hitler's claims of Aryan superiority in athletics were a crock. In fact, Meretsky was one of 13 Jewish athletes who won medals at "Hitler's Olympics." Meretsky also found time to befriend another athlete whose dominance irked the German leader — black American track star Jesse Owens. Owens did his part to discredit white supremacy by winning a then-record four gold medals. Team Canada assistant coach Julius Goldman also managed to get 140 autographs from various medal-winning athletes onto one very valuable photograph. Rather than profit from the memento, he later donated it to the Olympic museum at Colorado Springs.[29]

As the Canadians boarded a train for England and the eventual ocean liner trip home, the satisfaction of a silver medal was tempered by thoughts of what might have been. What if the court hadn't been a sloppy mess? What if they had gone to the zone sooner to slow down that darned giant Fortenberry?

The Ford Motor Company of Canada had a crazy idea that wouldn't change the outcome but would certainly cause a frenzy in Windsor. They scheduled a rematch, this time under "good weather conditions." The series would be played at Kennedy Collegiate, and with the world auto giant backing the showdown, it didn't take long for the Universals to agree to make the 3,700-kilometre trek across 10 states for the highly anticipated match.

Twelve-year-old Gino Sovran, an aspiring local player, was among the crowd that packed the Kennedy gym for the two-game total points series. He remembers that even without Joe Fortenberry and Willard Schmidt, the Americans still posed matchup problems for the Canadians. "The U.S. team won, their tall center getting the jump that was required after each basket," said Sovran.[30]

Oh, that pesky centre jump! The Americans had so much height at all levels of basketball that Naismith's rule could lock up his adopted country's basketball dominance for decades to come. Surely there must have been some way to level the playing field!

Canada's hopes, and those of the rest of the world, lay with American Julius Goldman, who was not only a loyal Ford V8 but also, most conveniently, Canada's representative on the International Rules Committee for basketball. The rules meetings would set the framework for future tournaments in the new Olympic sport. They also put the adopted Canadian on a collision course with the adopted American and inventor of the game.

James Naismith made a point to sit in on the Berlin meetings and, much to his dismay, realized that Goldman was proposing to consign his treasured centre jump to the dustbin of history. Dr. Naismith had borrowed the centre jump idea from football, where he believed the kickoff added suspense to the game.[31]

Naismith was even more dismayed when every single delegate, no doubt aware of their countries' height disadvantage vis-a-vis the United States, supported Goldman's motion. Naismith proposed several compromises, including having the referee toss the ball high or rotating players for the jumps, but to no avail.[32]

Japan then went after the Americans again, bringing back the idea of height classes. Though the Asian power was on the verge of war with Europe, the two were allies in that committee room as they isolated the Americans by agreeing on a six-foot-four cut-off for a first division, called class No. 1, of the Olympic tournament. Any team with taller players would be forced to enter class No. 2, and the rule change was to take effect for the 1940 Olympics. Prior to the meetings, the other nations had already agreed to enter all of their teams in class No. 1, and Goldman realized the implications for his country of birth. "The result would be only the U.S.A. would enter class No. 2. None of other teams had players taller than [six foot four] so class No. 2 would wither away," he wrote on the 60th anniversary of the Berlin Olympics.[33]

The Second World War led to the cancellation of the 1940 and 1944 Olympics, and the idea of height classes was later rescinded, potentially paving the way for America to run roughshod over the rest of the world unless Team Canada — or the International Rules Committee — could stop them.

The game of basketball had come full circle during that gold-medal basketball game on August 14, 1936. Canada and the United States had such a head start on the rest of the world that it appeared they could battle it out for Olympic gold for years, maybe decades. On the women's side, the Edmonton Grads had barely lost to Americans or anyone else for 25 years. Their dominance seemed to be a sign that Canadian women would continue a stranglehold over the sport that would be the envy of their male counterparts.

But Berlin in fact marked the start of a split in the basketball destinies of these two North American neighbours, who would pursue wildly different paths in the postwar era. It turned out that elite basketball was nearing a peak in Canada, while south of the border it was just getting started. Nineteen thirty-six was as close as Team Canada would ever get to gold at the Olympics or the Worlds in the 20th century and well beyond.

CHAPTER 6

– JACK'S BIG DREAM –

Canada showed so much success in international basketball in the 1920s and 1930s that one would have thought a century of dominance was a foregone conclusion. The Edmonton Grads cast an imposing shadow over women's basketball, going undefeated in four Olympic exhibition tournaments and posting an unprecedented 502–20 record. The 1936 Olympic men's team, fed by players from the twin hoops capitals of Windsor and Victoria, had won a silver medal and posed the biggest threat to the emerging American hoops juggernaut. But by the 1950s it was clear that the game had passed Canada by.

In the postwar era the national team repeatedly found itself falling short in the early rounds of the Worlds and the Olympics as hemispheric and European rivals began challenging for medals in the suddenly wide-open international scene. The United States men's team, meanwhile, was untouchable as they steamrolled to seven consecutive Olympic golds from 1936 to 1968, failing to drop a single game.

The proliferation of professional leagues around the world had left Canada at a disadvantage in major international tournaments as they made do with a revolving door of hastily built senior amateur teams. One by one, countries such as Brazil, Mexico, Uruguay, and the Soviet Union began to run past Canada in world basketball, with the Soviets becoming the world's second-strongest hoops power by the late 1950s. The U.S.S.R. routinely routed Canada at the Olympics as well as the World Championships where Canada made its debut in 1954 with a 2–7 record. Among its losses in '54 was a defeat at the hands of the Philippines, which went on to win bronze for the best showing by an Asian team in the history of the Worlds.

The Filipinos had vaulted past China and Japan to take control of Asian basketball, buoyed by its wildly popular MICAA industrial league.

After a ninth-place finish in 1956 in Melbourne, Australia, the bottom fell out for Canada in 1960 as the national champion Tillsonburg Livvies failed to finish in the top five of the qualifier in Bologna, Italy. Canada had missed the Olympic basketball tournament for the first time, and its national-team program couldn't even be seen as floundering because the program didn't actually exist.

The Canadian Amateur Basketball Association (CABA) was mainly focussed on national championships and regulatory matters, giving little time or money to its other mandate to field Olympic teams. Paul Thomas, player-coach of the 1952 national champion Livvies, remembered comparing notes with rivals at the Helsinki Olympics that year only to find that even the most destitute nations were outspending Canada when it came to basketball.

"We were given a daily stipend of $2 a day," he said. "India got $12 a day. The poorest countries in the world like India had far, far more than we ever did. But this was Canada's approach."

Practice time was another luxury that Canada simply couldn't afford, a fact that the world media discovered when they interviewed the young coach in Finland.

"They said 'how long have your been practicing for the Olympics?' I said three. They said 'three what? Three years? Three months?' I said no, three practices."

Compare that to the Argentineans, who had reportedly completed a months-long training camp in the Andes mountains in hopes of giving them an aerobic advantage in relatively low-altitude Helsinki. Though Argentina finished just out of the medals in 1952, it was clear the South American country was heading in a very different direction than Canada where basketball was concerned.

While Canadian championships had previously filled major arenas and Olympic anticipation captivated fans across the country, sports officials thought so little of basketball by 1964 that they were prepared to skip the Games in Tokyo altogether. The national champion Toronto Dow Kings faced the cold, hard reality of indifference when members contacted the CABA to ask about the pre-Olympic qualifier in Yokohama, Japan. Officials said that they'd be happy to support the transpacific trip as long as the Dow Kings raised the $35,000 travel bill all by themselves, proof positive that Canada's postwar boom hadn't trickled down to the world of basketball. But the Dow Kings were undeterred, and each of the players chipped in $1,500 while persuading corporate sponsors to back them up. The CABA agreed to refund the money if the Dow Kings qualified, and with the promise of repayment lifting their spirits, the Toronto boys travelled to Japan and went 7–2 to make the field for Tokyo.[1]

But once the Games tipped off, the euphoria died off as the thermometer rose in the scorching Pacific rim heat, and the red and white quickly found themselves overwhelmed by better-organized and better funded opponents. Canada didn't even have a full-time coach, with 30-year-old University of Toronto alum Ruby Richman doing double duty as player and bench boss. Canada lost its first seven games in Tokyo, including a 21-point shellacking at the hands of host Japan and two losses to Hungary. Their 1–8 record placed them 14th out of 16 teams — Canada's worst-ever showing at the Summer Games.

Things got even worse as Canada failed to qualify for the 1968 Games, prompting the CABA to introduce some stability that had been sorely missing over the previous three decades. Nine different coaches and more than 100 players was simply not a recipe for success, so officials approached long-time University of British Columbia men's basketball coach Peter Mullins, an Australian-born member of the 1959 national team and a proven winner on the university scene. He was named as the program's first permanent, full-time coach and he immediately set about putting together a squad to qualify for the 1970 World Championships in Ljubljana, Yugoslavia. For the first time, players across Canada had a shot at glory, and Mullins picked Maritimers Rod Cox, a University of New Brunswick legend from Saint John, and six-foot-five Dalhousie centre John Cassidy, a mainstay in the Nova Scotia Senior Men's League. Tillsonburg Livvies legend Barry Howson of London, Ontario, became the first black Canadian ever to wear the red and white. To those semi-pro stars Mullins added six members of his high-powered and undefeated UBC national champions, including creative All-Canadian Ron Thorsen. The California-born, Prince George–raised playmaker was a spiritual precursor to Steve Nash, dominating with his "quick driving, accurate passing, ability to score points and his unselfish team play."[2]

Unfortunately, history repeated itself for Canada's first truly national team, which found itself overmatched in Yugoslavia. They dropped the first five games, including a nine-point loss to Korea, and lambastings at the hands of Brazil (by 53 points) and even Cuba (by 33). Though Mullins's crew rallied to win its final three games, they ended up in 10th place — their third consecutive finish in that spot or lower at a World Championship.

The following year, Mullins again led Canada at the 1971 Pan-American Games, where the top two finishers automatically qualified for the 1972 Olympics. But Canada only managed an eighth-place finish, and Mullins's days on the bench seemed to be numbered.

The program was on the verge of missing two consecutive Olympics for the first time in its history, and the timing couldn't have been worse. Montreal had beaten out Moscow and Los Angeles for the right to host the 1976 Olympics, and Canadian sports officials realized that basketball was one of many sports that needed a shot in the arm if there was to be any hope of winning medals on home soil. All of the national sports organizations were moved to a building in suburban Ottawa and their budgets were beefed up.

For the first time in its history, the Canadian Amateur Basketball Association had money to bring in a top-flight coach and try to build a winner. This time, officials were prepared to cast a wide net as they sought their saviour. They even contacted basketball's world governing body, FIBA, hoping for a bite. Job postings were also mailed south of the border to tap into that seemingly bottomless pool of coaching talent that had been nurtured in the exploding college basketball scene that James Naismith set in motion 70 years earlier at the University of Kansas.

John Patrick "Jack" Donohue was a coaching lifer who had known his calling even before he graduated from Fordham University in Manhattan. He did an undergraduate in economics and a Master's in health education, but his extracurricular time spent as a volunteer basketball coach was an indication of where his heart really lay.

He would have been ready to jump full-time into coaching upon graduation in 1952, but Uncle Sam had other ideas and the 19-year-old was drafted into the U.S. Army and sent over to Korea to repair tanks.

Upon his return home in 1954, Donohue found a teaching job at an elementary school before he got right back to realizing his dream, coaching basketball at St. Nicholas of Tolentine High School in the Bronx. The wins started piling up, and by 1959 the 28-year-old was head coach at Power Memorial Academy, an all-boys Catholic school in Manhattan. It was the perfect spot for this Irish Catholic boy from Yonkers, and his hard-driving style mixed with life lessons for the youngsters led to plenty of wins.

A favourite saying of Donohue's came from his father, John Joseph, who told him "if it is important enough to you, shoot for the moon and if you come up short you're still in the stars." He also put his own spin on his father's optimistic mantra, telling players to "dream big dreams."

It was a great slogan for an overachiever, and the young coach had built Power Memorial into a formidable force even before ninth-grader Ferdinand Lewis Alcindor joined the varsity squad, sprung up to seven foot two inches, and became the best player in America. With Alcindor swatting shots in defence and lofting elegant hook shots on the other end, Power won 71 games in a row and three city titles, with the undefeated 1963–64 team later earning the title "Team of the Century" in a vote by U.S. sportswriters.

Donohue, who ran a popular summer basketball camp in the Catskill Mountains, was by then well-known in cast coast basketball circles for his winning ways as well as his wit and self-deprecating manner. He would often deflect accolades with the same line: "God is good to dumb Irishmen."

Alcindor graduated and moved on to UCLA, becoming one of the dominant players in college basketball history before repeating his excellence in the NBA, where he converted to Islam and changed his name to Kareem Abdul-Jabbar. Donohue, meanwhile, had taken a job in 1965 at Holy Cross University in Worcester, Massachusetts, a once proud program that had slipped off the national radar. After a 10–16 first season, Donohue reeled off six consecutive winning campaigns, but by 1971 his combative style began to rub his bosses the wrong way, according to his biographer, Quebec basketball coach Mike Hickey, whose tender, hilarious, and loving Donohue biography *Dream Big Dreams* was published in 2006.

"He was having a lot of trouble with Holy Cross, the administration," said Hickey, who, like Donohue, is an Irish Catholic originally from the New York City area. "One thing that Jack was not good at was having bosses. As the head coach he sort of ran his own thing."

When the administration refused to let Donohue upgrade the Crusaders program by scheduling games against bigger schools, Donohue was miffed. When his bosses nixed a planned California trip that would have pitted the Crusaders against college powers UCLA and USC, Donohue was positively steamed. Relations between the head-strong 40-year-old and the administration became poisoned, and it was clear that Donohue wouldn't be long for the Massachusetts school. Jack started to look around, and was considering a job offer from the Florida Institute of Technology (F.I.T.), when a colleague stopped by his office at Holy Cross and passed along an unusual job posting.

"[He] dropped an ad for the Canadian National Team on my desk and said that I would do a good job coaching a country," Donohue later recalled.[3] He put it in his desk and forgot about it. Canada? Do they even play basketball up there? But he later came across the piece of paper and decided to apply, since he knew the 1971–72 season would be his swan song in Worcester.

His main focus was the F.I.T. offer, and he and his wife Mary Jane went down to Melbourne, Florida, for some house-hunting. But Canada wanted him more than he realized, and upon his return to Worcester, he received a call from Ottawa asking him to come in for an interview. Not missing a beat, he asked them how many people were applying for the job. Not impressed that he was among 25 candidates, Donohue told them to call him back when he was higher on their list.[4]

Mary Jane knew that Florida, despite the warm winters, wasn't for her Jack. It was a Division II school, after all, a step down from Holy Cross. And what's more, those persistent Canadians called Jack up to Toronto, where he was one of three finalists for the job. Of the nearly 200 resumes the CABA received, only Americans made the final cut — Donohue, Robert Samaras, who coached the University of Windsor to five national titles but is originally from Michigan, and Gilbert "Gib" Chapman, who won the 1971 CIAU Championship with Acadia but is originally from Houlton, Maine, on the New Brunswick border.

Selection committee member Murray Swayze, a long-time coach and referee from Saskatchewan, remembers that Chapman was impressive, Samaras was distracted by a sick daughter, and Donohue absolutely blew the committee away with his quick wit and vision.

"Jack was very convincing," said Swayze. "The minute I opened the door and he came into our room he had a trench coat on and no sport jacket, very Jack Donohue. He really impressed us and then we went back to the board and recommended him."

John Hudson, a track coach who was also on the committee, said Donohue had done his homework and knew the challenge he faced. "I was impressed because he knew about Canada and where we stood in the international picture," said Hudson. "He recognized that it wasn't going to be an easy job, and you could tell he possessed a lot of basketball knowledge."[5]

Jack was hired just a few weeks later, and all that was left was to inform Mary Jane that they would be moving north of the 49th parallel. "I am going to coach the Canadian national team. It's a country above Maine," he told her.[6]

She was perplexed — they only lived eight hours from the border, but for a woman who had spent her entire life on Long Island, Canada might as well have been 8,000 miles away.

Jack Donohue's ability to coax more out of his players than even they believed possible was just what Canada needed to rebuild its moribund program, but the results weren't immediate. The eighth-place showing at the 1971 Pan American Games forced them to try to crash the Olympic party through a qualifying tournament on the eve of the Munich Games in '72.

As the new coach travelled the country scouting for players, he immediately earned the respect of long-time national team veterans such as John McGibbon, a theology student who had played on the 1960 and 1964 Olympic teams before retiring from the sport. When he heard the famed American coach had taken over, he decided to lace up his sneakers for one more go.

Though he didn't end up making the team, he knew Donohue was about to shake things up. "I represented the 'old school CABA' when things were done half-heartedly," said McGibbon. "Now basketball was being taken to a new level by bringing in one of the best coaches around. I experienced firsthand as a player the difference between pre-Jack and post-Jack and it was quite a change."[7]

The summer of 1972 was more of an extended tryout than a bid for the Olympics. Donohue knew he didn't have enough time to build the kind of team he wanted, but training camps in Montreal, Borden (Ontario), and Courtenay (B.C.) gave him a chance to assess the talent pool. Donohue would take the "A" team to Mexico and Europe prior to the Olympic qualifier while his assistant Paul Thomas, the former national team player-coach, would take the "B" team to China.

Donohue liked what he saw at camp, particularly the play of two forwards who played NCAA basketball. Six-foot-five Albertan Phil Tollestrup had just completed four years at Brigham Young University in Utah, leading the Utes in scoring with an inside-out arsenal of moves. Seventeen-year-old Ontarian Jamie Russell, a six-foot-seven centre, had averaged an impressive 22 points per game in his freshman season at Colgate University in upstate New York. But with little time to prepare, Canada fell short at the qualifier as teams such as England, Sweden, and Poland advanced ahead of them, dealing a tough blow to start the Donohue era.

He shook it off and returned to Canada, booking a national tour to sell the game of basketball and scout out talent. It soon became clear that Canada's problem wasn't a lack of players but a lack of passion. The people he spoke with didn't expect to win on the international stage, a view Donohue certainly didn't share. More than anything, the New Yorker was taken aback by the indifference toward the sport and his plans to rebuild the national-team program. "There wasn't a bad attitude; there wasn't any attitude at all," Donohue told a journalist years later. "If you like Jack Donohue, fine. If you didn't like Jack Donohue, fine. But if you don't care about Jack Donohue, that's awful."[8]

Armed with a four-year contract in the late summer of 1972, Donohue set about drumming up excitement for his team and for basketball in general. He was a dynamo in internal meetings at head office in Ottawa, and just as charismatic when he travelled to schools and community centres to sell the sport he loved. He even irked hockey aficionados in 1973 when he said basketball would be the most popular sport in Canada within 10 years. The vitriol that was heaped his way only showed him that he was on the right track; he had gotten media attention for a sport that was usually ignored in the press, now he needed results to back up his talk. "You can believe the impossible dream and it can come true in sports," he said. "But dreaming is not enough. There has to be an awful lot of sweat behind it."

To that end Donohue set about making as many friends as he could in the coaching fraternity, and he did it by putting them to work. Every coach in the country had an open invitation to Team Canada training camps, where anyone seen sitting on the sidelines would quickly be given a whistle and put to work.

Donohue had no plans to answer to anyone as he rebuilt Team Canada, and he tried everything he could to remake the organization from behind the scenes. Donohue was accustomed to high school and college basketball where the coach doubles as general manager, vice-president of communications, and just about everything else. He already had the title of technical director, and when CABA's executive director quit in 1973, Donohue lobbied intensely for his team manager, John Restivo, to get the job, which he did. Donohue brought in former Acadia University star and fellow New Yorker Steve Konchalski as his assistant in the summer of 1973, and he remained colleagues and friends with the younger coach for the rest of his life.

Donohue made sure to build relationships, even with the players who he cut, knowing that some of them could help him down the line. One such player was Billy Robinson, a sweet-shooting guard from Vancouver's Simon Fraser University, a team that eschewed the CIAU in favour of the U.S.-based NAIA division. A native of tiny Chemainus, on Vancouver Island north of Victoria, Robinson's incredible shooting range forced defenders to guard him anywhere inside half court, as college and national teammate Alex Devlin recalled. "In my opinion, Bill Robinson was the greatest shooter Canada ever produced. His shot was incredibly unique in the tremendous amount of backspin his follow-through put on the ball. One Sunday when we were shooting in the SFU gym and he hit 44 shots in a row … he was standing 10 feet above the top of the key. I would like to see anyone else in the world repeat that feat."[9]

Robinson could not only get his shot when he wanted but he was known for having an uncommon passion for the game that would be echoed decades later by another Vancouver Islander, Steve Nash. One of the top Canadian backcourt aces of the 1970s, Robinson was also a counterculture figure who refused to cut his hair and insisted on doing things his way. The six-foot guard's iconoclastic ways had so irked Team Canada officials prior to Donohue's arrival that one of the coach's first marching orders was to make sure never to pick Robinson for his teams. Donohue promptly ignored the order, quickly realizing that Robinson might be his best player. But when a knee injury slowed the guard at camp, Donohue relegated him to the B team, an offer the fiery Robinson refused, opting instead to quit. He would not be going to China with the A team despite the fact that he thought he was the most talented player in the program. Swayze, a member of the committee that hired Donohue, and later named an assistant coach, was stuck with a very tense exit interview, as Robinson fumed and let loose a stream of curse words over what he saw as a sign of disrespect. "He said 'Donohue, that son of a bitch, he told me my hair was too long, he told me I had drugs, I had girl problems, I had money problems, and he doesn't want guys on the team with all those problems,'" Swayze recalled.

Robinson figured his career was over and decided to end it in a blaze of glory. He drove his car out to the waters of the Georgia Strait, dumped his shoes, shorts, and jockstraps on a makeshift raft, doused the whole thing with gasoline and set it on fire, watching as the tower of flame floated away.

But extinguishing his fire for 'ball would prove much more difficult. Billy Robinson longed to play in the NBA, years before such dreams were realistic for Canadian players, and he knew that Donohue provided his best chance of getting there. When he called the coach in the off-season to ask for another chance to try out for the team, Donohue agreed, but with a caveat: the British Columbian had to cut his hair, and pass the ball into the post rather than jack up shots.

Though the two continued to butt heads during the 1973 prep year, Robinson realized that Donohue's strict approach, which included marathon three-a-day practices and constant team meetings, was the only way to turn a losing program into a winner. "You could see the military approach to the way he did things and it was needed," said Robinson.

Donohue, as always, found humour in his contentious relationship with Robinson. "It was a love-hate relationship," the coach was often heard saying. "I loved him and he hated me."

The core of the team started to meld together during those tough summer sessions in 1973, capped by a European tune-up tour that would test their preparedness, as well as Donohue's patience with officials. Donohue worked the refs like any other coach, though the conservative Catholic avoided the sort of chair-throwing outbursts that made Indiana University coach Bobby Knight infamous. Tolerating officials on the court was one thing, but bunking with them was another matter entirely. The CABA's perpetual financial problems forced Donohue to share a hotel room in Italy with Ron Foxcroft, who had become Canada's top basketball official earlier in 1973 when FIBA certified him to referee their games. FIBA member countries paid for their own officials to travel overseas, but Foxcroft's per diem was miniscule and the bureaucrats didn't want to spring for separate lodging. That meant Donohue was stuck with Foxcroft, an arrangement that wouldn't have normally caused any conflicts on the court since he wasn't allowed to referee any of Canada games to avoid a conflict of interest. But Donohue and Foxcroft were placed on a collision course when, just before one of Canada's games, an official got hurt and the Hamilton native was the only replacement they could find.

Once the ball was tipped, Foxcroft's refereeing partner started burning Canada with one lousy call after another, turning Donohue's face several shades of red. The coach insisted Foxcroft level things out by making some calls in Canada's favour. When the young ref refused, Donohue stormed onto the court and screamed bloody murder, prompting the Canadian to whistle him for two technical fouls and give him the toss. At least no one would be able to accuse the Canadian ref of bias against his home country, but his neutrality came at a price. "I got back to my room and he had locked me out," recalled Foxcroft. "I said 'Jack, it's Ron.' He said 'I know.' And I slept in the hall until seven in the morning when our bus left for Venice."

It made for a frosty bus ride, but Donohue soon let things pass and the two remained lifelong friends, though they made sure to book separate rooms from then on.

Team Canada's next big test would come in 1974 at the World Championships in Puerto Rico. Billy Robinson was the team's top guard along with Alex Devlin, an NAIA All-American.

Up front, Donohue had a deep and tall mix of players. Aside from Tollestrup and Russell, there was six-foot-ten marksman Lars Hansen, a four-year starter from the University of Washington who later won a championship with the NBA's Seattle SuperSonics, and Ken McKenzie, a physical force and the team's tallest player along with Hansen. There was also Mike Moser, a CIAU superstar at the University of Waterloo who was a load down low and could also step out and knock down jumpers.

The team jumped out to a promising start in Puerto Rico with a 2–1 record, advancing to the medal round of the Worlds for the first time in program history and drawing rare media attention back home. But the team ran into a U.S.A. wall in the fourth game, losing by 21 and finishing out the tournament with one win and five losses to end up in eighth place.

Their 3–6 record didn't do justice to the team's competitiveness, however. Canada lost by one point to Cuba, beat rising power Spain by 13, lost by a single point to Brazil, and were edged out by just three to Yugoslavia, who at that time were just as powerful as the Soviets. Canada's eighth-place finish was their best placing in a World Championship in 20 years. Billy Robinson played under control and made the All-Tournament team while Jamie Russell, just 19 years old, had led Canada in scoring at 14 points per game. Donohue, stressing an egalitarian approach, had four players average double figures in scoring. He knew that the team was coming together beautifully, which Canadians got to see firsthand the following year in a game against the powerful defending Olympic champion Soviet Union team at an Intercontinental Cup at Maple Leaf Gardens in Toronto.

It took some cloak-and-dagger to make the game happen, since arena owner Harold Ballard hated the Soviets and didn't want them playing in his building. Basketball officials had to organize the game when Ballard was on vacation. In the biggest upset in program history, Canada beat the Soviets 86–84, and one highlight came after the game when Prime Minister Pierre Trudeau's sports minister, Iona Campagnolo, rushed across the court to give Donohue a big hug.

It turned out that Campagnolo was a big fan of the stocky New Yorker, who had used every bit of his Irish charm on cabinet ministers and other government officials to wrest more money for his growing program.

But while hard-core partisans and players were elated, media and most sports fans had the same indifferent attitude they had always shown to a sport that they considered to be an American phenomenon. "We have 21,000 fans watching us but unfortunately 18,000 were disguised as empty seats," Donohue quipped after the win.

Now it was time to deliver the goods, and with the world gathering in Montreal in July 1976, Billy Robinson, Jamie Russell, and Team Canada would have a chance to make history and vault their sport to a level that even the skeptics wouldn't be able to ignore. Donohue wasn't interested in a mere a solid showing and a pat on the back — he told everyone who would listen that Canada would win a medal. But they would have to do it without their starting centre, as they had lost Ken McKenzie to a blown-out knee during a 10-point exhibition loss to the United States in Plattsburgh, New York.

Donohue shrugged off the injury setback, replacing McKenzie with veteran alternate John Cassidy. He made sure to keep the guys focussed on the task at hand, namely an opening game against the Asian champions from Japan. It worked, as Canada hammered Japan 104–76, but when a reporter asked Donohue if he still had designs on a bronze medal, he made it clear he was aiming higher: "I never said anything about third place."

Centre Lars Hansen had paced the red and white with team highs of 16 points and seven rebounds but didn't seem impressed after trouncing the shorter and slower Japanese. "I thought the whole team should have played better because of our height advantage," he said.

This time the fans had showed up in droves, spurred on by enthusiastic media predictions of a possible gold medal. Four thousand people had crammed into the 5,000-seat Étienne-Desmarteau Arena to watch the game, and crowds would grow steadily throughout the tournament.

The second game against Cuba was a chance for redemption, since the Caribbean 'ballers had humiliated Canada by 30 points at the '74 Worlds. The Cubans were the defending Olympic bronze medalists, but that wouldn't matter in Montreal as Phil Tollestrup bullied his way to 26 points, Jamie Russell tore down 14 rebounds, Canada won 84–79, and

The Gazette's Dick Bacon waxed poetic about the wire-to-wire victory. "Canada's medal-minded men's basketball team is beginning to make believers of most Canadians," he wrote.

Donohue, meanwhile, laid out the stakes for his team. "All we have to do is win two out of three to get to the medal round," he noted.

Up next were the dreaded Soviets, villainous Cold War foes not only for Canada, but also for the United States and the entire western world. Slowing down six-foot-nine Soviet muscleman Aleksandr Belov, who had scored the controversial gold medal–winning basket against the U.S. in '72, would be key for Tollestrup and Hansen. But Belov had his way with Canada's front line, especially in the first half, and seven-foot-three, 310-pound teenager Vladimir Tkatchenko finished the job with 22 points, all from point-blank range, as the Soviets cruised to a 108–85 win. Canada quickly shrugged it off, moving past Australia and Mexico to make the medal round for the first time since their silver medal–winning performance in 1936.

From this point forward, there would be no easy games, and the Americans and their acclaimed coach, Dean Smith from the University of North Carolina, were out for blood. It had taken a refereeing fiasco in Munich to rob them of their eighth straight gold medal in 1972, with three restarts on the final possession giving Belov a chance to hit a winning layup that would go down in hoops infamy. This time around, the States had restocked its squad with 10 future NBA players, blitzing through the preliminary rounds with a 6–0 record, but looked beatable after close wins against Puerto Rico and Czechoslovakia. Donohue's job was to convince his players that they could deal the U.S. its second loss in Olympic history.

Canadians, whether athletes or not, have an inferiority complex vis-a-vis their giant neighbour to the south that can manifest itself in bizarre ways. Canadian attitudes toward their American cousins can run the gamut from idol worship to derision and a mocking, critical tone that sometimes comes off as desperate. The Canadian inferiority complex certainly extends to the world of basketball, where America took a sport invented by a Canadian and ran away with it, building the world's best basketball factory — one so attractive that half of Canada's roster, not to mention its head coach and top assistant, had ties to the U.S. system.

Although the Americans might have been looking ahead to the

gold-medal game against Yugoslavia, the normally dignified Smith's quotes about Canada in *The Gazette* were nonetheless shocking. "Three great teams are left. Canada is an average team that got there through the luck of the draw. If they had been in B section, they wouldn't have won a game," the newspaper quoted Coach Smith as saying.

He vehemently denied ever making the statement to *The Gazette*, and he was so outraged that he threatened to sue the newspaper. But the damage was done, and Canada had potential bulletin-board material that would be augmented by a capacity crowd of more than 16,000 who watched the game at the Forum on July 26, 1976.

Donohue gave an especially strong pre-game speech, though it didn't do much good when the ball went up, as the U.S ran off to a 13-point halftime lead. The Canadians missed easy layups, made unforced turn-overs, and generally seemed rattled by the cat-quick Americans and their All-American guards Quinn Buckner and Phil Ford.

Konchalski said the guys were nervous. "[They] got so worked up and carried away with the crowd that they forgot our game plan and started to run with the U.S. We just can't do that."

Smith also noted the nervousness of the Canadians, telling reporters, "I thought we had a psychological edge going into the game."

The final score was 95–77, denying the Canadians a chance to win gold but leaving them with a shot at bronze. They would now face an equally tough opponent if they hoped to advance.

Yugoslavia managed to knock off the Soviets in a semifinal result that was nearly as disappointing to the Americans as it was to Canada, who would now have to beat the Russians if they hoped to claim bronze. Donohue, in a nod to the controversial Soviet win over the U.S. four years earlier, told reporters, "I'm an American citizen ... and quite frankly I'm upset that the U.S. is not playing the Soviet Union."

The States would be denied their revenge while the Canadians would have to find a way to slow down Russian centre Tkatchenko, who they had nicknamed "Lurch" for his alleged resemblance to the towering Frankenstein-like character from the 1960s TV sitcom *The Addams Family*.

While Canada did manage to hold Tkatchenko to eight points, Aleksandr Belov torched them for 23 and 14 as the Soviets cruised to a 100–72 victory and a bronze medal.

Canada had finished an impressive fourth — their best Olympic showing since 1936, but the media and fans weren't impressed. The Canadian 'ballers got caught up in a wave of disappointment as Canada managed only 11 medals overall, with no golds, despite a substantial investment in coaching, facilities, and player subsidies.

Perhaps the harshest language came from Brent Russell, a sports psychologist with the Canadian swimming team, who said "there is a national system of choking here."

Konchalski wasn't having any of it, insisting that Canada would have won a medal if they had had just one key player in their lineup. "Losing [Ken] McKenzie cost us a medal," he said of his fallen big man. "He was the one guy that could bang and hold his own against the Yugoslavian, American, and Soviet post players."[10]

Donohue, for one, was thrilled with the turnaround. Canada had gone from a basketball afterthought that hadn't qualified for two straight Olympics to a budding world power that was perhaps one torn knee away from a top-three finish. Phil Tollestrup and Bill Robinson were fantastic from start to finish, with Tollestrup finishing fourth in the tournament in scoring with 21.3 points per game. "I've never been prouder of them than I am right now," the coach told reporters after the Soviet loss. "I've had undefeated teams in the U.S. … I've had teams with a lot more talent, but I've never been associated with a greater bunch of kids."

What he said next was a sign that he, Mary Jane, and their young family had made the Ottawa area their home over the previous four years. "I'm proud to be living in Canada."

It's perhaps a little-known fact that Donohue wore two hats as he steered the men's team toward Montreal. He also coached the women's team for a year, taking over in 1974 when previous coach Darlene Curry suddenly quit amid a rebuilding effort. Donohue picked up the pieces, embarking on a cross-country scouting trip where he selected players from Ontario, Quebec, British Columbia, and Nova Scotia.

The young women took to his personal style even more than the men, and gushed about him for decades afterward. "For the first time I felt like someone was coaching the national team that really cared for me as a person and a player," said Kathy Shields, who later went on to win eight championships as coach at the University of Victoria.

Donohue also wasn't above some crazy stunts to motivate a group of women unsure whether they'd be able to make a good showing in Montreal. Following a loss on the road, one of the players received a call from Donohue. "I'm stuck in the phone booth," he said.

Word quickly got around and the women sprinted downstairs just in time for the coach to burst out of the phone booth wearing a Superman suit. As jaws dropped, Donohue explained that he had changed his identity and expected the players to do the same if they wanted to start winning games.

Donohue built a 12-woman unit and emphasized team play, though he certainly made note of the talent that would be key to making a run at a medal. Guards Carol Turney and Beverly Bland stood out in training camps and exhibitions, as did Sylvia Sweeney, a 17-year-old phenom from Dawson College, a prep program coached by one of Donohue's former players, Richie Spears.

Sweeney grew up in a well-off musical family that included her mother, music teacher Daisy Sweeney, and her world-famous uncle, jazz pianist Oscar Peterson. Sylvia became such a talented pianist in her own right that McGill accepted her into their classical piano program, but her real love was basketball. She made sure to stretch out her studies through the 1970s to play as much elite basketball as possible, becoming a star on the McGill Martlets team before moving on to Concordia and Laurentian.

One of Donohue's other picks was mercurial Elizabeth "Liz" Silcott, one of the most dynamic — and tragic — figures in Canadian basketball. Silcott grew up on Mount Royal, in the working-class neighbourhood of Côte-des-Neiges, just a few kilometres from Sweeney. Like Sweeney, Silcott's father was a railroad worker and both women had West Indian roots, but the similarities ended there. Schooled on playgrounds instead of gyms, Silcott was combative where Sweeney was diplomatic, reckless where Sweeney was conservative, and volcanic where her fellow Montrealer was controlled. Rocked by the brutal murder of one of her three brothers, Silcott was standoffish and withdrawn, providing a challenge for her coaches but a risk worth taking since she was also unstoppable on the court.

Sweeney became one of the best women's players in Canadian history, but she doesn't miss a beat when asked about Silcott's skills. "She was the best player ever, I mean ever," says Sweeney, quickly deflecting attention away from her own lofty accomplishments. "She was the best wing player in the world."

Silcott led the University of British Columbia to back-to-back CIAU championships, leading the team in scoring both years. At five foot six, but with incredible strength honed by playing against guys back home, Silcott was too quick and strong for women to stop on drives, and yet her shooting ability forced defences to play her close, opening up her driving game. But with the blessings came the curse — Silcott's unwillingness to take direction, frequent screaming fits, and violent mood swings made her a feared figure among teammates and even coaches. Sweeney recalls one scrimmage on the Quebec provincial team where Silcott decided to undercut her on a layup. Most players, even guys, were afraid to mess with the volatile and well-built superstar, but Sweeney was incensed at the dirty play and retaliated by kicking Silcott in the ribs.

"She turns around and there was a look in her eye that just told me that I was in trouble," said Sweeney. "It was a crazed look that I decided 'okay, let me run out of this gym.'"

In 1975, Donohue handed the reins of the team to fellow New Yorker Brian Heaney, who was left to try to manage Silcott's talent and temper. She showed her brilliance by winning MVP of a pre-Olympic tune-up tournament featuring Czechoslovakia, Spain, and Russia. Canada beat Russia in the tournament final, one of the great upsets in the program's history; but that was as good as it would get for the red and white. Heaney kicked Silcott off the team weeks before the Olympics, and the women finished 0–5, good for last place.

Heaney soon followed Silcott out the door, but Sweeney and the rest of the core picked by Donohue two years earlier stuck together and approached the top of women's basketball, winning a bronze medal at the 1979 World Championships. Sweeney won MVP of that tournament, the only Canadian 'baller of either gender to be so honoured at a World Championship or an Olympics. "[Donohue] was the one that got the women's team going in the direction of winning," Sweeney recalled.

Donohue's attachment to his adopted country explains why he turned down several European offers in favour of a creative deal to stay on as Team Canada's coach. There was no way the CABA could afford to match the salary offers from the top European teams, but a white knight came in to set things straight. Carling O'Keefe breweries agreed to hire Donohue and lend him to the national team, in exchange for internal pep talks to O'Keefe staff. Donohue would also give outside speaking engagements and keep the fees — a win-win for everyone involved. It was a deal that would keep Donohue on the sidelines for Team Canada for the foreseeable future.

The 1980s brought with them a new name for the CABA, which rebranded itself as Basketball Canada, and new hopes, with a talented young generation of players itching to get into the medals for the 1980 Summer Games in Moscow. Simon Fraser guard Jay Triano, from Niagara Falls, and six-foot-eight wing Leo Rautins emerged as potential program cornerstones.

Rautins, a Toronto native whose brother George played for Canada in the early 70s, first turned heads in the summer of 1977 when he was just a gangly teenager from St. Michael's College in the city's west end. Able to play guard or forward despite his towering height, young Leo was inexplicably cut from the Ontario provincial team but made up for the disappointment in national-team training camp, where he served notice of his skills by diving to the hoop on a fast break and dunking right over seven-foot centre Jim Zoet. Later that summer, the 17-year-old scored 19 points against Italy and a game-high 21 points in a memorable upset of Yugoslavia. Rautins, Triano, and Zoet would lead Canada into the 1980 Olympic qualifier in Puerto Rico, a tournament that took place under a cloud of world events apparently unrelated to basketball but ultimately devastating to the program's progress.

Russia's invasion of Afghanistan in December 1979 led U.S. president Jimmy Carter to suggest western nations boycott the Olympics. The Canadian government held off on a final decision through the spring of 1980, and Team Canada took the court in April with a decision hanging over their heads. Donohue told his guys to ignore politics and just play. "We've stayed away from talking about Moscow even before the boycotting thing came up," he said in Puerto Rico. "I don't believe in giving my players two goals at the same time. For two weeks, all we want to think about is the American section of the Olympic qualifying tournament. That's been our only goal for the past two years."

The team kept the blinders on with spectacular results, rolling to a stellar 5–0 record to earn a spot in the Olympics. But just before their final game against Puerto Rico, their government announced that Canada would join the U.S. and keep their athletes at home.

Canada had played their way into the Olympics at the Americas tournament for the first time ever, and it was all for naught. The squad was 12-deep, loved playing together, and had two future NBA players (Rautins and Zoet). The ensuing years haven't dulled the certainty that Canada would have come home from Moscow with a medal, if not for politicians' insistence on making a statement by depriving athletes of a once-in-a-life-time experience. "I am certain that this team would have won an Olympic medal had we attended. It was truly special," said Team Canada shooting guard Varouj Grundlian.

The strong showing in 1980 only strengthened the players' resolve to chase the country's first hoops medal in nearly 50 years. Scoring guard Eli Pasquale and bruiser Gerald Kazanowski, members of Ken Shield's dynasty at the University of Victoria, strengthened the unit and helped to craft the program's magnum opus — a gold medal at the 1983 World University Games in Edmonton.

In the semifinals, Canada beat a U.S. team that featured future NBA legends Charles Barkley and Karl Malone. Their gold-medal win over Yugoslavia was watched by an international television audience on the CBC and CBS. The enduring image of the dream run was the moment when the players hoisted their beloved coach on their shoulders after the final buzzer sounded.

One of Donohue's last major accomplishments at the helm of Team Canada was a fourth-place finish at the heavily boycotted 1984 Olympics. It turned out to be the squad's finest hour in the modern era. A lack of funding, talent, and star power left the national team mired in mediocrity, anonymity, and accusations of racial and geographic bias in roster selection.

The men's program floundered after Donohue retired in 1988, failing to qualify for the Olympics in 1992 despite the presence of NBA veterans Rautins and Bill Wennington, and they were knocked out of the Americas qualifying tournament by a less-talented Venezuela team.

Donohue assistant Steve Konchalski had taken over the team in 1995, struggling under stagnant budgets and a lack of NBA talent. The squad failed to qualify for the 1996 Games and posted a 1–7 record at the 1998 World Championships without the services of an injured Steve Nash and two unwilling NBA vets in Rick Fox and Bill Wennington. Konchalski says he returned home and didn't hear from his bosses for two months until he received a phone call saying he was fired. He went to the press, accusing Basketball Canada of letting him go despite the fact that he had met the terms of his contract by finishing in the top 12 at the Worlds. Donohue predicted dark days ahead for his old team. "It will take a near miracle for Canada to qualify for the (2000) Olympics," the retired coach told The Canadian Press, "and the only guy with a hope to do so was Steve."

Fortunately, Donohue's own former captain proved him wrong. Jay Triano was hired in time to qualify for the team's first Olympics in 12 years, guiding the red and white to a surprise fifth-place showing in 2000 with the help of a revitalized and brilliant Nash. But Triano's tenure lasted just six years, and he was inexplicably let go in 2005 despite the fact his star was rising as an NBA assistant coach. The decision to replace Triano with Leo Rautins infuriated Nash, who never played another game for Canada, and the bottom predictably fell out as the team failed to qualify for three straight Olympics for the first time in program history.

For all the criticism Jack Donohue received for his roster choices or Canada's failure to medal at an Olympics or a World Championship, the inescapable fact is that Canada qualified for every Summer Games under his watch, finishing fourth on two occasions and sixth another time. No other Team Canada coach has come close to that kind of success in the modern era, and aside from James Naismith himself, perhaps no one did more for basketball in Canada.

But Donohue's legacy was about more than just wins — his boundless optimism was contagious, even currying favour among Canadians who normally don't give a hoot about basketball, not the least of whom were people in the hockey establishment.

Chicago Black Hawks coach and general manager Mike Keenan had heard about Donohue's skill as a motivational speaker and brought him in to talk to the team in the early 90s. By then time the former coach was well into his second career on the speaking circuit, touching on his favourite themes of team-building, a positive outlook, and setting high standards in life. Every speech was peppered with one-liners that often featured his loyal wife, Mary Jane, who he referred to as a "religious cook" because of her frequent "burnt offerings."

His favourite subject was basketball, and he remained close to the game as a personal coach and consultant, even helping to train the world's tallest basketball player, seven-foot-nine North Korean Myong Hun Ri in the summer of 1997. He kept up a busy schedule until a Florida vacation in January 2003 when he was too tired to swim. By the time he returned to his adopted hometown of Ottawa, where tests revealed liver cancer, Donohue's health was failing quickly. He died surrounded by his family on April 16, 2003, eliciting a flood of reaction across Canada and down to the U.S. east coast. Notably, several local, provincial, and federal politicians issued statements, a rarity when a member of the basketball community passes away. *Toronto Sun* columnist Steve Simmons reminisced about Donohue's legacy after cancer claimed the coaching giant's life. "He was always there, with a handshake, a story, a cup of coffee, another story and always a stain on his shirt," Simmons wrote, adding that Donohue was "The American who loved Canada more than most of us."[11]

Kareem Abdul-Jabbar, by then a six-time NBA Most Valuable Player, called Donohue "an extraordinary basketball coach and an even more remarkable human being." Donohue was honoured before the Ottawa Senators game and the House of Commons even adopted a resolution noting the American's impact on his northern neighbour. Yet again, Jack Donohue was able to get basketball onto the front pages of sports sections, if only for a few days. As the memories faded and basketball once again resumed its typical spot away from the spotlight, its small but loyal Canadian fan base was left to look back with nostalgia at the days when a fiery Irishman from Yonkers gave them a reason to dream big dreams.

CHAPTER 7

— MINOR PRO —

The death of the Toronto Huskies in 1947 sparked a love-hate relationship between Canadians and pro basketball that continued for decades.

With the Canadian Senior A league fading into obscurity by the 1970s, a massive void emerged for basketball fans that only pro hoops could fill. But the modern history of the pro game in Canada is a tragicomic tale of broken promises, fly-by-night operations, and shattered dreams for fans who just want to get a basketball fix in their own backyards.

A dizzying array of Canadian franchises have lived and died since the early 1980s, with more than 40 teams lasting a few seasons at best or else folding before playing a single game. As the NBA reached unprecedented heights on the backs of Larry Bird, Magic Johnson, and Michael Jordan, Canada remained one of the few nations in the western world not to have a domestic professional league, an entertainment option that you can even find in such places as Albania, Luxembourg, and Cameroon.

But if Canada has been a pro basketball wasteland, it wasn't for lack of trying. Even when clubs have drawn large crowds, their shaky leagues rarely lasted more than a few years before biting the dust, leaving franchises with no choice but to close up shop.

The modern era of Canadian professional basketball kicked off in October 1980 when the Alberta Dusters opened play in Lethbridge, Alberta, as part of the Continental Basketball Association (CBA), which had played second fiddle to the NBA since the late 1940s.

There were no Canadians on the Dusters roster, but that didn't stop more than a thousand fans from turning out to watch, despite the team's 11–31 record. The 1981–82 season saw a slight improvement as the Dusters sported 12 wins against 34 losses, but the CBA team folded when owner Pat Shimbasi said rent was too expensive.

About a year later, across the country in Toronto, the city's small but loyal group of basketball fans had their hopes stoked by Ohio business-man Ted Stepien, who was having a whale of a time getting fans out to see his sad-sack Cleveland Cavaliers. The team was hemorrhaging money, and Stepien issued a public announcement that he was ready to move the club to Toronto. He even came up with a name — the Toronto Towers — which persuaded some fans in Hogtown that he was serious.

But Stepien's braggadocio might have been more of a bargaining tool than a real threat, given that Toronto's history of supporting pro basket-ball was even less impressive than Cleveland's. In the end, Stepien ended up selling the Cavs for $20 million in 1983, but he gave Toronto a con-solation prize — a CBA basketball team called the Tornadoes.

CBA finances were a pittance compared with those of the NBA. Stepien paid the CBA $180,000 for the rights to set up the Tornadoes, an amount that wouldn't have covered two months of Magic Johnson's salary.

Home games for the 1983–84 season would be played at aging Varsity Arena, a 6,000-seat facility that would prove difficult to fill. But Stepien told his inaugural news conference that he only needed to sell 2,500 tickets a night to break even, and his plan was to entice Torontonians with dirt-cheap prices. Tickets started at $3 and a floor seat went for just $7.50 a pop.

As for who would actually take the floor for opening night, Stepien initially remained mum despite the fact the Tornadoes had drafted three NBA prospects. Robert Smith, Calvin Garrett, and Terry White were still in NBA training camps as the Tornadoes prepared for their home opener and it wasn't clear if any of them would bite on CBA salaries that maxed out at $400 a week.

Stepien had much less difficulty luring Canadians to his fall tryout. As their Huskies forerunners had done decades earlier, the Tornadoes brought in two Canadians to appease the home fans. Seven-foot-one Montrealer Ron Crevier had been a fourth-round NBA draft pick by the Chicago Bulls the previous summer following a career as a backup at Boston College. Training camp also featured another towering Canadian, Ontarian Jim Zoet, who had had a short stint in the NBA the previous season. Zoet was cut before the start of the season and Crevier was kept on as a reserve.

Just when it seemed the Tornadoes might be undermanned for their debut, Stepien realized his hopes of landing NBA prospects by signing Robert Smith on the eve of the home opener after he was released by the San Antonio Spurs.

Also making the roster was defensive specialist Dudley Bradley, once credited for a then-record nine steals in an NBA game. Up front were former NBA and ABA centre Larry McNeill and forward Walter Jordan, who once played for Stepien's old team, the Cavaliers.

Riding substantial buzz (for basketball, at least), the Tornadoes just surpassed Stepien's break-even point, welcoming 2,613 fans into Varsity Arena on December 4, 1983, for the home opener against the Bay State Bombardiers.

The minor-league surroundings didn't discourage a healthy media presence that included Paul Patton from the *Globe and Mail*, who said that the game marked the "rebirth of pro basketball in Toronto."

Unlike the final Huskies' home win against the Knicks 36 years earlier, the Tornadoes fell to their American rivals 112–108, but there were clear signs that things had changed among basketball fans in Hogtown. Spectators were on their feet throughout the thrilling contest, with the *Globe* noting that fans gave "frequent standing ovations, a far cry from Toronto's usually reserved audiences."

Scalpers gathered outside the arena to peddle tickets for the city's newest sports franchise.

Toronto guard Carl Nicks, best known for being a college teammate of certain blonde-haired Indiana forward named Larry Bird, said he felt sorry about being unable to deliver a win. "'The fans were so great, they deserved a win," he said after delivering 23 points for his side.[1]

The goodwill soon wore off, as Toronto proceeded to lose six of their next seven games. The decades-old home arena also did little to encourage healthy crowds. The facility on Bloor Street west of Yonge was built in 1926 and had often been cited for fire-code violations. The building also suffered from a lack of proper insulation, which was no help on chilly winter evenings as the Tornadoes piled up the losses and crowds dwindled.

Varsity Arena was so cold prior to one game against the Albany Patroons that the visitors stayed warm by wearing T-shirts under their jerseys, at least until a referee nixed the idea, saying the garb violated the league's dress code.

The Tornadoes finished their inaugural season with a 16–28 record, good for last in the division. Worse were reports that the franchise was deep in the red by its second season, with the *Globe* reporting that Stepien lost $466,838 in 1984–85 against just $83,381 in ticket sales.[2] Profits would have been even worse had the Tornadoes not rallied to finish with a 26–22 record.

The improved on-court performance didn't help crowd support, as average attendance dropped to around 1,000 a game, a fraction of what the Maple Leafs were drawing despite recording even fewer wins than their basketball cousins.

By May 1985, Stepien was openly floating the idea of relocating the team to Florida or Memphis. He admitted that operating a Canadian team from his home south of the border presented problems. "It's difficult running a franchise from another city," he said, also casting blame on his staff. "Our front office was not doing its job selling season tickets."

Just 273 season ticket packages had been sold for the 1985–86 campaign, prompting Stepien to move the team to Pensacola, Florida, mid-season after he lost $700,000 on his Toronto venture. It was yet another failure among a long and growing list of basket cases on Canada's tattered pro hoops landscape.

Hopes for a long-awaited breakthrough shifted back west in the late 1980s. The World Basketball League (WBL), which featured players six foot five and under, emerged from the short-lived International Basketball Association (IBA) in 1988. Founded by Ohio drugstore magnate Michael Monus, the new league began play in the fall of 1988 and its charter teams included franchises in Calgary and Vancouver. The league also had a big name on board. Former Boston Celtics legend Bob Cousy was an adviser for the Memphis-based outfit that would feature players, such as Cousy, who were able to excel despite being average in stature.

Armed with loads of cash from Phar-Mor, Monus's chain of discount pharmacies, and buoyed by a television deal with Sport Channel America, the WBL was ready to launch the latest bid for the middle market of pro basketball.

The Calgary 88s, named for the Winter Olympics held in town that year, played their games in the city's biggest venue, the Saddledome. The Vancouver team, known as the Nighthawks, chose cavernous BC Place as their home base.

The 88s were a smashing success right from the start, averaging 4,000 fans a game. Led by former American collegiate stars Jim Thomas and Sidney Lowe, the 88s blitzed through their inaugural season, finishing in a first-place tie with the Las Vegas Silver Streaks.

The league's Sixth Man of the Year that season was sharpshooting 88s guard Chip Engelland, a former member of the Duke University Blue Devils. Though born and raised near Los Angeles, Engelland adopted Calgary as his own, working hard to fit in in the booming oil town. "It was such a vibrant town — gosh, how lucky was I?" Engelland told the *Calgary Sun* in 2005.[3] "We were in the community so often, doing camps, clinics, speaking engagements, anything to get involved."

One of his great memories was participating in a wrestling broadcast in the days when Calgary was the centre of wrestling development through Stu Hart, father of the famous Hart brothers of the World Wrestling Federation. Engelland was also a regular at Peter's Drive-In, a local institution that has been serving shakes and burgers since 1964. The WBL was so impressed with the show that Calgary had created that it chose the city to host the league's inaugural all-star game. Some 7,000 fans showed up, making it one of the largest crowds ever to watch a basketball game in Western Canada.

The game presented the Vancouver Nighthawks with one of its rare bright spots as guard Jose Slaughter was named Most Valuable Player of the game. His team finished at the opposite end of the standings from Calgary, sporting an 18–36 record and folding after just one season. Calgary went on to lose a heartbreaking 109–107 decision to the Chicago Express in the league semifinals but bounced back in 1989 to record a league-leading 31–13 record and a berth in the WBL championship. They lost in the two-game total points series to the Youngstown Pride, a bitter disappointment to fans, but the franchise had solidified itself as the most successful professional basketball team in Canadian history.

Under the leadership of All-League performers Engelland, Carlos Clark, and Andre Turner, the 88s never finished lower than third in the WBL, including two first-place finishes in 1989 and 1991, the year they made their second trip to the finals.

Meanwhile, other Canadian franchises, buoyed by Calgary's success, joined the WBL. The Saskatchewan Storm debuted in 1989 and were wildly successful, drawing 8,279 fans to Credit Union Centre for opening night and gaining modest success in the standings.

Across the country in Fredericton, businessman Mike Doyle was watching the Canadian expansion and dreaming of bringing semi-pro basketball to the Maritimes. He had cut his teeth as an executive with the Halifax Citadels of the American Hockey League and by 1990 he still hadn't seen a pro basketball game in person.

To get a feel for the game, he drove eight hours east to Montreal for a rare NBA pre-season exhibition game at the Forum between the Washington Bullets and the Philadelphia 76ers. The October 1990 contest drew about 13,000 people for what was then little more than a novelty item in a hockey-mad city. The NBA teamed up with local promoters to put on a pre-game show with dancing girls and trick-shooting wizards that Doyle was certain would work in Halifax.

Once the ball went up at the Forum, the frequent scoring caught Doyle's attention. Whereas a hockey crowd would cheer every few minutes for goals, fights, and big hits, Doyle noticed that the Forum crowd was making noise every 20 to 30 seconds when a bucket was scored. He was convinced, and gained league approval for a WBL expansion franchise for the 1991–92 season. The team was called the Windjammers, after the world-famous cargo sailing ships that were a frequent sight at the port of Halifax in the 19th and 20th centuries.

More Canadian teams followed Halifax, with the Winnipeg Thunder making its first WBL appearance in 1992. That same year, Hamilton, Ontario's Ron Foxcroft decided to make the jump from referee to basketball owner.

Foxcroft was one of many Canadian basketball aficionados who had migrated to the United States to make a living, and he remains the only Canadian ever to referee an NCAA tournament game. He spent decades officiating games south of the border and overseas, and one of his proudest moments came in July 1976 when he refereed the men's basketball final between the United States and Yugoslavia at the Summer Games in Montreal.

By 1992, Foxcroft was the highest-profile Canadian referee in basketball history, and had returned to Canada to pursue his other passion — business. Aside from a transportation company, Foxcroft tirelessly marketed the Fox 40, a pealess whistle that has since made him a fortune worldwide.

He drummed up some money, founded a team called the Hamilton Skyhawks, and jumped aboard the WBL train when Michael Monus and his pharmacy chain still seemed to be on the up and up. "We had all this sponsorship money coming in from Phar-Mor, plus ... we got $150,000 from Sport Channel America. And CHCH Hamilton did our games every night," Foxcroft recalled.

He signed a lease with Copps Coliseum, the NHL-ready arena in downtown Hamilton, and fans showed up in droves. The gritty industrial town an hour west of Toronto was one of the few Canadian cities where basketball had a stronghold. A strong high school hoops scene, coupled with perennial men's and women's powers at McMaster University, had fed a loyal fan base that Foxcroft was all too eager to mine. The maker of the world's first whistle without a pea had another winner, it seemed.

Those who didn't attend Skyhawks games could watch two matches a week on television. Monday evening games were broadcast on CHCH, the city's top-rated local television station, and Friday night games appeared on Sport Channel America. "We set a record for 14,000 people opening (night), largest crowd in WBL history," said Foxcroft, who added that the team averaged 7,000 fans a night.

The secret was to sell the Skyhawks as wholesale entertainment, appealing not only to hard-core fans but also to average Hamiltonians who wouldn't normally watch basketball but just wanted an inexpensive night out on the town with the family. "The thing that I stressed was that ... we were in the business of entertainment, not basketball, so we had mascots and chickens and dancers and music and lights. The city really got behind it. It was fabulous."

Media jumped on board and the Skyhawks became the next-best sports story in town after the beloved Tiger Cats of the Canadian Football League.

But while WBL franchises north of the border showed promise, the story at league office in Memphis was a train wreck. In the summer of 1992, Phar-Mor's CEO accused WBL co-owner Michael Monus of embezzling $350 million from his own company, at the time the largest scheme of its kind in U.S. history. A *Newsweek* article said Phar-Mor execs believed the Ohio magnate "had been cooking the books like a master chef for at least three years."[4] Monus promptly vanished, leaving WBL officials, players, and tens of thousands of fans in the lurch.

The dominoes started to fall, with Florida and Jacksonville disbanding by June 1992, Erie exiting on July 20, and Dayton done by July 31. Calgarians also lost their beloved 88s to the carnage.

On August 1, 1992, unable to pay its teams, the World Basketball League suspended operations. According to estimates, the league owed the Canadian franchises more than $100,000 each. The WBL had joined the ranks of dead North American basketball leagues, a list that had close to 100 names by the turn of the 21st century.

But rather than keel over and accept their place in history, the remaining Canadian owners did a strange thing just one day after the WBL died. While orphaned American teams packed up and went home, the Canadians banded together and tried to find a way to rise from the ashes.

Once it became clear the WBL was going belly up, Doyle got on the phone with his counterparts and discussed an idea that was as unlikely as it was unprecedented — to start up an all-Canadian pro basketball league.

The television deal had evaporated with Phar-Mor's cash, but the owners planned to approach the NBA and set themselves up as a farm league. All of the Canadians jumped on board — except Ron Foxcroft. "I said 'we can't survive without TV.' And I closed with money in the bank. I'm still a businessman first and a basketball guy second."

Foxcroft realized that a sports league can only be successful if fans know that it exists, which has been the Achilles heel of every pro operation not called the NBA.

No television network worth its salt would ever sign with an outfit that isn't likely to survive the life of the deal, and minor-pro basketball leagues are notoriously short-lived.

Even the venerable Continental Basketball Association, which had survived name changes and franchise turnover for 55 years, was on life support by the early 1990s after the NBA abruptly ended a player-development deal with its old rival.

Foxcroft was out, but the Hamilton Skyhawks would live on. He sold his team to a new group of businessmen and the fledgling league set about trying to boldly go where no sports league had gone before in Canada.

The owners chose to go with the name National Basketball League (NBL), not the most original choice, since no fewer than five previous pro leagues in the United States had carried that moniker. All had since collapsed, with none lasting longer than 11 seasons.

Partnership talks with the NBA went nowhere and the owners decided to go ahead with a spring-summer schedule in 1993 and some surprise additions. Canada Basketball, fresh off a disappointing failure to qualify for the Summer Games in Barcelona, had decided to set up a permanent, in-season national team. Two major Division I conferences in the NCAA even jumped on board, with the Atlantic 10 and the Big East providing all-star teams to fill out the schedule. Also on the schedule was Athletes in Action, a barnstorming team made up of top-level Christian players.

The owners were confident that with teams in most major Canadian cities, the NBL could continue the WBL's momentum and garner much-needed television and sponsorship deals.

Opening night was set for May 1, 1993, in Halifax, perhaps the strongest market in the league. What's more, fans across Nova Scotia had an intense rooting interest since the Windjammers would be taking on their new cross-province rivals, the Breakers, from the eastern mining town of Cape Breton.

The game was played at the Halifax Metro Centre, the city's flagship facility with 10,000 seats. With owner Mike Doyle handling the show and former American college stars such as Steve Burtt and Willy Bland wowing the crowds, things got off to a rousing start. The underdog Breakers won the game in a 98–94 thriller. Alex J. Walling, a long-time sportscaster based in the harbour city, recalls the sales job that Doyle pulled off to persuade Haligonians that a Windjammers game was the place they ought to be. There were the Windjammer dancing girls and colourful public address announcer Rick Anderson ("over the top, but he fit," recalled Walling). Fans flocked to the Metro Centre to take in the show. "Mike Doyle caused a buzz," Walling said. "Mike Doyle was entertainment and show, Mike Doyle had the brains enough to let the coach manage the team, but he managed everything else." The Windjammers ended up leading the league in attendance and were clearly carrying the banner for the new league.

Meanwhile, two provinces away in Montreal, long-suffering basketball fans were pinching themselves when they heard about the newest show in town — the Dragons. Businessman Francois Tremblay had launched his team against perhaps the tallest odds in the WBL. The professional basketball wave that swept through much of North America over the past century largely missed the mainly French-speaking metropolis of Montreal. As recently as 1990, not one of Quebec's four French-speaking universities had an intercollegiate basketball team.

So it was with cautious excitement that 4,000 fans packed Verdun Auditorium on May 7, 1993, for the Dragons' home opener against the Windjammers. Adding to the excitement was a surprisingly talented roster stocked with well-known former U.S. college stars including centre George Ackles of the 1990 NCAA Champion Nevada-Las Vegas Runnin' Rebels. The Dragons were coached by Californian Otis Hailey, a former state high jump champion who went on to coach five Canadian minor-pro teams, likely a unique feat in the country's hoops annals. Dragons fans were stoked by the presence of two local legends, forwards Wayne Yearwood and Dwight Walton, both successful professionals from Montreal who the owners had persuaded to join the roster to pique hometown interest. But fans were doubly disappointed on opening night — not only did Walton and Yearwood ride the bench for the entire game, the Dragons lost 117–110.

While the Nova Scotia franchises were drawing healthy crowds, and the Winnipeg-Saskatoon rivalry showed potential, Dragons fans had the rug pulled out from under their feet. Tremblay's team was reported by the *Montreal Gazette* to be on the verge of financial collapse just two weeks after opening night, and the debt-ridden franchise folded after just 17 games. The Hamilton Skyhawks, Ron Foxcroft's former franchise, didn't survive that first season either, moving to Edmonton as the team had lost all of the momentum it had generated in the halcyon WBL days. By the time the NBL began its second season in May 1994, the writing was on the wall. The league only survived about 20 games before it folded. The embarrassing exit left fans wondering if they'd forever be forced to live vicariously through their American cousins to get their pro basketball fix.

It was a bitter pill; another punishing blow to a pro landscape that had seen far more failure than success.

Hailey, who coached on both sides of the border prior to his death in 2010, had a first-hand look at the myriad failure stories and chalked it up to poor sales jobs. "It's been the business plan," Hailey said in a 2004 interview. "People do not know how to market pro basketball in Canada."[5]

Hailey wasn't deterred, coaching teams in Montreal, Vancouver, St. Catharines, Calgary, and Saskatchewan despite meagre paycheques that didn't reflect his multiple job titles. He was among a handful of Americans who used their guile, experience, and old-fashioned hustling skills to try and peddle a sport invented by a Canadian to a country that had long since given its heart to hockey.

In Winnipeg, just as the beloved Jets flew out of town, another pro hoops operation tried to steal hearts with the help of yet another American. The Cyclones played in the International Basketball Association from 1995 to 2001, garnering a measure of success largely because of the buzz generated by co-coach Darryl Dawkins, a hulking former NBA dunking machine who was part of the Philadelphia 76ers dynasty along with the legendary Julius "Dr. J" Erving in the 1970s and 1980s. Dawkins, a born showman, drew attention as much for his bombastic pronouncements as his colourful suit-and-tie combinations. His tireless promotion of the team helped attract media attention that often eluded franchises in other cities.

Further to the west in Saskatoon, former Tornadoes owner Ted Stepien and British Columbia businessman and politician Tom Tao founded the Saskatchewan Hawks, which began play in the IBA in 1999 and were coached by Hailey. The Hawks made it as far as the division finals two seasons later, but they and the Cyclones suffered the same fate as so many Canadian teams that had potential but no league to back them up. The IBA folded in 2001, taking the Cyclones with them into oblivion.

The Saskatchewan Hawks, meanwhile, joined the slumping Continental Basketball Association (CBA), where they compiled the league's worst record and folded after just one season.

While the NBA was soaring, in part on the back of the Toronto Raptors' young superstar Vince Carter, minor pro basketball across North America was unstable as ever.

The CBA had declared bankruptcy shortly before the IBA folded, and while the two leagues relaunched under the CBA banner later in 2001, the reconstituted league sputtered and died a merciful death in 2010, ignored by fans and media alike.

A third minor league, the USBL, also called it quits in 2001, a triple dose of failure that was perhaps no coincidence, since 2001 was the year the NBA had decided to debut its own minor league to develop talent and conveniently squeeze out potential competitors.

The National Basketball Developmental League, known as the NBADL or the D-League, not only had the financial backing of the world's top hoops juggernaut but the direct affiliation with the NBA meant that top North American players who weren't in Europe lined up for a chance to join the pipeline. That spelled disaster for any businessman trying to break into the middle market in pro basketball, and Canada once again became a backwater for anyone who wasn't a Raptors fan.

It wasn't until 2004 until someone else tried to make inroads in the tough Canadian market, and Calgary was chosen as the testing ground. The American Basketball Association (ABA), which had formed back in 2000 and had already folded once, had relaunched with a new business plan. Anyone — absolutely anyone — who had $10,000 to plunk down for a franchise fee could mail a cheque to league CEO Joe Newman in Indianapolis for territorial rights to start a franchise.

Calgary businessman Spero Kokkans bought in, persuaded Newman that he could get a team up and running for the 2004–05 season, and brought in Otis Hailey as his co-owner, president, and general manager. Kokkans managed to secure the Stampede Corral, a 7,500-seat venue where you're more likely to take in a rodeo than a basketball game. Hailey, for one, was positively bullish on the prospects for hoops in Cowtown, declaring that "calls and emails have been overwhelming" and that "we'll have one of the best operations in the league."

Unfortunately, advance media buys and aggressive publicity campaigns weren't part of the budget, and the Drillers debuted in November 2004 with a low profile and even lower attendance. Most Calgarians missed the nightly aerial act by hyper-athletic Drillers forward James Penny, who nearly kissed the rim on some of his dunks. Unfortunately, when the team folded prior to the conclusion of the season, the Drillers' death also went woefully underreported.

But Joe Newman wasn't deterred, announcing expansion plans for Vancouver, Toronto, and Montreal, where entrepreneur Serena Locker-Coles announced in the summer of 2005 that she would be running a team from Virginia, where the former Montrealer had relocated some years earlier.

Her husband, Melvin Coles, already owned two ABA teams in the United States as well as franchise rights for prospective teams in Ottawa, Quebec City, and Wilmington, Delaware, a feat that would have been outlawed in any major professional league but which posed no problem whatsoever for Newman and the ABA.

The owners secured a municipal facility in east end Montreal and hired former college player and local hoops mainstay Pascal Jobin as the team's first coach and general manager. In another attention-getting move, Locker-Coles partnered up with former Raptors favourite Jerome "Junkyard Dog" Williams as a co-owner.

The inaugural news conference attracted plenty of local media attention and the team chose the name Matrix, capitalizing on the apocalyptic science-fiction franchise that was filling up movie theatres at the time.

The home opener against the Buffalo Rapids drew a sellout crowd to the Centre Pierre-Charbonneau on Remembrance Day, 2005. The day was indeed a memorable one as the home team thrilled the capacity crowd with dunks, hustle, and an all-important victory as they blew away Buffalo 94–74.

Supporting a roster that featured seven local players, most of whom turned in stellar performances, 2,200 fans showed their love with constant cheering, chanting, and foot stomping, and team captain and senior-league scoring champion Bobby Miller choked back tears in interviews with reporters after the game. "Who would have thought this would happen in Montreal? It touched my heart," said Miller, who remembered the bitter disappointment of the Dragons flameout back in 1993.

But behind the scenes, tensions were quickly evident between Locker-Coles and Jerome Williams, who was gone by December. Jobin also had his own personality conflicts with the former Montrealer, and he was dumped first as GM, then as coach.

The personnel changes, coming so soon after the start of the season, were a red flag for *The Gazette*, which in a December 23, 2005 article noted that the bevy of personnel changes had left the Matrix looking like "a very different franchise" since its previous home game.[6] Locker-Coles fended off allegations that she was an absentee owner, insisting that "failure is not an option" and assuring fans that the Matrix would be in town for the long haul.

Bobby Miller and his teammates battled all season long and finished with a 14–16 record, qualifying for the round of 16; not a bad result considering they played for three different coaches, three general managers, and didn't receive all of their cheques on time. What's more, the team's star centre, Nigerian-born Sani Ibrahim, didn't have a U.S. work visa and couldn't travel with the team. At least the Matrix lasted the entire season, unlike a third of the ABA's teams, which had either folded or never played a game.

Newman raised eyebrows for continuing to pocket the "franchise fee," which was no guarantee that fans in a given market would ever see a team take flight. Some neophyte owners reportedly emptied their bank accounts to cover the entry sum only to realize that start-up costs were up to 10 times the amount they had paid.

Down east in Halifax, negative reports about ABA fiascos didn't dampen the spirits of jilted Windjammers fans, who were chomping at the bit when the league announced in August 2006 that it was coming to town. Former local CIS star Jadranka Crnogorac had returned home from Toronto with her American friend and co-owner, Detroit native Andre Levingston, with whom she had jointly plunked down $20,000 for the rights to revive pro hoops in one of Canada's healthiest basketball markets.

Levingston is yet another American cog in the Canadian hoops wheel, having first made his name as an auto detailer in Toronto. A former collegiate basketball player in California, Levingston had dabbled in various business interests but dreamed of owning a pro basketball franchise. The enormous Greater Toronto Area seemed the logical place to set up shop, but Crnogorac, or "Jan," as friends called her, told Levingston that Halifax was a hidden hoops treasure. Levingston admitted that he had never heard of the city while growing up on the streets of Detroit in the 1970s.

But Crnogorac knew the town was a winner, having starred at point guard for the St. Mary's Huskies from 1993 to 1998, where she once hit a record nine three-pointers in a game. Halifax is one of the few cities in Canada where organizers know they can draw a crowd to watch basketball, and the CIS took advantage for years, hosting its Final 8 National Championships at the Metro Centre.

Levingston also banked on fan interest when he made the risky move of bringing the ABA all-star game to the Metro Centre in January 2007, months before opening night. The game was a success, and though local media complained about poor public relations and disorganized events planning, sports pages provided months of enthusiastic coverage of the only pro sports outfit in town.

Fans had chosen the Rainmen name in a contest, with Crnogorac explaining that "Halifax gets a lot of rain, and in terms of basketball it's great to market around raining threes."[7] Amazingly, a fifth of respondents chose the nickname Explosion, strangely unmoved by the fact that thousands of Haligonians had been killed in a cataclysmic 1917 munitions blast that levelled much of the city. With inappropriate nickname ideas out of the way, Levingston announced plans for a 36-game schedule and opening night was set for November 15, 2007, against the Boston Blizzards. Things got off to a rousing start before more than 4,000 fans as the home team topped the Blizzards 136–103. Though the Rainmen finished their inaugural season with a losing record, there was every reason to believe the second incarnation of pro basketball in Halifax would be an overall winner — as long as the ABA survived.

Franchises such as the Rainmen, which tried to run a stable operation and fill out a full schedule, found themselves stymied by the ABA's ever-changing stable of teams, including those that existed in name only. Imagine running a sports franchise and not being sure your adversaries will even show up for your home games! Well, that's exactly what the Rainmen had to put up with in their first season.

In one case, an opponent showed up in Halifax with only six players after the others were turned back at the Canadian border because of criminal records. Then there was the time that a team called the Bahama All-Pro Show failed to show up for a doubleheader at the Metro Centre.

Alex Walling, the Halifax-based sportswriter, said he tried to write a positive column about the ABA in 2008 but found the task nearly impossible once he actually began interviewing former players, coaches, and executives. "They had 80 teams in the league, some divisions had only two teams," he recalled. "They charge you $25,000 to $40,000 to come in. Joe Newman ... he may even mean well, but boy, he's the only guy who made money from the ABA."

One U.S. writer estimated that the league had seen over 170 teams come and go from 2001 to 2008. Fed up with the circus, Levingston, Quebec City Kebs owner Real Bourassa, and Ian McCarthy from the Mill Rats left the ABA following the 2007–08 season to join a new league that included other disgruntled former ABA teams from the United States. The Premier Basketball League (PBL) vowed to present a more stable product to fans, but eventually suffered some of the same problems as the outfit it had left behind.

First was a lack of owners with deep pockets.

The PBL required a maximum six-figure payroll, ostensibly to prevent owners from spending themselves into oblivion, but in fact the league's real problem was an inability to generate cash flow beyond gate receipts and meagre local sponsorships.

Aside from financial concerns, the PBL was faced with other operational problems that would eventually chase its Canadian franchises out of the door. For one thing, conflict-of-interest controls were conveniently ignored right from the start, as the owner of the PBL team in Rochester, Dr. Severko Hrywnak, was also the owner of the league.

Hrywnak's dual role led to accusations that his team, the Razorsharks, had the referees in their pocket at key points in the 2010–11 season, most notably during the championship game against the Lawton-Fort Sill Cavalry. The Razorsharks rode a 37–17 foul discrepancy to a championship in the decisive game of the title series, leading Levingston to immediately withdraw from the league, saying he was "appalled by the officiating that took place during the playoffs" and that he was "ashamed of the PBL's operations this season."

Though his team had no league in which to play, Levingston insisted that "there will be professional basketball in the city of Halifax next season."

Bourassa, Levingston, and Mill Rats owner Ian McCarthy gathered in Halifax to plot their next move. Fans were expecting them to take the court for the following season, but first they needed other Canadian owners to jump on board, preferably in population-rich Ontario.

After securing letters of intent from businessmen in Moncton, New Brunswick, and the Ontario cities of Kingston, London, Oshawa, and Barrie, the three charter franchises held a news conference in Halifax to announce their plans to create the National Basketball League of Canada, the second professional basketball league in the country's history. "Today is a great day for Canadians," McCarthy told reporters. "The NBL will embody the virtues of Canadians through conducting business in a responsible, democratic, and objective manner."

The league was only missing a full slate of teams, a television deal, a title sponsor, and a commissioner, but fans' expectations were so low by the spring of 2011 that any news was good news. Levingston, for one, was determined to make basketball work in his adopted country. He demanded that every owner hand over $100,000 up front to show that they were serious about fielding a team. Revenues would be shared among franchises and the salary cap would be set at $150,000 per team. He figured the bevy of former Canadian college 'ballers would provide a tantalizing talent pool. "You can't tell me that there's not enough talent in this country to play at the highest level," he said. "All we have to do is put it into place to help these guys grow as basketball players and give them the opportunity." But in the end, owners decided that their teams would only be required to have three Canadians on their rosters.

Oshawa, Charlottetown, London, and Moncton decided to field teams for the inaugural NBLC season, and Levingston and his partners rented out the lounge at the Rogers Centre in Toronto for the league's first draft, a choice venue aimed at spurring media interest in the country's biggest market. The idea worked, as most national media attended the August 2011 event that saw several CIS players drafted, along with a number of obscure American players from small colleges south of the border.

The NBLC began play in October 2011, still without a television deal or a full-time commissioner, but local sportswriters provided generous coverage, no doubt aware of just how precarious the entire NBLC operation would be without a gentle nudge.

Attendance ranged from a league-high average of 3,000 in Halifax to as low as 800 per game in Quebec City, where the owner had to rely on money from the league to finish the season before his team moved to a Montreal suburb in the summer of 2012 and quickly folded, giving way to the league-owned Montreal Jazz. Canada's second-largest city has the dubious distinction of playing host to six minor pro teams in less than 20 years.

It probably came as no surprise to the NBLC's first commissioner, John Kennedy, that sponsors weren't exactly falling over themselves to jump on board, but the sheer magnitude of his new job must have seemed daunting to the Los Angeles–based, Windsor-raised marketing man accustomed to closing deals. "It's a competitive marketplace out there where hockey is our game, so we've got a huge uphill battle," he told reporters near the beginning of the first season. "There are some mornings I feel like Sisyphus…. The rock is always at the bottom of the hill."

But the fact that the operation survived its first two seasons had to be seen as a victory for the upstart league, which was a tiny blip on the Canadian sports scene but yet managed to draw as many as 3,000 fans to Credit Union Place in tiny Summerside, Prince Edward Island. More than 5,100 people flocked to London's John Labatt Centre for the 2012 championship game between the Rainmen and the hometown Lightning, who won the first of two consecutive league championships.

The NBLC beat expectations simply by finishing out one season, which even many American-based leagues hadn't done in the previous 115 years of professional basketball. "[NBLC] kept their problems under control and they didn't fold," said Walling. "Compared to what we've seen … teams folding, not coming, this was incredible for a basketball league. I give them credit for starting; I give them credit for surviving."

Survivors indeed. The Rainmen were one of the longest-lived pro basketball teams in Canadian history by 2012, outliving two leagues and co-founding a third. The Saint John Mill Rats also survived through two defunct leagues and had solid fan support.

For a brief period, at least, Canada had joined Albania, Cyprus, and Luxembourg in the category of "Countries with Professional Basketball Leagues."

CHAPTER 8

– HOMEGROWN –

A tiny liberal arts college near the shores of the Detroit River ended up being ground zero in the modern era of Canadian college basketball.

Windsor, Ontario's Assumption College didn't even have its own gym or library in 1961, sharing both facilities with the local high school, but when the nation's athletic directors gathered in Montreal that year to decide the site of the first-ever CIAU National Basketball Championship, the school's pedigree as a hoops power put it in the driver's seat.

Assumption had been beating all comers in basketball on both sides of the border since the 1930s, producing Olympians and NBA players while piling up Ontario, Eastern Canadian, and Canadian Senior A championships.

The Canadian Intercollegiate Athletic Union (CIAU) decided that Assumption would host the first two national championships, in 1963 and 1964, but the tournaments were considered "experimental," a result of the still untested and uneasy new partnership between universities of various sizes that had been scattered in regional associations for decades.

Infighting had led to the breakup in 1955 of the old CIAU Central, and with intercollegiate sports expanding in size and scope from coast to coast, the hodgepodge of regional athletic unions was simply not up to the task of overseeing athletics in the far-flung nation.

Delegates to the 1961 athletic directors' meeting in Montreal, and a separate expansion meeting in Toronto, decided to lengthen schedules, increase travel budgets, and have everything culminate in national championships. Queen's University in Kingston was chosen as the site of the first national hockey championship and Assumption got the basketball tournament.

The national event would be a great test for Assumption's newly appointed head coach, Bob Samaras. A Greek-American high school coach from Detroit, Samaras swore by a high-octane offensive style called "Blitz Basketball" that involved playing all 12 players and pressuring the opposing team to generate lots of steals and fast-break points.

During his initial job interview, Samaras made an admission that would have been fatal to most coaches' employment prospects: he informed athletic director Dr. Richard Moriarty that his frequent substitutions would leave Assumption trailing at halftime of most games! But Samaras explained that the 12-man rotation would leave his team fresh in the second half while the other team and its shorter rotation would be out of gas and unable to finish the job.

Moriarty ended up picking Samaras over two local candidates, but it took until the end of their season opener to convince local critics the right man had been hired, as the athletic director recalled years later. "Assumption had a large lead but lost it by halftime as all the players were played," he said. "There were many skeptics rushing into my office at half-time, exclaiming, 'What kind of coach did you hire? He doesn't know who his good players are!' Fortunately, the second half was played, as he said, and the team was triumphant."[1]

No defence could slow down Samaras's blitz and he led Assumption to a conference championship and a berth in the inaugural CIAU championship to be played on campus at St. Denis Hall. The old facility held more than 1,500 people, enough to fit Assumption's entire student body five times over. But with media, local fans, and visitors in town, filling the building wasn't a problem for a tournament that included western champions University of British Columbia, Acadia from the Maritimes, and Loyola University from the Ottawa region.

Acadia beat UBC while Assumption topped Loyola, setting up a championship match that the home side won 53–50 before a crowd of 2,100 that likely violated fire code. Assumption, later renamed the University of Windsor, repeated the feat in 1962 and won five of the first seven championships in the 1960s before the balance of power shifted to the east and west coasts.

UBC was Canada's next great basketball powerhouse under the tutel-age of Australian-born Peter Mullins, who took over the team in 1962 and lost in two finals in the 1960s before breaking through on the strength of scoring machine Ron Thorsen. Originally from San Jose, California, Thorsen was quick, had a sure shot, and possessed ball-handling and passing ability that made him arguably the best guard in the country from the time he first suited up for Mullins in 1968.

By 1970 Mullins had guided the Thunderbirds to the National Championship, boasting an undefeated record against Canadian teams capped by a 21-point drubbing of McMaster in the title game. His teams won 36 in a row against CIAU competition from 1969 to 1971, claiming a second title in 1972. Mullins went on to coach the national team and took several of his star players with him.

While the national network of member schools slowly grew, the CIAU nerve centre remained a tiny outfit based in the office of Major Danny McLeod, athletic director at Royal Military College, and surviving with no full-time staff. But the group began to jell with the help of the federal government, grabbing ever-larger cash amounts from the Fitness and Amateur Sport budget aimed at promoting high-performance athletics.

The opportunity to play in a new national network of basketball leagues against the best college players in Canada immediately began to catch the attention of players in the hoops heaven south of the border. Americans had dominated the rosters of many CIAU schools right from the inaugural 1963 title game between Assumption and Acadia in which six players on each team, plus both head coaches, hailed from the United States.

The flow of American expatriates intensified toward the end of the 1960s as the war in Vietnam became increasingly intractable and Washington introduced a draft in 1969, prompting many to get out of dodge and head to Canada. The draft dodgers, coupled with other American ball players who had migrated north to study and play sports, were a treasure trove for coaches but a nightmare for less-talented Canadians trying out for some CIAU teams.

John Dore, a young guard from New York, migrated to Montreal in 1971 after a short and unhappy college experience in Georgia and remembers feeling right at home when he suited up for Sir George Williams University, which later became part of Concordia University. "When I first came in 1971, 11 of the 12 guys on the team were from the States," said Dore, who later became head coach at Concordia and won a national title with the men's team in 1990.

The same year as Dore landed in Montreal, St. Mary's University in Halifax developed a distinctly American flavour when another New Yorker, Brooklyn's Brian Heaney, was appointed as head coach. His first star recruit was an unsung guard from Forest Hill, Queens, named Mickey Fox.

Legend has it that coach Heaney stumbled upon Fox while on a recruiting trip back home in New York to scout out a pair of high school players. It was soon made clear to the young coach that the two targets were already locked up by NCAA schools and it seemed he had made the trip for nothing. But Fox, a skinny bench player, scored 21 points that day and Heaney made a point to meet the young man, beginning a relationship that led Fox to commit to St. Mary's and change the course of the program for the rest of the 1970s.

The six-foot-two, 185-pound recruit became perhaps the finest player in the history of the CIAU on the strength of his smarts, jumping-jack athleticism, and unparalleled shooting ability. In his first year in Halifax, though just 18 years old, Fox averaged 20.3 points per game, which would be the lowest scoring output of his five-year career.

Anchoring a roster with several other Americans, the New Yorker led the Huskies to a title run in 1973 in which he won the game's Most Valuable Player, though the performance captured the attention of CIAU top brass for another reason: the preponderance of American players on the sport's biggest stage. When St. Mary's and Lakehead took the court for the championship final at the University of Waterloo, nine of the ten starters at the jump hailed from south of the border, recalls journalist Alex Walling. The young reporter had travelled to Waterloo to cover St. Mary's for Halifax radio stations CHNS and CHFX and recalled that the lack of Canadians in the final led to swift action by CIAU officials. "The CIAU put in a new rule, only limiting teams to three Americans," said Walling. "That was the result of having … Lakehead with five Americans and St. Mary's with four."

Heaney was central to another rule change brought about by his tactics in the opening game of the 1975 CIAU championship, which was being held at Waterloo for the third straight year. Heaney knew that Waterloo fans had a tradition of standing and banging drums until the home team scored their first point. Heaney had a plan to make them stand for so long that they'd be too tired to make a peep the rest of the game.

He told centre Lee Thomas to win the tip and instructed his Huskies to hold the ball for as long as possible, taking advantage of the fact that there was no shot clock. His men did as they were asked. "Heaney kept the ball for eight or ten minutes before he shot the ball," recalled Walling, who noted that the halftime score was 6–2 and home fans were exhausted and furious, just as Heaney had wanted. Officials made note of Heaney's hold 'em strategy, and later introduced a shot clock that had been commonplace in American college basketball for 30 years. Waterloo ended up winning the low-scoring opening game against the Huskies despite a season that might have crushed a less-resilient squad.

Before tipoff of every game at those 1975 nationals, Waterloo introduced just four starters despite the fact they sent out five men like everyone else. They were honouring their star centre, Mike Moser, perhaps the greatest player in the program's history who had recorded six of the top 10 single-game scoring performances in a Warriors uniform. The young centre from Kitchener, Ontario, was so talented that Team Canada head coach Jack Donohue had picked him for the national team that ended up finishing eighth at the 1974 World Championships.

The six-foot-six centre's outside shooting ability and great hands made him an unstoppable force during the '74–'75 season as he recorded double figures in points and rebounds in nearly every game. He led his squad to a 13–2 record on both sides of the border, including an undefeated mark against CIAU competition heading into the Christmas break. Head Coach Don McRae had organized a trip to western and central Florida for exhibitions against Division II and III schools, but Moser didn't play in any of the four games after he started running a fever before the first match against Eckerd College in St. Petersburg.

Moser had checked into a hospital in St. Petersburg while his team went on to lose three of four, but none of the tight-knit group could have prepared for the news that came down following their loss to Rollins College: Mike Moser was dead, a victim of an inflamed heart. "I can't believe he's gone," teammate Phil Schlote told the local Waterloo newspaper when the stunned team returned home. "I keep thinking this is some sort of mistake."[2]

No one would have blamed the squad for taking the year off to regroup after the death of their best player, but the team knew it had to continue to honour Mike, and they didn't miss a beat. Led by forward-centre Art White, who led the team in scoring for the remainder of the season, Waterloo went undefeated, culminating in a come-from-behind victory in the National Championship against Manitoba, making up a nine-point deficit with six minutes to go.

Phil Goggins, a reserve centre, was the surprising hero, hitting the winning basket with four seconds left, and Warriors fans poured onto the court to celebrate the first championship in program history.

Decades later, Coach McCrae still wasn't quite sure how his team managed to overcome the loss of their leader and best player mid-season and play even better after he died. "I honestly don't know how they held it all together," he said. "This was such a good group. You could trust them. They played fast and hard."

And how would they have played with Moser in the lineup? "If Mike would've been with us, we wouldn't have needed to play the national championship game. They would've mailed it to us," said the coach.[3]

Following Waterloo's heavy-hearted win in 1975, the balance of CIAU basketball power shifted decisively to the east and west coasts, where teams began to equal, and then surpass, their Central Canadian counterparts in terms of budgets and recruiting. Teams from Atlantic Canada and the West won every CIAU championship from 1976 to 1989, beginning with Manitoba's bounce-back title in the Olympic year following a loss in the previous year's final.

CIAU Player of the Year and national team member Martin Riley led Manitoba to that 1976 championship before the east coast took over with three consecutive titles beginning with Acadia in 1977 and a second title for Heaney and Fox's St. Mary's Huskies in 1978.

Heaney had returned to Halifax the previous year following a stint as head coach of the women's national team for the Montreal Olympics, and he couldn't have arrived back east at a better time. His school was hosting the CIAU championship and the tournament would be held at the brand-new Halifax Metro Centre, a 10,000-seat facility that was the crown jewel of the port city. Folk icon Gordon Lightfoot had just inaugurated the arena with a concert, and basketball would be the second act in the new building.

Heaney turned the promotional campaign into high gear, and fans came out in huge numbers to watch St. Mary's march toward a finals matchup with Heaney's alma mater, the Acadia Axemen, bitter inter-provincial rivals from up Highway 101 in Wolfville. A capacity crowd at the Metro Centre watched the hometown Huskies win the first of their back-to-back titles. The Huskies' second straight championship came in 1979 over the Victoria Vikes.

The Vikes were a relatively new basketball program that had steadily rose up the ranks under Ken Shields, a young coach from Prince Rupert, British Columbia, by way of tiny Beaverlodge, Alberta. Shields was a noted perfectionist with a reputation as a grinder all the way back to his high school days on the Queen Charlotte Islands on the upper B.C. coast, when he led Prince Rupert High School to the 1964 provincial title, the only team from their region ever to win a championship. It wouldn't be the last time the intense and introspective hoops fanatic would take a program where it had never gone before.

By the mid 1970s the University of Victoria had several choices to make as college sports began to explode in popularity. There were at least 30 potential varsity sports from which to choose, but newly appointed president Howart Petch realized that the school's money would be best spent on a few sports with championship potential rather than a scatter-gun approach that would breed mediocrity. He commissioned a task force that reached the same conclusions, and UVic adopted a lean and mean athletic model centred around soccer, rugby, field hockey, rowing, swimming, golf, running, and basketball, much to the relief of hoops coach Gary Taylor. Petch's "Tradition of Excellence" philosophy paid off as Vikes programs went on to win 25 National Championships in his 15 years as president.

Another key decision, soon to become standard at basketball programs across the CIAU, came when the school elevated the men's basketball head coach position to a full-time job. Taylor, who was in his fifth year in 1976, was a school principal by day while coaching the Vikes part time. He still managed to field a competitive team, albeit one that was unable to break through to the nationals. Shields, who in 1970 had been named head coach at Laurentian University at just 25 years of age, was brought into Victoria for an interview and impressed top brass with his vision to

Vikes Athletics and Recreation, University of Victoria.

Ken Shields coached the University of Victoria Vikes men's basketball team to seven straight CIS Championships from 1980 to 1986. He won four CIS Coach of the Year awards and later served as head coach of the Senior Men's National Team. In 1998, he was appointed as a Member of the Order of Canada, and a year later he was inducted into the Canadian Basketball Hall of Fame.

146

win through hard work and tactical competence. Petch hired him prior to the 1976–77 season, not just as basketball coach but also as athletic director, a dual position that he had also held at Laurentian.

The young coach would inherit one of the top players on the west coast in Robbie Parris, who had begun studies at the University of Victoria in 1974 after wrapping up a stellar high school career just five kilometres away at Oak Bay Secondary. He had quarterbacked his team to back-to-back BC High School championships under the legendary Don Horwood, who went on to become the winningest coach in the history of University of Alberta men's basketball.

A five-foot-eight ball-handling whiz, Parris had been one of the cornerstones of the young UVic program under Taylor, propelling the Vikes to their first-ever Canada West final in his first year and ending the season with a 14–6 record. But the Vikes slumped to a third-place conference finish in 1976.

Parris knew things would be different under Shields's leadership from the very first practice when, instead of standing to the side with whistle and clipboard, his new 31-year-old coach grabbed a ball and dove right into scrimmages. "Our scrimmages and pickup games became so intense," Parris recalled, adding that Shields combined blind intensity and a solid shooting touch to set a personal example for a young team that he knew hadn't yet reached its potential. "When Ken arrived, it was just incredible, his passion for the game and his desire to get better, his desire to learn, and he just instilled that in all of us."

Not everyone could handle Shields's hard-driving style, and that was apparent in tryouts when players dropped out, realizing that focussing on studies might be a better option. But with a solid core of Lee Edmondson, Jim Dudderidge, and Parris, the Vikes made it back to the Canada West finals and were on the verge of a breakthrough that came the very next season when they qualified for their first-ever berth in the CIAU Championships, losing in the quarterfinals.

By the 1978–79 season Shields had a stranglehold on Canada West, but he wouldn't be satisfied until he held that precious championship trophy. Led by conference all-stars Parris and Billy Loos, a high-scoring big man from Rhode Island, the Vikes made their first appearance in the finals to face off against the east coast powerhouse Huskies for the 1979 title.

The defending champions had been the dominant team of the 1970s on the strength of Mickey Fox, a five-time conference all-star and four-time All-Canadian who remained in the Huskies lineup despite the fact he could have parlayed his 1975 draft selection by the Detroit Pistons into a pro career.

The Huskies were in the midst of a spectacular season that included wins over NCAA stalwarts St. Joseph's and Boston College. Assembled media and basketball observers expected the Huskies to pull out an easy one over the unknown upstarts from the west coast, and Fox befuddled the Vikes with a flurry of points off of his unstoppable jumper. Parris and backcourt mate Reni Dolcetti held their own, however, and with Loos manning the middle, the Vikes held close heading into the final minutes. But a turnover on the last possession killed their chances and St. Mary's, paced by Fox's 37 points, became the first back-to-back CIAU champions since Windsor turned the trick in 1967. "We just couldn't handle Mickey," Parris recalled. "He was an incredible player."

Fox, reflecting on his brilliant final game in a Huskies' uniform, deflected attention to teammates such as Ross Quackenbush and Tom Kappos, saying, "I get all the glory because I'm the shooter but this team might have been the finest basketball team ever assembled in Canada."

As Shields shook hands with his east coast opponents, he silently fumed. He was losing Parris to graduation, but with Loos and leading scorer Reni Dolcetti returning, he had the makings of a powerhouse.

He built his dynasty one practice at a time, demanding precise execution, rarely smiling, and handing out compliments even less frequently. He also put in extra time after practice for individual player development, realizing that bench players would need to spell starters and could play key roles at unexpected moments. His personal touch was life-changing for reserve guard Ian Hyde-Lay, who arrived on campus the same year as Shields. Apprehensive and uncertain of how he would fit in on the team, Hyde-Lay found Shields tough and un-compromising but willing to work with him on the finer points of shooting and ball-handling. "Other than my parents, he's had a greater influence on my life than any other person," said Hyde-Lay, who went on to work as an assistant for Shields. "I was a very, very poor to average basketball player when I walked into UVic … certainly by no stretch of the imagination a top-level player, but I became a credible, functional CIAU player."

Shields's personal workouts boosted the young guard's confidence and in the 1979 final, coach counted on his walk-on to do what no one had managed for the entire decade — slow down Fox. The American superstar torched Hyde-Lay, but that was no different than most of Fox's other victims over the years, a fact that wasn't lost on Shields. "He pulled me aside and said that I had played well," Hyde-Lay recalled of the "completely surprising" comment from a man who typically equated losing with misery.

The loss did in fact eat away at Shields and his guys all summer long, but it also gave them a clear target to shoot for, and they responded like gangbusters. In 1979–80 the Vikes became the first team in Canada West history to post a 20–0 record in a year in which the conference had an incredible six teams in the CIAU top 10 at various points during the season. Forward Billy Loos became the Vikes's second All-Canadian and guard Rene Dolcetti scored 20 points and hauled in 13 rebounds in a 73–65 win over Brandon to give Shields his first championship.

The Vikes, paced by a steady stream of All-Canadians including Loos, Dolcetti, and Eli Pasquale, went on to establish a stranglehold on Canada West, winning seven conference titles in a row and taking the national championship every season from 1980 to 1986. Shields had such a stable of talent in Victoria that in 1981, five of his players made the senior men's national team.

Legendary Vikes stars such as six-foot-nine forward Gerald Kazanowski and sharpshooting guard Eli Pasquale became mainstays on the national team and would have been household names had they reached similar status in the United States, though of course they were completely anonymous in Canada outside of basketball circles. Vikes games could be seen on local television but hockey-obsessed Canadian networks have never made Canadian basketball a staple of their sports programming. Shields spent several years as Jack Donohue's assistant before Canada Basketball hired him to replace the legendary New Yorker in 1989, a job he held until 1994, during which time he even moved the national-team program to Victoria.

Shields didn't have to go far to talk hoops, since he was just one half of Canada's first couple of basketball. Kathy Shields arrived in Victoria in 1978 and propelled the Vikettes to the top of the heap in women's basketball almost immediately, winning the first of three straight championships in just her second season at the helm. Together with her husband, she re-established Victoria as Canada's basketball capital, a title it had held unofficially along with Windsor in the first half of the 20th century. The Shields monopoly over college basketball later extended to the national level when Kathy became head coach of the women's national team while Ken was still in charge of the men. But while their careers were mirror images, their coaching styles couldn't have been more different.

Ken, ever the perfectionist, was likely to tear a strip off of a player who was slacking off during suicide drills or failing to execute his carefully crafted game plan. Kathy preferred the diplomatic approach. "She's almost the antithesis of me," Ken told the CBC in 1994, just before he resigned from Team Canada. "Sometimes, I think she's too tolerant."

Kathy, who was sometimes aghast at the screaming and yelling during her husband's UVic practices, held her ground. "He could try and encourage a little bit more rather than demand constantly."

UVic's second of seven consecutive championships was won at the University of Waterloo in 1981, and Eli Pasquale (#13) was the MVP.

Different styles, but the same results, as they combined for ten CIAU championships and were both named to the Canadian Basketball Hall of Fame. In the process, the Shields family dynasty served as an inspiration for their players, many of whom went on to become coaches in a country where making a living on the court was a tall order.

The quality of CIAU basketball was at an all-time high by the 1980s, what with the number of college players donning the red and white for the Canadian national team that Donohue had built into a world power. A dozen CIAU players were even drafted into the NBA, in part because of the exposure from the Olympics and World Championships, but broadcasters were slow to jump on board. Regular season and championship games were relegated to local cable-access channels or regional broadcasts just as Magic Johnson and Larry Bird's epic 1979 championship matchup helped to put NCAA basketball in prime time, and into the public consciousness, south of the border.

But some big changes in Canada's television landscape provided the CIAU with a chance to rise from obscurity. Canada's broadcast watchdog, the CRTC, opened the door for a bevy of specialty channels to fill the cable grid in 1984, and the Labatt's brewery founded The Sports Network (TSN) to showcase pro sports. Amateur sports wouldn't be, and never has been, a major priority for the new outfit, but the CIAU was able to persuade TSN to broadcast the Final 8 men's and women's championship by the early 1990s. The championships had returned to the Metro Centre beginning in 1988 because of the town's love for the sport and the ability of organizers to pack the building with as many as 10,000 people for a game. It made for a raucous environment that translated well to television.

The CIAU changed its name to the CIS in 2001 and intensified its efforts in marketing and promotion. But if the product looked good, the viewers weren't catching on. Ratings for the Final 8 lagged behind more established products such as CIS football despite the fact that a second powerhouse had emerged that rivalled Ken Shields' Vikes and were led by a man cut from the same cloth as the take-no-prisoners west coast icon.

No matter whom you talk to about Dave Smart, one word keeps coming up — competitive. All you have to do is watch him work the sidelines, for example at the 2012 CIS Final 8, where he established himself as one of the most dominant winning machines anywhere in world basketball by taking his eighth national championship in 10 years, eclipsing Shields for most titles by one coach in CIS history.

In the 2012 quarterfinal, Smart's Ravens team was in a familiar position: up by 15 points against a tough opponent that was looking overmatched against his powerhouse squad. With just seven seconds left in the game, a berth in the semifinals all sewn up, one of his players deviated from his finely tuned game plan.

WHACK!

The sound of Smart's hand smashing the press table hard enough to cause journalists in the front row to jump back in fear and amazement; fear that perhaps someone had fired a gun in the arena and amazement at the realization that Smart was unable to enjoy an imminent inevitable victory for even one second of game time.

Winning comes at a price in Dave Smart's world, but his hard-driving ways were perhaps the only hope for glory for a basketball program that was little more than an afterthought among CIS powers.

Dave Smart's fiery intensity, attention to detail, and indomitable work ethic transformed the Carleton Ravens from a CIS afterthought into the greatest dynasty the college game has ever seen.

Photo by Murray McComb Photography.

Carleton University, nestled on the banks of the Rideau Canal south of downtown Ottawa, had nationally renowned journalism, law, and political science schools but no sports tradition to speak of when Smart took over the anonymous Ravens program in 1999. By that point no Ravens program had ever won a national championship in any sport.

On the hardwood, the Ravens men's basketball team had been thoroughly overshadowed by conference powers Western, McMaster, and Waterloo, breaking through to the nationals in 1968 and 1988. Ontario conference titles and national title game appearances continued to elude them, but that changed in a hurry as Smart, accustomed to starring on the court and obsessed with execution and planning, imposed his iron will on practices, promptly beginning the kind of winning habit that hadn't been seen in the CIS since the Shields era.

Peer into Dave Smart's past and you find a biography quite different from other historical figures in the Canadian game. Born in Kingston and raised in Ottawa, Smart loved hockey as a youth, only switching to basketball at Nepean High School in grade 10 when it became clear that the NHL wasn't in his future. He enrolled at Carleton in the mid 1980s, but a knee injury cut short his season and he soon left school. However, it turned out that Smart loved coaching even more than playing, enjoying the chance to execute a game plan and mentor young men with tangible results. "After I started coaching, I never really wanted to play again," he said in a 2008 interview. "I was coaching 350 games a year. All I was doing was coaching. I wasn't taking school seriously; I wasn't taking any kind of work seriously."[4]

He was completely undeterred by the fact that no high school in Canada would pay anyone more than a stipend to coach basketball exclusively — Smart threw everything he had into the job and rewarded Nepean high with a 1989 juvenile boys provincial championship.

Not satisfied with just one coaching job, Smart ran clinics across Ontario and the United States for the next two years before he finally decided to enrol at Queen's University, where his older brother Robert Sr. had once played basketball and later coached. He quickly rediscovered his love for the game, especially practice, excelling at shooting and becoming unguardable for the Golden Gaels. Smart seared his name into the Gaels record book from 1991 to 1994, recording the highest

153

career scoring average (26.6) and single-game scoring explosion (43) in program history. He seemed a shoo-in for the head coaching job that came open in his graduating year but Queen's administrators decided to pass on him and he returned to Ottawa to start up a club basketball program called the Guardsmen.

Carleton head coach Paul Armstrong persuaded Smart to join his staff in 1997 and the veteran coach resigned two years later, knowing that he was turning the program over to a perfectionist with a work ethic that was second to none but who wouldn't tolerate pretty-boys who refused to work. Smart's hard-driving style had driven four players right off the team — and that was just when he was an assistant! Basketball might not officially be seen as anything more than an extracurricular activity on Canadian college campuses, but don't tell that to the man who has taken the sport to never before seen heights. "As soon as someone says, 'it's only basketball … well then, I don't want them,'" said Smart who, like Ken Shields, was very stingy with compliments but quick to lose his temper over unacceptable mistakes.

Carleton made it to the OUA east final in Smart's first season, but in 2000–01 he led the Ravens to their first appearance at the nationals in more than a decade, and his All-Canadian starting shooting guard was none other than Rob Smart Jr., his brother's son. The six-foot-four deadeye shooter stayed around long enough to help his uncle usher in the longest sustained run of dominance in Canadian college basketball history.

The Ravens recorded a 21–1 record in 2002–03 and edged out Guelph 57–54 for their first national championship and the first for any Carleton team. They made it back-to-back titles in 2004 with another close win in the final against St. Francis Xavier, capping a season that saw them continue their record 50-game winning streak against CIS competition. By that time Rob Smart had given way to two of the coach's other nephews, guard Mike Smart and inside-out forward Aaron Doornekamp, related to Dave Smart through his sister. Guard Osvaldo Jeanty joined the pair to form an unstoppable core, and the Haitian-born sparkplug was the first player in CIS history to win Most Valuable Player of three consecutive championship games. The Final 8 shifted to Carleton's home base of Ottawa for 2008 and the Ravens machine actually slowed, with Acadia breaking the defending champions' streak of five straight titles by edging them out 82–80 in overtime. Carleton bounced back with a 10-point win over UBC in 2009. Smart eventually eclipsed Shields's longstanding record of titles, winning his ninth National Championship with a 50-point blowout over Lakehead in 2013. His streak included a 92 percent victory rate as well as an 87-game winning streak between 2003 and 2006.

The parallels between Smart and Ken Shields's Victoria dynasty are unavoidable, and it starts with the two men at the top, says Shields's former star guard Robbie Parris. "Really great coaches like Smart and Shields, they all have this ability to really make players accountable and really have a drive to make yourself better," said Parris.

His thoughts are echoed by Leo Rautins, a onetime national team coach who hired Smart as an assistant in 2005. "Ken Shields, who, like Dave Smart had a run of national championships — it's really been only the two of those guys who've had those kind of runs," said Rautins, who remembers Smart staying up all night watching game film of upcoming opponents.

Smart is living proof that Canadian college hoops can hit the big time through the will of one man who's able to make his players an extension of his own brilliant basketball mind. His Ravens are one of the few amateur

Courtesy of Carleton University Athletics.

Nine national championships in 14 seasons make the Carleton Ravens the greatest basketball dynasty on either side of the border. The 2008-09 team, pictured here, won the school's sixth championship in seven seasons.

sports shows in Canada that can lure up to 10,000 fans into an arena, the kind of exposure that can make a U.S.-minded Canadian 'baller think twice about heading south of the border. It's a testament to the allure of Smart's program that Doornekamp and several other Carleton stars turned down Division I scholarships to stay home and win championships.

While Smart has steadfastly refused to take credit for the greatest dynasty in CIS history, his players know better, as Doornekamp told reporters upon landing in Ottawa after beating Brandon for the 2007 title. "He's the best in the country by far, best in North America by far," said the forward. "Nobody works even close to as hard as he does, and it shows. We're an average group of guys and he makes us pretty special."[5]

Smart gave himself every advantage he could muster, including on the recruiting end, where he transformed his Guardsmen youth program into a feeder for the Ravens, echoing a model that Percy Page had used to build his Edmonton Grads women's hoops monster in the early 20th century.

And while the CIS isn't known as a pro breeding ground, several of Smart's All-Canadians have also gone on to play for money, including Doornekamp and Jeanty, the best guard in program history, who went on to Germany's first pro division in 2008.

Smart's success notwithstanding, the talent drain to the United States remained an intractable problem for the CIS into the 21st century, and the status quo simply wasn't good enough for some schools in the West and in Atlantic Canada, who had grown tired of butting heads with the central Canadian establishment over the issue of "full-ride" athletic scholarships of the type offered in the NCAA.

The scholarship debate created a deadlock that caused traditionalists in Ontario and Quebec to dig in their heels for fear that expanded scholarships would create a pro-style system of jocks eyeing the pros while paying lip service to their classes. Programs on both coasts, which had joined the CIS more recently and were less tradition-bound, wanted to grow their athletic programs and gain a recruiting advantage. Such programs also typically faced less resistance from administrators than their brethren in Ontario and Quebec.

Facing pressure from the coasts, the CIS by 2001 allowed for partial scholarships to athletes, but only for those who entered school with an 80 percent academic average or better. By 2010–11, CIS basketball players were getting an average $3,500 in annual scholarships to offset tuitions that were about $5,100 a year on average. About half of all players received the money, but athletic departments were limited to covering tuition and fees and could only offer scholarships to 70 percent of the members of any one team. What's more, budget-conscious athletic directors at some schools only allowed their basketball coaches a few scholarship players per team.

Compare that to NCAA Division I schools, which had as many as 13 scholarships per team and could offer a top player fully subsidized tuition plus money for food, lodging, and books, in a deal worth tens of thousands of dollars a year.

Also weighing on a Canadian high-schooler's mind was the massive television exposure offered to "high-major" basketball and football in the six so-called Power Six conferences — the SEC, ACC, Big 10, Pac-12, Big East, and Big 12. By 2011, ESPN was broadcasting or webcasting most regular-season basketball and football games in the Power Six, offering pro scouts a chance to scope out new talent from the comfort of their homes, if they so desired. Any games the scouts missed were conveniently archived for their viewing pleasure.

For top Canadian basketball players, especially young men with their eyes on the pros, it's an easy decision — head south for the winter. The results were predictable — the tallest, most talented, and most athletic Canadians were scooped up by Division I schools like never before. By 2005 an average of 80 Canadian men and 50 women were playing for Division I schools every year, plus as many as 100 others who played at U.S. high schools, junior colleges, and NCAA Division II schools, the latter of which also offered athletic scholarships.

It's a frustrating situation for CIS coaches who would often watch superstar local players at their high school games with full knowledge that the young men never seriously considered staying home. The talent drain also led to a sense of defeatism among some Canadian coaches, according to players, who wondered why CIS coaches never bothered to show up to their games.

Such was the case for Leo Rautins, one of the greatest Canada has ever produced. Athletic and standing six foot eight, but with unusually refined guard skills for such a large man, the Toronto wing caught Jack Donohue's eye in the summer of 1977 after the youngster was inexplicably cut from the Ontario provincial team. Canada's Mr. Basketball before Steve Nash, Rautins was good enough to start for Donohue while still a high-schooler, and he later starred at Syracuse University before being picked 17th in the first round of the 1983 NBA draft by the defending champion Philadelphia 76ers. Rautins, who went on to become a commentator on Toronto Raptors broadcasts, has long wondered why CIS coaches never so much as called him with an offer to stay home and play in front of family and friends. "When I was coming out of high school I was recruited by everybody in the States. Name the school and they recruited me. I had one Canadian school go after me. One," he told an Ottawa newspaper, referring to Simon Fraser, which played in the U.S.-based NAIA division at the time.[6]

Staying home might seem at first glance to have been an absurd notion for a player of Rautins's talent since CIAU schools had no schol-arships to offer him in 1978, but he insists he would have at least listened to a pitch from a Canadian program. The problem, as Rautins sees it, is an "unchallenged level of mediocrity" by CIS programs that annually lose dozens of players to the ultra-competitive U.S. basketball industry. It's a basketball machine that continues to churn out greater amounts of cash every year, fuelled largely by lucrative broadcasting deals that attract young players from around the world, even to high school programs that routinely get airtime, in HD, on ESPN and other networks.

The biggest earner is the Southeastern Conference (SEC), whose programs earned $91.6 million in 2010–11, largely from broadcasting deals for football. Much of the money is dumped back into the pot to fund non-revenue sports, but power conference basketball and football head coaches also get a huge cut, with annual salaries averaging more than $1 million.

Watching all of this closely from north of the border was the University of British Columbia, which was aggressively expanding its sports facilities in the early 21st century while eyeing new revenue streams. UBC athletic director Bob Philip was also a vocal critic of the CIS's go-slow approach to full-ride scholarships. Philip was even prepared to abandon the only sports association his school had ever known to get a bigger piece of the pie.

By the turn of the millennium, UBC offered 29 intercollegiate sports and boasted a new multipurpose arena, two new artificial turf soccer fields, a renovated football stadium, and a multimillion-dollar scholarship endowment fund. Philip knew that his school's facilities already rivalled those of many NCAA sports programs, but at that time NCAA bylaws forbade non-American members.

A surprise meeting with NCAA vice-president Bernard Franklin at an athletics conference gave Philip the opening to prod a little further. "Could there ever be a circumstance where UBC could compete athletically in the NCAA?" Philip asked Franklin, to which the American answered "yes."

His answer lit a spark that posed the biggest threat the CIS had seen since its founding a century earlier. In January 2008, largely because of Philip's lobbying, the NCAA announced a 10-year pilot project to accept foreign schools for memberships into its ranks for the first time, and Simon Fraser, UBC, and the University of Alberta publicly announced they would consider the idea.

A 2009 UBC review committee report, based in part on enthusiastic recommendations from Philip's department, said a move to the NCAA "would protect the level of competition, attract more community and student support and [have] no negative impact on UBC's academic mission."[7]

Philip said UBC brought academic credibility to the NCAA and that the higher profile and increased scholarship packages would keep athletes on the lower B.C. mainland from fleeing south. "That was by and large the biggest reason athletes chose to attend school in the States," Philip said on the eve of the school's final decision in April 2011. "We currently have about a million dollars that is spread amongst all of our student-athletes. If we join the NCAA, we're looking to immediately raise that figure to two million."[8]

Getting the NCAA to open the door to Canada was just half of the battle — now Philip and his staff would have to sell the idea at home. On-campus consultations revealed a split between administrators who were ready to grow UBC's athletic department by making the seismic move and students and professors who invoked patriotic reasons why UBC should stay put. Varsity football player Nathan Kanya said the CIS needed all of its parts if it planned to grow. "We need CIS and Canadian sports to get better," he said, adding that "moving to the NCAA would be letting down the CIS and Canadian athletes."[9]

CIS president Clint Hamilton and fellow executives Leo MacPherson and Marg McGregor met with UBC president and chancellor Stephen

Toope on March 14, 2011, to discuss UBC's impending move. It would clearly be a devastating blow to the CIS, especially in football and basketball, which would no longer have UBC's mainstay programs to use as leverage when negotiating its relatively modest television deals.

In a March 28, 2011 letter to Toope, CIS executives reminded him of his school's storied history in Canadian sport while refuting allegations that the governing body was dragging its heels on scholarships and quality of competition in Canada West. Hamilton reminded Toope that UBC wasn't yet maxing out its CIS scholarship allotment, suggesting that Philip had the means under the current system to further entice basketball players who were thinking about leaving home. "As CIS prepares to celebrate its 50th anniversary, we sincerely hope UBC chooses to remain a member and to work with us as we address pressing issues and grow CIS into the future," the letter concluded.

In the end, Toope decided to stay put, announcing on April 26 that UBC would hold off on an NCAA move despite the fact that the CIS had yet to resolve key issues. Part of what convinced UBC to stay home was the resolve to create a CIS super league and significantly beef up scholarship packages that could spur unprecedented growth in the CIS and open up new marketing opportunities.

College athletics found itself at a crucial point in its history, torn by the potentially conflicting promise of new revenue streams against core values of academic integrity. Any aggressive move to grow the CIS would also put intense pressure on the organization's tiny staff in Ottawa, who would have to police potential athletic and academic fraud that could become a larger factor amid a chase for dollars.

The CIS says it "provides student-athletes the best there is to offer in Canada," but it's facing pressures from its much larger American cousin. UBC, the runaway bride who finally chose fight over flight, pledged to take a leadership role in financial and competitive reforms that could, ironically, bring the CIS closer in vision to the NCAA than it has ever been.

CHAPTER 9

— LOOSE BALLS —

Cleveland's sad-sack NBA franchise, the Cavaliers, shocked more than a few observers when they selected an amiable, lanky teen from Brampton, Ontario, as the fourth pick in the 2011 draft as they tried to replace former franchise player LeBron James. Cleveland was still reeling from James's departure a year earlier, a move seen by locals as pure betrayal.

The departure of "King James" to Miami sent the Cavaliers into a free fall from powerhouse to doormat. The team suffered an unprecedented 40-win decline, including a 26-game losing streak that was the longest in North American professional sports history. Though James would never receive thanks for it, the debacle did come with a silver lining: Cleveland's league-worst record put it in a position to snare not one, but two top talents in the 2011 draft, with the first and fourth picks.

Six-foot-nine forward Tristan Thompson had already been tipped off that the Cavaliers would pick him number 4, making him the highest born and bred Canadian draft selection up to that point. Decked out in a dark double-breasted suit, spotted tie, and brown shoes, Thompson was calm and collected when NBA commissioner David Stern called his name on June 23, 2011, at the Prudential Center in Newark, New Jersey.

His grandmother wasn't quite as placid. Seated with Thompson in the "green room," where top draft picks wait to hear their names called, she let out a scream that could be heard halfway across the arena floor. Thompson hugged her, donned a Cavaliers cap, and began his slow walk up the stairs to shake hands with Stern, whose league has been the ultimate destination for Thompson and countless other Canadian kids who dream of NBA glory nearly impossible to attain in their home country.

Thompson, a former paperboy, had become another of Canada's basketball vagabonds whose parents entrust their children's lives to professional coaches employed by prep schools that feed the NBA's unofficial farm system — college basketball. Legions of mostly black teenagers from Canada are all chasing one big prize — the coveted "full ride" scholarship to a university whose team competes in the National Collegiate Athletic Association (NCAA). The one-year package covers tuition, lodging, food, and books for some of the top amateur players in the world. If the "student-athlete" performs up to expectations, the scholarship is renewed. If not, they lose their athlete status but are free to continue on as students — on their own coin, of course.

Amateur basketball is big business in the United States. Just about every North American NBA prospect comes from a relatively small number of "high-major" Division I programs that can each generate between $5 million and $15 million in annual profits for their schools. The NCAA's crown jewel is the wildly popular Men's Basketball Tournament, dubbed March Madness. The three-week whirlwind pits 68 teams against one another in a single-elimination thrill ride that culminates in the National Championship in early April. The property is so popular that CBS and Turner Sports paid $10.8 billion in 2010 for 14 years of exclusive TV and Internet broadcast rights. Not part of the equation are the billions more that are gambled away in office tournament pools and gambling rings around the world.

March Madness offers the greatest platform for would-be NBA stars. College players make up more than three-quarters of the 60 athletes drafted into the NBA every year. Kyrie Irving, the top pick in the 2011 draft for Cleveland, was guaranteed $5.3 million in his first season, with teammate Thompson pocketing $3.8 million as the fourth pick. It's a journey perhaps only Thompson thought was possible.

He's the oldest of four boys raised by Trevor, a truck driver, and Andrea, a school bus driver, who were among a generation of West Indians who immigrated to Canada in search of jobs and financial security that are scarce in tiny Caribbean nations. The Thompsons initially lived in Toronto but eventually settled in Brampton, a sprawling west-end bedroom community that has swelled in size as former city dwellers flee downtown and its sky-high housing prices. Basketball was an afterthought for Trevor and Andrea, whose fellow Jamaicans usually gravitate to track, cricket, and soccer, but the lure of hoops was irresistible to young Tristan. By grade five he was tall for his age and eager to emulate the college and pro stars whose exploits are featured regularly on slickly produced American sports broadcasts. Andrea remembers her son hopping with glee after school one day when he heard the Brampton Warriors, a local club team, were looking for players. "He said 'Mummy, mummy, I really want to go try out for this basketball.'"[1]

Tristan excelled through elementary school and into middle school and soon sprouted well past six feet. Brampton-based Tony McIntyre, who coached Thompson in the Blue Devils club program, said the young athlete's work ethic set him apart. They would work together in the gym for hours on end and Thompson never seemed to get enough of the chance to improve his game. "By the time grade 8, grade 9 got around, you knew there was something special because his development really started to take off. He started to work out a little bit harder; you started to see that he was a kid who was special."

That was in 2003, when Raptors superstar Vince Carter virtually owned Toronto and the NBA. Thompson, like many Canadian kids, was smitten by the NBA star's flashy dunks, but even at 13 he knew he would have to excel at a U.S. college before he could ever star in the big show. Andrea recalls: "I remember when he was in the seventh grade, he said, 'Mummy, I want to be in the NBA.' I said 'Why?' He said, 'Mummy, the life is so nice. The only thing you have to do is work out hard in the gym, relax, go back and play.' I said, 'That's the life you like?' He said 'Yes.' I said 'Go for it.' He predicted that this is the life he wants."[2]

Thompson left home for Newark, New Jersey, in 2007, where he enrolled at St. Benedict's Preparatory School, a Catholic academy of 8,000 students that has sent dozens of basketball players to big college programs. Andrea Thomson admits to some reticence about letting her baby go at the ripe age of 15, but she says Tristan was always wise and responsible beyond his years. He had a paper route at 14 and always took care of business at home. "He always made sure … his room is clean, all his duties were done and [then] go take the bus and play basketball, so he's very independent," she said. "Before he even went to St. Benedict's he did all his research. When I spoke to the coach, he said, 'you know when I interviewed your son he knows everything about me.' I said wow. Tristan was so advanced. You could just know that he was ready."[3]

He knew where his bread was buttered when a reporter at the draft asked him who should take the credit for his success. He immediately blurted out the names of his parents, who had instilled in him the same work ethic they lived by as they built a new life in their adopted country. They're among a wave of West Indians and Africans who have arrived in Canada since 1961, when Ottawa changed immigration rules to allow for more skilled labourers from non-European countries. The new arrivals sponsored siblings, children, and spouses, changing the face of Toronto, Montreal, and other cities. Canada's black population, just 31,000 in 1961, swelled sevenfold to 239,000 by 1981 and had doubled again to 504,300 by 1991. That was the same year that Andrea gave birth to Tristan, who is part of a generation that increasingly prefers blacktop courts to ice hockey rinks. All you need to play basketball is a pair of athletic shoes and a ball — no expensive equipment and no teammates, if you want to work on your game solo.

Not only is basketball inexpensive, but it's got another quality that matters in the streets — it's cool. "Basketball has become synonymous with everything else that is urban," says former player Wayne Dawkins, whose All-Canada Classic brought together some of the best high school players from across Canada for several years. "The rap music, the clothing, that whole culture that calls every black person. You don't even have a choice but to like basketball and rap or people say 'you're not black,'" he adds, laughing.

By the 1970s, outdoor courts in Toronto's west end Jane and Finch neighbourhood and Montreal's north end Côte-des-Neiges borough were packed with young kids who had visions of NBA lights dancing in their heads. The odds were against them — only eight Canadians had ever suited up in an NBA game since the league's creation in 1946 until the early 1980s. What's more, all of the Canadian draftees up to that point had been white — U.S. coaches hadn't yet tapped into Canada's inner-city talent pool. That all changed when two Caribbean-Canadians, Montreal's Bob White and Toronto's Ro Russell a decade later, helped to showcase young urban players to American suitors while making mortal enemies at home.

Rohan "Ro" Russell arrived in Canada from Jamaica at the age of four in the early 1970s. He grew up in the multicultural, poverty-ridden Jane and Finch area, where he learned the game on street courts and became a successful player in the late 1980s, attending two small U.S. colleges before returning home to coach the young players who came behind him. Russell founded a summer basketball program in 1992, and was one of the first coaches in Canada to take travelling all-star teams to the States to compete in summer Amateur Athletic Union (AAU) tournaments.

The AAU circuit is a loosely regulated collection of private club teams controlled by coaches and outfitted by the big sneaker companies. The industry is centred on the talents of aspiring young pros who peddle their skills before college coaches in gyms from Orlando to Las Vegas. "You can dominate in Canada, but the true litmus test doesn't come until you do it in America," said Russell, who has seen scores of players from his Grassroots Canada program move on to play university basketball. "There's a huge difference in how they market and expose top athletes."[4]

And in AAU basketball, exposure is the thing. Teams play in a dizzying array of tournaments from May to August. Five or six games a day is not unheard of for hungry young athletes looking to land scholarship offers and rise up the online player rankings. Shoe companies are also looking for exposure of their own, having realized decades ago that they could gain huge visibility by outfitting entire teams from head to toe. One Canadian AAU coach recalls arriving at a tournament in Virginia where players were lined up by the hundreds to receive a motherlode of athletic wear. "Gear was arriving by the busload," he recalled, listing off shoes, headbands, and even flip-flops. "It was crazy. Probably over $1 million of gear exchanged hands between programs and kids. Box loads, box loads. It was like a factory line."

The pioneering figure on the sneaker circuit was shoe company executive Sonny Vaccaro, who created the first high school tournaments and all-star games in the 1960s in Pittsburgh and Chicago. In 1984, Vaccaro signed budding NBA superstar Michael Jordan to his first contract with Nike, ushering in a new era of sports apparel and endorsements. By the 2000s, high school basketball had become a billion-dollar business as Nike, Adidas, and Reebok scrambled to sign deals with amateur basketball teams and their coaches. Critics say corruption was quick to follow.

One AAU figure says high school coaches who are signed with one shoe company often discourage their players from joining summer teams sponsored by a rival firm. Worse are the rumours that some AAU coaches are paid under the table to steer players toward certain colleges. Ro Russell dove headlong into the amateur basketball business and the rumours, criticism, and innuendo that came with it. By 1995 he found himself competing for players on his home turf with Dawkins, also a former scholarship athlete with his own summer program. "Mine was called Toronto Elite Development and his was Elite Toronto Development," said Dawkins, noting the irony of the near-identical names. Both men soon realized it was time to combine their talents and conquer American basketball under a new moniker — Grassroots Canada.

Grassroots, comprised almost entirely of Toronto-area blacks, made an immediate impact on the AAU scene. It was the only travelling team in the Greater Toronto Area at the time and Russell and Dawkins had their pick of the top players. "When we travelled anywhere, it was a dozen Division I players," said Dawkins. "Coaches used to call us and say 'just give me a Grassroots player.' They didn't ask who, because they knew every single person on our roster was a Division I player." Sometimes Russell and Dawkins didn't even wait for summertime before taking their teams south of the border. They irked their Toronto coaching brethren in 2001 when they formed an in-season travelling team that showcased top city players at major U.S. winter tournaments. That triggered a whisper campaign that questioned their loyalty to Canada, with suggestions that they were profiting personally whenever a player signed a D-I scholarship.

"People started accusing us of all kinds of stuff [like] 'they're selling kids,'" said Dawkins. "People couldn't understand how we could take a group of inner-city kids and go all the way to France. How do you take a group of inner-city kids and you're travelling to U.S. tournaments all the time?" He says the reality of AAU fundraising at Grassroots was far more innocuous than the naysayers want to believe. He remembers sending his players out into the street to wash cars by hand to pay for an upcoming tournament. They scraped together enough money to embark on an international tour in the summer of 2001, led by muscle-bound forward Denham Brown, who once scored 111 points in a high school game for West Hill Secondary in the east end Toronto borough of Scarborough. Brown's strength, athleticism, and scoring touch propelled Grassroots to wins over several world powers including an

Argentinean team that featured future NBA All-Star Manu Ginobili. Grassroots later lost a close match in France to a star-studded U.S.A. squad led by forward Carmelo Anthony, who went on to become an NBA superstar.

But while Grassroots touts itself as "Canada's #1 Student Athlete Development Program," rival coaches say Russell's rise to the top has left its share of victims. Faced with a lack of financial support in Toronto and dogged by badmouthing from a coaching fraternity that kept him on the sidelines, Russell decided to join the Americans instead of beating them. In 2009, following a short stint at a Pennsylvania prep school, he moved to Creedmoor, North Carolina, where he was named head basketball coach at Christian Faith Center Academy. The school's stated mission is to "impact the lives of today's students for Christ" and to "minister and reach children from low- to mid-income households and dysfunctional back-grounds." Russell adopted the nickname Ro the Rev while stocking his new team with Grassroots players and proceeding to ruffle some feathers in Canada's basketball establishment.

Former Toronto hoops legend Leo Rautins, an NBA draft pick and long-time broadcaster and coach, refused to discuss Russell directly. But he took a thinly veiled shot when asked about Russell's impact on the basketball scene. "There's a lot of people that love to get their hands on the kids for selfish means," said Rautins, who was named head coach of the Canadian national team in 2005. "There's a way to make money off of these kids, these kids are being put into all kinds of prep schools. Some never graduated, as a matter of fact a large percentage have nothing to show for their time that they have played and that's the thing that scares me." Rautins says that many of the players are raised by single mothers who don't understand the system and have "blind trust" in AAU coaches. "If I come up to you and say 'Hey, I've got this cell phone right here. Give me $1,000 bucks for it.' Are you just going to give me $1,000 bucks for it? Find out who you're dealing with."

Russell insists he got into coaching to help disadvantaged kids get an education as well as a shot at pro basketball. He rejects any suggestion of nefarious motives. "That troubled me, really hurt me," he says. "I'm taking the time and effort, leaving my family, playing father, uncle and social worker to these kids and people don't appreciate it. The kids and parents love you, but the coaches don't. This was totally confusing and hurtful to me. I'm doing a service and the basketball community is negative about it. They are saying, 'Ro is making money off the kids,' rather than seeing that I got a kid a scholarship worth $100,000. No, there is no graft, no evidence of anything."[5]

The spotlight shone even brighter on Russell following the success of Tristan Thompson, who joined Grassroots at age 15 and quickly made noise on the summer circuit. The west ender teamed up with sweet-shooting east end guard Cory Joseph of Pickering, and the wins piled up. Their crowning achievement came in the summer of 2008 when their 17-and-under team, coached by Russell, won the Adidas Super 64 tournament before a bevy of Division I coaches in Las Vegas. Their double-overtime victory over Los Angeles powerhouse the Compton Magic was touted as the biggest win by a Canadian amateur basketball squad on U.S. soil. A country that rarely produced NBA players and was known as a puck power had beaten the mighty Americans at their own hoops game. Thompson and Joseph parlayed the victory into scholarships at the University of Texas and they later became the first Canadians to declare for the NBA draft after just one year of college. Joseph was a surprising late first-round pick by the San Antonio Spurs in the same draft as his running mate.

On the eve of the draft, Thompson made no bones about his allegiance to Russell. "He's the man behind everything," the young forward told Toronto reporters following a workout with the Raptors. "He's given me the opportunity to really go down to the States, been a mentor to me and decide which college choices I should make. He's done a lot for me and my family and I've got to give him all the thanks." Russell was one of Thompson's exclusive guests in the draft green room on that momentous night in New Jersey. When his two Grassroots mainstays heard their names called, the 42-year-old coach might have wielded as much influence in the sport as any Canadian on the planet.

In central Canada's other metropolis of Montreal, another Canadian basketball lifer with West Indian roots has also made friends and foes by shuttling young athletes south of the 49th parallel. Bob White says he has given young, poor, inner-city black youths a chance at success in athletics that he claims is denied them at home because of their skin colour.

Race and racism are frequent topics in the world of White, son of a Jamaican storeowner and a proud native of Little Burgundy. The working-class neighbourhood of row houses and shops is the historic heart of Montreal's English-speaking black community. It's home to descendants of 19th-century slaves and more recent West Indian immigrants in a mainly French city where being English causes its share of problems while being a visible minority can be a double whammy. That was certainly the case in the early 20th century, when many black men, unlikely to find work in department stores or on the St. James financial strip, were relegated to the railways, where they worked as sleeping-car porters and freight-train loaders. But it wasn't all heartache — black Montrealers were Canada's jazz music pioneers, led by national treasures such as pianists Oscar Peterson and Oliver Jones. Noted Philadelphia jazz bassist Charlie Biddle adopted Montreal as his own in the 1940s and raised several children there who went on to become successful jazz artists in their own right. Hockey and baseball were also favourite pastimes and blacks had their own hero to idolize on the baseball diamond when Jackie Robinson broke the sport's colour barrier with the Montreal Royals in 1946. Young blacks also dabbled in hockey on outdoor rinks, but buying equipment was out of the question. "Remember *Life* magazine? We used to fill our clothes with those for padding," recalls one Montrealer who grew up in Burgundy in the 1940s.

The city's black population was small in the pre-war era, numbering just a few thousand, and everyone knew each other, often by name. Many were on a first-name basis with grocer Benjamin White, who was legendary for handing out freebies to new arrivals at his corner store. He enrolled his children at the local YMCA on Stanley Street to help them stay out of trouble, instilling in his kids a spirit of racial pride that doesn't seem to have dimmed in his son Bob's intervening 60 years. Free-swearing and blunt, Bob White recalled his father's work in founding the Veteran Taxi Association to provide jobs for black Canadian soldiers who were stung by racism when they returned to Montreal from overseas tours. "The trains came in to Windsor Station carrying the soldiers, and the band would be playing," said White. "As soon as they see the black guys, the band stopped. The veterans couldn't get jobs."

By the late 1960s Little Burgundy was in a steep decline. Many blacks had moved to Ontario amid declining job prospects, and swelling French separatist sentiment added a linguistic layer to longstanding racial tensions. Many who remained in Burgundy struggled to finish high school and avoid a life of crime. More recent community portraits paint a depressing picture.

A 2004 Quebec health department analysis found that nearly a third of Caribbean families in the province were headed by a single parent, usually a woman. Poverty and unemployment were more prevalent among black women than others, and while racism was difficult to quantify, interviews with blacks suggested it was a reality of life. "They experience prejudice as women and as blacks and … because they are poor, single-parent women or immigrants," said the study. "The percentage of low-income black households is double that of the Quebec population as a whole."

White says he did what he could to help local kids through his specialty — athletics. White founded the West End Sports Association in 1976, and basketball, which by then had displaced baseball as the game of choice in Burgundy, was the featured attraction. All that the WSA was missing was a place to play — the parks in Burgundy didn't have basketball courts. So White rigged up nets by filling tires with cement, sinking poles into the base and attaching a rim and backboard. By the winter of 1976, White was renting local school gyms for pickup basketball games where young players could hone their skills. The early stars were a trio of skinny pre-teens named Trevor Williams, Wayne Yearwood, and Tommy Kane.

All three became major local standouts by the late '70s, but Kane was in a class by himself. Standing five foot nine and weighing just 160 pounds, Kane excelled at track, hockey, and football as well as basketball. Legend has it that Kane outplayed future NHL immortal Mario Lemieux in a midget hockey game at the old Forum. Kane, who could dunk a basketball from a standing start despite his short stature, led Dawson College to a national championship in 1983, with Yearwood and Williams playing key roles. White says he quickly realized that big-time American sports were Kane's ticket out of poverty. The young man had been raised by a single mother and his father wasn't part of his life. "I am a realist," says White, "I went through it, and there's no hope down there [in Burgundy] because there's no help when you come from dysfunctional families."

White's solution was the same one that Ro Russell would hatch 15 years later — load young protégés into a van, drive them to major American basketball camps and tournaments, and let the talent speak for itself.

White's plan worked. Kane secured scholarship offers for basketball and football at Syracuse University in upstate New York, opting for football when he was forced to choose between the two. Yearwood (West Virginia) and Williams (Southern University) followed their ex-teammate to the NCAA. Kane and Yearwood both obtained their degrees in 1988, the same year that Kane was drafted by the Seattle Seahawks of the National Football League. "[Tommy] was the first Quebecer ever to go to the NFL and play," says White, and Kane remained loyal well after others dismissed White as an overbearing self-promoter.

"Without Bobby I'd have never got out of Little Burgundy," Kane said in a 1990 interview, before adding ominous words: "There's a good chance I could have ended up in jail like a lot of my friends."

After a two-year stint with the Seahawks, Kane went on to play in the Canadian Football League before injuries curtailed his career. He later drifted into depression and drug use and was sentenced to 15 years in prison in 2004 for the beating death of Tamara Shaikh, his ex-wife and mother of his three children.

White, meanwhile, remains as fiery as ever, accusing the Canadian establishment of ignoring his good work in Little Burgundy for one simple reason — racism. "When you say basketball, what ethnic origin do people think [of]?" White asks rhetorically. "Black," is his answer. "They didn't want to have a basketball court down in Burgundy. You've got to keep the kids off the streets. They didn't want that. They want to fill the jails with the kids."

Love them or not, Bob White and Ro Russell's Canadian travelling basketball teams made U.S. programs wise to the talent pool north of the border. By the mid 1990s it was common to see dapper millionaire Division I coaches crowding into tiny Canadian high school gyms to try to snatch the next hidden northern gem. Pretty soon Canadian players started bolting for the States even before they graduated high school, preferring the intensely competitive U.S. prep school system that could offer a direct route to Division I basketball.

By 2000, the Canadian talent drain had become a deluge.

When gregarious Toronto guard Myck Kabongo isn't smiling, it seems as if a grin is never far from his lips. In 2010, the Congo-born athlete had even more reason to break out in a grin when he had a chance to take over from fellow Canadians Tristan Thompson and Cory Joseph at one of America's top prep programs. Kabongo replaced them as the cornerstone talent at Findlay Prep, an elite program affiliated with The Henderson International School, a private academy outside Las Vegas, Nevada. His basketball voyage had taken him from Toronto's Eastern Commerce High School down to St. Benedict's in New Jersey and then on to Findlay, which needed him more than he needed them. He had already committed to play at the University of Texas before he landed in Sin City. Findlay assistant coach Anthony Johnson said it only made sense to keep tapping into the Canadian hoops pipeline. "When you get a good thing, you gotta keep going with it," said Johnson. "Cory and Tristan were great players for us. Myck was kinda like their baby brother. So we've got to kinda keep going that Canadian route and hopefully keep getting wins."[6]

Kabongo is more comfortable than most teens when speaking to adults, and upon landing in Nevada got right to work making acquaintances in the suburban neighbourhood where Findlay players room together. Before he even walks through the front door, Kabongo stops on the steps to chat. "I'm new to the neighbourhood," he blurts out to a man shepherding a toddler in front of the house next door. Kabongo continues: "Nice to meet you. Myck."

"Mark," the neighbour replies. Kabongo, without missing a beat, smiles back. "You guys take care."[7] Then he enters his third home in three years.

It's a good thing Kabongo makes friends quickly, since he didn't stay in one place for long after he left Toronto at age 16. He had only been at St. Benedict's for a year before he bolted when head coach Danny Hurley left to take a job at a Division I school. Kabongo joined a Findlay Prep program moulded in the image of its hard-driving coach, Michael Peck. Peck is a tanned, dark-haired man who rarely smiles, is not above swearing to get a point across, and runs his squires through gruelling two-hour practices. He has the ultra-intense demeanour of a man who lives and breathes basketball and treats it like the business that it has become. Peck's attitude rubs off on his players, who often use business terms in interviews and seem fully aware that they're unpaid workers in a lucrative basketball industry.

Aside from Kabongo, Findlay managed to secure the services of two other promising Canadian talents for the 2010–11 season, notably barrel-chested Brampton native Anthony Bennett, who was left without a team following the closure of Mountain State prep school in West Virginia. The six-foot-seven, 240-pound power forward is quietly confident, and says coming to the desert was a "good deal" brokered by his AAU coach back home. He echoes the opinion of most Canadian high school players who want a piece of the potentially lucrative basketball pie. "Findlay Prep's Canadian players are developing and getting better, and us Canadians, when we're back there, we see that," said Bennett, who, like Kabongo and Thompson, came south before graduating high school. "Everybody back home is talking about 'Oh, they want to come to Findlay Prep.' But not a lot of people can make that happen. So when I got the chance, I jumped on it."[8]

Smaller but equally bold is guard Nazareth "Naz" Long of Mississauga, located just west of Toronto. Brash and full of gusto, Long uses a military analogy to explain the extent to which the Canadians have bonded thousands of kilometres away from family and friends: "I'm ready to go to war," says Long, his Canadian accent laced with a slight American twang after several years in the States. "If you go in the game … your brothers are depending on you. I just gotta go out there and fight for my brothers like my brothers will fight for me."[9]

Kabongo echoes Long's sentiment, but in somewhat gentler terms. "It was like a family atmosphere, a brotherhood," he said. "I look at everybody on this team as my brother away from home. And I gotta look out for them 'cuz I know they gotta look out for me at the end of the day."[10] But Nazareth Long didn't finish out at Findlay. He lasted just one season in Nevada before transferring to another prep school, his third in three years. He eventually finished high school back in Canada, but still realized his dream and signed with Iowa State.

Findlay doesn't have its own school building or gym, but still has emerged as a top prep program that graduated most of its players. The same can't be said for many other schools in the loosely regulated industry whose poor academic track record ensnared one of Canada's top players in the mid 2000s. Brampton big man Theo Davis was touted as an NBA prospect by several U.S. scouting services after a star turn at Cardozo

High School in Queens, New York, in 2004–05. But he was declared academically ineligible during his senior year and transferred to Lutheran Christian Academy in Philadelphia to get eligible for Division I. The school had a stellar reputation as a basketball factory but an equally questionable academic record lurked beneath the surface. A 2006 *Washington Post* investigation revealed Lutheran didn't have a building or classrooms and "operates out of a community center in a ragged North Philadelphia neighborhood."[11] Its only full-time employee, Darryl Schofield, also founded the "school" and doubled as basketball coach and Lutheran's only teacher. Once he got to Lutheran, the six-foot-nine Davis was declared ineligible a second time, this time for admission to Iowa State University, and bounced around several schools as his skills stagnated and his NBA draft stock crumbled.

The game of academic musical chairs irks basketball analyst Jack Armstrong, who recruited Canadian players as head coach at Niagara University in Niagara Falls, New York. He says many Canadian players who head to American basketball academies are buying into a myth. "The thing that I think is absolutely insane right now is the concept that a player in southern Ontario or anywhere in Canada has to go to the United States to play at some scam basketball academy," said Armstrong, who coached at Niagara from 1988 to 1998. "People are saying 'Well the coaching isn't good enough [in Canada], the competition isn't good enough, and therefore you're not going to develop.' I think that's a crock." The Brooklyn-born coach says the Canadian system might be smaller than its cousin to the south, but it's also cleaner. "The atmosphere is more pure, it's less tainted, kids don't have their hands out," said Armstrong. "It's on the up and up.... I want to deal with those types of players, those types of families, and those types of coaches in the recruiting."

But with the talent drain accelerating by the year, there are fewer big-time Canadian players to choose from. High school rosters in Montreal and Toronto have become depleted as dozens of players leave the country annually, sometimes after the eighth grade. You would think Kevin Jeffers, head coach of Kabongo's former Eastern Commerce team, would be insulated from that exodus. Jeffers runs perhaps the finest high school basketball program in Canada, boasting multiple provincial championships and dozens of players who went on to Division I programs. He can

Courtesy of UK Athletics.

Jamaal Magloire, from Toronto's Eastern Commerce High School, drew mainstream media attention when he signed with the University of Kentucky in 1996. The six-foot-eleven centre was an Honorable Mention All-American in 2000 and a first-round NBA draft pick the same year. "Big Cat" was an NBA All-Star in 2004, scoring 16 points and hauling down eight rebounds in the game.

even point to photos of the school's greatest alumnus — 2004 NBA All-Star Jamaal Magloire. But all of that history wasn't enough to keep Kabongo and other aspiring stars from leaving town. Jeffers says things have become so chaotic that some Toronto coaches don't even know if they'll finish the season with a complete roster. "A lot of kids walked in our doors in the beginning of September and went to prep schools," says Jeffers. "With the prep school situation down south it's difficult. I hear some teams this year lost six or seven guys and those are key players."[12] Dawkins says those same big-time coaches who used to flock to Canadian gyms are now skeptical about a local players' exploits against the diluted talent pool.

While some lay the blame on men such Bob White and Ro Russell, critics of the Canadian game say that the hate is far greater than any will to provide real options for young players at home. The choice to pack up and leave then becomes a no-brainer.

Rouel Hidalgo, an AAU coach in Montreal, says that even an injection of cash into the system wouldn't sway the minds of most young players. "That mentality is pretty much embedded into the top players' minds that they're going to have to play in the U.S.," he says.

Canadian basketball has become a victim of its own success. Steve Nash and Jamaal Magloire both graduated from Canadian high schools and were the first two from their country ever to be named NBA all-stars. But their success has convinced ever more players to flee south at increasingly younger ages, adding to the number of loose balls bouncing through an American system that's all too happy to finish what Canada started.

CHAPTER 10

— THINKING BIG —

Some 4,000 people jammed into the main hall at the Prince Hotel Takanawa in Tokyo on September 18, 1990, as IOC president Juan Antonio Samaranch walked up to the podium to end years of speculation and announce the host city for the 1996 Summer Games.

At that moment, on the other side of the world, about 1,500 people gathered at Toronto's SkyDome stadium to watch the live feed, confident that their city would finally get to join Montreal and Calgary as the only Canadian cities to host an Olympics.

Samaranch opened an envelope, paused for 10 seconds that must have seemed infinitely longer to the breath-bated bid teams, and declared, "The International Olympic Committee has awarded the 1996 Olympic Games to the city of ... Atlanta!"

The IOC boss's announcement sent well-dressed American delegates into a frenzy, while in Atlanta thousands whooped and hollered beneath a shower of balloons and fireworks in the downtown square. It was quite a different scene at SkyDome as Torontonians slowly filed out of an arena that suddenly felt like a tomb, the bitterness welling up behind grim faces.

The city, which hadn't hosted a major international sporting event in the modern era, had just had its collective hearts broken by the rich Americans, who used big money to convince the European sports barons to award their country a second Summer Games in just 12 years. Not to mention the fact that Atlanta, unlike Toronto, hadn't had to deal with the legions of vocal social advocates who said bringing the Olympics to Toronto would be an orgy of excess amid more pressing needs such as social housing and food banks.

Little did Toronto sports fans know that the bitter setback in 1990 would set in motion a chain of events that would culminate just three years later in the birth of the Toronto Raptors, a monumental event in the country's hoops history that reversed the tide of pro basketball failures that had dogged the sport for decades.

The key figure in the NBA's return to the Queen City was one of the angriest members of Toronto's defeated Olympic bid team. Thirty-year-old businessman John Bitove Jr. had been certain that his hometown's soaring skyscrapers, diverse population, redeveloping waterfront, and efficient transportation network would win over IOC delegates. Bitove resolved right then and there that if Toronto couldn't get the Summer Games, at least he would bid for, and win, world championships for two showcase Olympic sports.

"I told everyone I was teed off when we lost our Olympic bid … and became determined to go after track and basketball," he said in 1992. "I was embarrassed through the Olympic-bid process, where we claimed we were a world-class sports city but had never held a major international event. I looked at the sports that were available and worthy of pursuing, so they could impact on the true sports fans."[1]

He put his personal touch to work on officials at the IAAF and FIBA, the world governing bodies for track and field and basketball, respectively. The IAAF was the first to bite, awarding Bitove's bid team the 1993 World Indoor Championships.

What's more, the track event would be held at SkyDome, site of the Olympic victory party that never was and also a facility where Bitove's family food business just happened to own a 40-year exclusive food services lease. The track event drew mixed reviews, with gold-medal performances by hurdler Mark McKoy and sprinter Bruny Surin offset by lower-than-expected ticket sales. But Bitove reported a small surplus and quickly turned his attention to the basketball championship, an event close his heart but presenting a much stiffer challenge.

Belgrade, Yugoslavia, had been awarded the 1994 World Championship, but an increasingly violent civil war prompted FIBA to reopen the bidding. Athens, another jilted 1996 Olympic bride along with Melbourne, Australia, was making a hard run at the hoops tournament, as was San Juan, Puerto Rico. But Bitove pulled out all the stops, enlisting hockey hero Paul Henderson as well as Montreal lawyer Dick Pound, a powerful member of the International Olympic Committee. They schmoozed FIBA delegates in the run-up to the vote in 1992. The Toronto team's shrewd leader also had an ace in the hole — the NBA.

It was FIBA that had recently decided to allow NBA players to compete in their events; they were actually enthusiastic about stacked U.S. squads destroying the rest of the world on the court, a short-term shot of pain for the long-term benefit of increased fan support and corporate interest, not to mention the lessons that non-American squads could learn by getting their butts kicked for awhile. Bitove knew that a thumbs-up from the NBA would be the tipping point for Toronto's world championship bid.

"I called Russ Granik, the deputy chairman of the NBA, and asked him if we could work together," said Bitove. "Granik called me back a week later and said the NBA would co-operate in making the 1994 world championship the best ever. The NBA also made it clear that players are prepared to come to Toronto, but not to San Juan or Athens."[2]

FIBA was won over and Toronto, thanks largely to Bitove, had landed two major sporting events in consecutive years.

The opening ceremony of the World Championship of Basketball was a stunning spectacle. In the player procession outside Toronto City Hall, U.S. superstar Shaquille O'Neal towered over his teammates, including six-foot-ten Derrick Coleman and Alonzo Mourning, as the 16 teams stood at attention during the pomp and circumstance preceding the start of play.

When the ball went up, "Dream Team II" was untouchable, winning every game by at least 15 points to take the gold medal. In seventh place were the host Canadians, headlined by NBA forward Rick Fox and 20-year-old college star Steve Nash, who played surprisingly well considering it was his first tournament on the big stage.

The World Championship drew decent crowds, but Bitove had even bigger dreams for frustrated basketball fans, though he would need to get NBA commissioner David Stern's attention to make them a reality. Stern was open to listening.

The NBA continued to eye Toronto as a potential foothold into the global market that Stern was eyeing as he tried to extend his burgeoning brand to foreign shores. By the early 1990s the league was at all-time highs in terms of popularity, buoyed by the success of Michael Jordan's Bulls and the superstar-laden Dream Team at the 1992 Summer Games. League-wide revenues, driven in part by the global surge in interest following the Barcelona Olympics, were skyrocketing and money started pouring in to most NBA teams. But more money didn't mean more profits for the poorly run Denver Nuggets, owned by satellite operator COMSAT, a telecom outfit that was a poor fit for the entertainment industry. In 1991 the frustrated Nuggets owners started scouting possible relocation sites, and a COMSAT lawyer called friend and Toronto attorney Joel Rose to quietly discuss relocation possibilities. Rose knew he would need lots of cash even to make a pitch to the NBA, and contacted his wife's cousin, construction magnate Larry Tanenbaum, whose Warren paving company was the largest asphalt firm in Canada. The two decided to contact Commissioner Stern directly to discuss the Nuggets relocation plans. Stern, always averse to instability in his league ranks, immediately quashed any relocation talk, as Rose recalled. "Ultimately, he said Denver is just on a temporary dip and it's going to get better in time, and he was right," said Rose. "[Stern said] 'be patient, and we are eventually going to have a competition for a team in Toronto.'"

Rose and Tanenbaum put together a marketing team, named themselves the Palestra Group, and began aggressively lobbying NBA owners, who, together with Stern, would have the final say on any deal. Palestra also showed they were serious by plunking down a non-refundable $100,000 application fee.

Toronto, despite earlier false starts in pro basketball, seemed a prime candidate for expansion in 1991. It was noticeably bigger than any of the four cities the NBA had chosen in its last expansion in 1986. The Blue Jays regularly filled the SkyDome and the Maple Leafs, despite their dismal winning percentage, sold out the Gardens every night. Toronto was Canada's financial and media capital, providing ample sponsorship opportunities, and despite their lack of familiarity with basketball, Torontonians were known for being lovers of entertainment, with a burgeoning theatre district and an array of longstanding cultural events.

Tanenbaum was so dogged in his pursuit of NBA executives that the league created an expansion committee of owners Jerry Colangelo of the Phoenix Suns, Harold Katz of the Philadelphia 76ers, Utah Jazz owner Larry Miller, Jerry Buss of the Los Angeles Lakers, and Portland Trail Blazers executive Bert Kolde.

They met in February 1993 at the NBA All-Star Game in Salt Lake City, Utah, and following the meeting Tanenbaum figured he was the clear frontrunner. "I'm convinced we've got this," he told reporters after meeting with Colangelo and wooing the NBA power broker with plans for a 22,000-seat arena in downtown Toronto.

But it immediately became clear that the NBA also wanted to hear from other interested groups from Toronto before making a final decision, opening the door for Bitove and a third, lesser-known consortium headed up by Bill Ballard, fellow promoter Michael Cohl, and a dramatic partner — NBA legend Magic Johnson, who had shocked the world 18 months earlier when he retired after announcing he had the HIV virus.

Tanenbaum had been lobbying the NBA for longer than the other two bidders, and Magic's group had a thousand-watt smile and bullet-proof popularity, but everyone seemed to be forgetting one thing about John Bitove Jr. The 33-year-old food services heir hated to lose.

He inherited his competitive streak from his father, John Sr., a son of Macedonian immigrants who wasn't afraid to drive a hard bargain as he grew an 11-stool lunch counter on Toronto's Avenue Road into one of Canada's largest food services companies.

Even the prime minister of Canada wasn't too big to get a talking-to from John Sr., who once reportedly made a direct call to Brian Mulroney when the entrepreneur's exclusive catering deal at Toronto's Pearson International Airport appeared in jeopardy. A new terminal was being built in 1988 and the 60-year-old businessman wanted to make sure his would be the only company to keep passengers' bellies full while waiting for planes at Canada's largest airport.

The elder Bitove had developed a reputation for turning to the courts to get his way, and a phone call from the food magnate carried weight, especially in the Progressive Conservative Party, where he was a powerful fundraiser.

Given his connections, it only made sense that the government allow him to extend his gastronomic hegemony from Terminals 1 and 2 to the new Terminal 3. The Bitove family had scored another victory in a game of business where their defeats are few and far between.[3] As the family patriarch entered his seventies, he gradually turned over the family business to his five children: Vonna, Tom, Nick, Jordan, and John Jr.

Trained in finance and law and schooled as an Ottawa bureaucrat, John Bitove Jr. emerged in the 1980s as the family deal-closer at The Bitove Corporation, founded by his father in 1987 to consolidate the clan's diverse catering and food services operations.

Bitove Jr. is a man who prefers personal, not long-distance, relationships, meeting prospective partners face to face to seal agreements with a firm handshake. His affluent background and exposure to success formed Bitove into a man who doesn't believe in limits, and there's another thing about the brilliant entrepreneur that would forever change one of Canada's most underdeveloped sports industries.

John Bitove Jr. is a rabid basketball fan. "Basketball is my true passion," he told *Toronto Life* magazine in a 2011 interview. "I played all through high school. I still go to a lot of games."

He was exactly what Canadian basketball needed: a multimillionaire who also loved the sport. The absence of both characteristics in any one person perhaps explains the country's corpse-littered basketball history, one that includes dozens of defunct pro teams including the '46–'47 Toronto Huskies. By the 1990s the Canadian game remained stuck in a catch-22 in which basketball lovers didn't have the cash to make a hoops venture work, while the country's wealthiest people didn't love the game enough to start or maintain a team. That was all about to change in February 1993 as the three Toronto groups began a six-month blitz to woo the NBA's expansion committee. They had six months to drum up league, public, and financial support before making final pitches in September.

Financial support would be key. The league, riding the crest of a decade-plus of financial growth, set the franchise fee at $125 million, nearly three times what they had charged Miami, Orlando, Minnesota, and Charlotte to join their exclusive club eight years earlier. Commissioner Stern and the owners were going to get top dollar for any new member of their cabal, whether the price was fair or not. As one insider put it, "The NBA overcharged for the franchise fee because they could get it." And the basketball titans weren't about to offer the Canadians a break on the exchange rate, which was at 80 cents to the U.S. dollar and falling, fast.

Toronto Basketball Associates, Magic Johnson's group, held a series of media events that featured their best asset: Magic Johnson. The retired star travelled to New York and Toronto to press the flesh, hold news conferences, and apply his infectious charm, telling Toronto reporters in June 1993 that he had historical and cultural reasons for bringing a team to their city. "I want to be an owner," he said. "There isn't enough black ownership in our game." He also made it clear he wasn't a mere showpiece, explaining that he would be in charge of basketball operations while partners would take care of the business side. Magic's partner, Bill Ballard, was planning to build a 30,000-seat arena at the Canadian National Exhibition on the southern edge of downtown.

Though Bitove was a latecomer to the race, he had lined up big names in politics, media, and finance, most notably former Ontario premier David Peterson, a brilliant public speaker and seasoned lawyer who shared Bitove's personal touch. The Bitove group also included Allan Slaight, a long-time family friend who owned several major radio stations through his Standard Broadcasting empire. Bitove rounded out his team by bringing in the Bank of Nova Scotia, which added a dose of financial gravitas.

Tanenbaum now realized he had a real fight on his hands with only seven months to go before the final decision. But with partners such as Labatt Breweries and the CIBC, Canada's largest bank, he still considered Palestra to be the front-runner.

"I never, ever discount competition," he said. "But they're going to have to have a real big kick. It took us 18 months to do all this."

Vancouver in 1993 was one of Canada's strongest sports markets despite having only two pro teams. The B.C. Lions of the Canadian Football League routinely filled BC Place stadium, but Vancouverites' true love were their beloved Canucks.

Media mogul Frank Griffiths had bought the expansion team in 1974 and the franchise endeared itself to fans despite meagre results on the ice through the '70s and '80s. Legends such as brawler Tiger Williams and sharpshooter Tony Tanti became cult heroes on the lower B.C mainland, and hockey-mad Vancouverites packed Pacific Coliseum year after year. When Griffiths' son Arthur graduated from university in 1980 and took a job in the Canucks' front office, securing a new arena to replace their aging home became a top priority.

After years of threatening to move the Canucks from Pacific Coliseum, Griffiths finally secured enough financing to break ground in 1993 on a $150-million, 20,000-seat arena across the street from BC Place.

The Canucks and big concerts would be the main spectacles, but Griffiths had another plan for his palace-to-be: NBA basketball. It might have seemed like an unprecedented stretch, but in fact Vancouver had hosted a team called the Hornets in the Pacific Coast league from 1946 to 1948. In 1980, local businessman Nelson Skalbania had tried to bring an NBA franchise to the picturesque city but couldn't raise enough money.

By 1992, Griffiths was serious about joining the Toronto NBA bidders, but he kept his intentions quiet, seeking out advice from NHL commissioner Gary Bettman, who was a former NBA vice-president. Griffiths also informed his own top executives about the major project. One of the first men he told was Dave Cobb, who was his vice-president of finance at Northwest Sports Enterprises.

Cobb said everyone was excited about the city's chances right from the start. "Those were Michael Jordan days and the league was incredibly popular, almost all the teams in the league we were told, were making money."

Vancouver was approaching two million residents and the large Southeast Asian population was certainly hot for basketball. Northwest began to put together a bid proposal that would emphasize Vancouver's picturesque sightlines and diversity to try to woo the expansion committee.

But to seal the deal, Griffiths would need big money. The NBA wasn't playing around financially, insisting on a $125-million franchise fee that Northwest couldn't pay for all by itself. Already facing a daunting bill for arena construction, Griffiths approached old family friends from Seattle, McCaw brothers John and Bruce, whose cellular empire was worth upwards of $11 billion and who were interested in branching out into sports as minority owners.

Money in hand, Cobb and other Northwest executives headed down to Seattle to catch a few SuperSonics games, and also flew to Orlando and Miami to meet executives with the expansion franchises. It was clear from those visits that Northwest would have a major sales job on its hands.

"We were larger than several NBA markets so it wasn't the pure size that was the issue, it was can we excite the population of the city," said Cobb. "We're a very diverse city ethnically and we thought if things went well we'd having a really good shot at making this a success."

The three Toronto bid groups and the Griffiths contingent flew down to New York for the presentations on September 20, 1993. Each team was given 60 minutes to make their case, and another 30 minutes to answer questions.

Palestra was first up, and Rose and Tanenbaum didn't take any chances. The paving czar set up a high-tech show featuring spectacular shots of the city. The presence of his partners from Labatt and the CIBC, plus the contacts he had made from two years of glad-handing NBA types, left him as confident as ever.

Next up was the Vancouver bid team, headed by Arthur Griffiths and David Cobb. They touted Vancouver as a foothold in the Asian market that the NBA was courting, and also mentioned their new arena and 20 years of experience running the Canucks. The clincher was a mind-blowing video montage showing Vancouver's spectacular skyline, the downtown surrounded on three sides by water with the magnificent Rockies in the background. When it was over, Philadelphia 76ers owner Harold Katz was moved to exclaim, "I live in a hole," and Cobb remembers expansion committee members joking about whether they could move their franchises to Vancouver should Northwest be turned down.

Magic's Toronto Basketball Associates were up next, buoyed by a backing letter from Ontario premier Bob Rae. The group's legendary front man led the presentation and reminded the owners that his Showtime Lakers put NBA basketball on the sporting map, a recipe he planned to replicate north of the border.

Last up were Bitove and David Peterson. Being last in a series of presentations can be a blessing or a curse depending on what kind of impression the first guy left with the decision-makers.

But Bitove used his spot in the batting order to his advantage after he heard about Palestra's whiz-bang show. He decided to revert back to what he knew best — the personal touch. Radio magnate Allan Slaight talked about his humble beginnings as a reporter and newscaster at CHAB radio in Moose Jaw as well as his dream to see pro basketball put smiles on the faces of hoops-hungry children.

Bitove focused on financial details including a plan to build an arena right next to Toronto's downtown Eaton Centre, a more central location than either of his rivals. For the finale he turned to partner Phil Granovsky, who 50 years earlier had founded a paper bag plant that he grew into one of Canada's largest packaging companies. Granovsky made an emotional plea based around his lifetime of philanthropic work and his burning desire to give an NBA team to the city that allowed his family business to flourish. "We totally humanized it," Bitove recalled. "At the end of the day, they're people, so we didn't come in with smokescreens and strobe lights."

The committee mulled it over for a week, and Bitove got ready to celebrate his 33rd birthday on September 30, 1993, an anniversary that became a lot more memorable when he received the phone call from league office informing him that he had the winning bid.

"What a great way to celebrate a birthday," said Bitove.

"I guess I'll just go back to building roads," said a dejected Tanenbaum.

The league held off on a decision on Vancouver until April of 1994, but eventually green-lighted the franchise, vaulting Canadian basketball to a level barely imaginable just a decade earlier. The Toronto-Vancouver axis would make for a tantalizing cross-country rivalry, and both teams agreed to stoke interest by hosting a pre-season matchup called the Naismith Cup, with the first game to be held in Winnipeg prior to the start of the 1995–96 season.

But the good cheer was mitigated somewhat by Stern's insistence that the NBA wouldn't allow the franchises to tip off unless provincial basketball betting lines were abolished. While Griffiths quickly appeased British Columbia by offering up $3 million in compensation for dropping hoops gambling, Ontario wouldn't bend quite so quickly. Basketball betting generated $20 million a year for Ontario's cash-strapped government, and Rae, whose government had backed Bitove's rival in the franchise bidding, triggered an ugly standoff by suggesting his New Democrats would maintain basketball betting as part of the Pro-Line lottery.

Stern, whose aversion to gambling has kept the NBA out of Las Vegas for decades, dug in his heels. He even set a "drop dead" date of February 14, 1994, a terrifying ultimatum that threatened to torpedo the whole deal in what would be the latest bitter setback for a sport that almost seemed cursed in the country of its inventor's birth.

Ontario and its lottery corporation hired labour lawyer Larry Bertuzzi to begin talks with the NBA that dragged on for months. Toronto mayor June Rowlands even got involved at one point, mentioning the obvious — that an NBA team would bring far more money to Ontario than a $20-million annual basketball betting haul.

But three days before the deadline, Stern, Bitove, and Rae held a joint news conference to announce a deal that would see the NBA and Bitove's group contribute $10 million to various charities in exchange for Ontario dropping basketball betting by October 1, 1995, right in time for the start of the Raptors' first training camp. "Premier Rae brought the ball up the court and sank a three-pointer right at the buzzer," Bitove told reporters at the Ontario legislature. "We all believe this is a win-win situation for everyone involved."

With the betting dragon slain, the Bitove group set out to pick a name. They opted for a national mail-in contest that eventually came down to the Dragons, Grizzlies, Bobcats, T-Rex, and Raptors, the latter two names a nod to the wild popularity of the recent *Jurassic Park* CGI blockbuster masterminded by Steven Spielberg. The smaller of the two dinosaurs won out, and the Raptors were introduced live on NBC during a playoff game on May 15, 1995. Bitove had ceded control of the details to the NBA's marketing machine, which quickly churned out jerseys, shorts, basketballs, and mugs stamped with a menacing, sharp-toothed red dinosaur dribbling a silver basketball.

Vancouver's name game was far more subdued, though Griffiths' team did run into a roadblock after executives opted to call the squad the Mounties, a nod to Canada's world-famous police force. The RCMP, in the midst of a national branding initiative, cried foul and the ownership team switched to the Grizzlies, well aware that the furry predators were in no position to object.

The naming contest was typical of the contrast between the Raptors' glitz and glamour and the more low-key approach taken by the Grizzlies. Toronto hired future NBA Hall of Famer Isiah Thomas as its vice-president of basketball operations while Vancouver opted for Stu Jackson, a relatively anonymous former head coach of the New York Knicks and the Wisconsin Badgers of the NCAA. Geography played a role in the contrasts as well. While the Raptors benefited from a massive population base and proximity to business giants, the Grizzlies had a far lower profile and far less coverage from national sports reporters, the lion's share of whom were located in the Raptors' hometown.

While the Grizzlies were to begin play at their new arena, christened General Motors Place, the Raptors were relegated to the cavernous SkyDome until their new building could be topped off. The home of the Blue Jays became the home of the NBA Draft for one historic day in June 1995, as Commissioner Stern christened his league's first foreign foray by moving the event from its usual spot in Greater New York.

Both Canadian teams knew they'd be locked out of the top five draft spots, a league expansion rule that put them at an immediate disadvantage.

Though Michael Jordan had proven that you didn't need a great centre to win championships, most NBA teams by the 1990s were still addicted to height. So when 15,000 people gathered at SkyDome for the draft spectacle, the boos that accompanied the home team's selection of five-foot-ten University of Arizona point guard Damon Stoudamire were unfortunate but not surprising. Fans considered Isiah Thomas's pick to be puzzling, especially since a player as short as Stoudamire hadn't dominated the league since Nate "Tiny" Archibald more than 20 years earlier, and Tiny was three inches taller than Stoudamire. Some wondered if Thomas's own success as a point guard hadn't clouded his judgment.

Vancouver had the very next pick, and went the traditional route. With big Joe Smith, Rasheed Wallace, and Antonio McDyess off the board, the Griz went even bigger, grabbing seven-foot, 285-pound pivot Bryant "Big Country" Reeves, a skilled mammoth of a man from tiny Gans, Oklahoma, who had dominated the Big 12 conference for Oklahoma State the previous three seasons.

Stu Jackson thought Reeves's massive frame could take the pounding that NBA centres were subjected to near the basket, and his soft scoring touch raised hopes that he could anchor the team in the paint for years to come.

Both franchises went with tough, low-key veteran NBA assistants as their first bench bosses. Brendan Malone was as much of a surprise pick to Toronto fans as Stoudamire. He had no previous head coaching experience, but he had put in a lot of years as an assistant on Thomas's "Bad Boy" Pistons teams of the 1980s and 1990s, building a reputation as a hard-nosed, defensive-minded coach. The Grizzlies' first bench boss, Brian Winters, had a similar reputation as an assistant with Atlanta and Cleveland, along with an impressive player pedigree as a two-time All-Star sharpshooter with the Milwaukee Bucks.

Fittingly, the Raptors' first pre-season game would be held at the Halifax Metro Centre, the country's basketball mecca and annual site of the CIAU National Championship for more than 15 years. Nearly 9,400 raucous Haligonians watched the diminutive Stoudamire dominate the Philadelphia 76ers to the tune of 25 points and an improbable 10 rebounds, prompting the *Toronto Sun*'s Frank Zicarelli to opine that he "played with the poise and fearlessness of a veteran."

The Raptors defensive anchor was former All-Star and All-Defensive selection Alvin Robertson, tough-as-nails and making a comeback from back surgery, who quickly emerged as the expansion team's leader. The three-time NBA steals champion and willing brawler locked up opposing guards, made timely outside shots, and got in opponents' faces when necessary.

Some scouts thought Stoudamire was too small to be an impact player, but the Oregon native was sensational right from the start, darting through defenders who all seemed a step slow, dishing an array of pinpoint passes and providing leadership that rookies rarely display so early in their careers.

The Raptors actually looked pretty good on paper, with the expansion draft providing veteran power forward Tony Massenburg, behemoth Croatian centre Zan Tabak, whose strong play persuaded Malone to pencil him in as a starter, and gangly John Salley, a wisecracking New Yorker who was a shot-blocking reserve on Thomas's back-to-back champion Pistons in 1989–90.

The crowd of 33,000 that gathered at SkyDome for opening night against the New Jersey Nets on November 4, 1995, had two reasons to celebrate. Not only was NBA basketball returning to the Queen City for the first time in 50 years, but the entire country had dodged a bullet just four days earlier when a slim majority of Quebecers narrowly voted No to a separatist bid that would have broken up the country.

The political climate added an extra dose of emotion when pop band The Barenaked Ladies belted out a heartfelt rendition of "O Canada", the cheers growing even louder when the Toronto musicians switched to French lyrics for the second half of the anthem.

The Raptors fed off the patriotic atmosphere right from the start. Forward Ed Pinckney won the opening tip, Stoudamire set up on the right, guarded by Kenny Anderson, the ball went into the right-side post to Tabak, whose skip pass to Robertson ended with a three-pointer from the left side, sending the crowd into a frenzy. "There it is, the first ever basket scored by a Toronto Raptor, a three-pointer," said CTV play-by-play man Rod Black.

The Raps beat the Nets 94–79 on the strength of Robertson's 30 points, and Stoudamire continued his strong play with 10 assists. "It was magical," recalled Leo Rautins, the legendary Toronto-born forward who was an analyst on the TV broadcast. "I remember looking around at SkyDome, seeing all the people in the stands, everybody here for basketball."

Bitove, who had invited Commissioner Stern as his special guest, could barely contain his pride at the achievement. A big section of the SkyDome was curtained off, and the sightlines were more suited for a Jays game than for basketball, but the potential was obvious and the crowd cheered constantly — even for the opposing team. Part of Bitove's job was to educate fans about how to cheer at a basketball game, but he quickly realized that even his crew would need some lessons.

The owner had personally instructed staff, most of whom were Canadian, to hand out noisemakers and foam noodles to distract Nets players during free throws. But something was lost in translation, as Stern pointed out to his aghast Canadian host. "David Stern leans over to me and goes 'Bitove, something new here? You're handing those out on the end that your team's shooting on.'"

Bitove scrambled to get a walkie-talkie, screaming at the guys to confiscate the noisemakers until the second half when the Nets would switch over to the basket.

Their cheering etiquette needed work, but Torontonians didn't need to be die-hard basketball fans to appreciate the whirling-dervish play of their flashy rookie. Far from having to adjust to the speed and pace of the NBA, veteran defenders were struggling to adjust to Stoudamire as he used his bowling-ball physique to pound into openings, while flashing the ability to change directions and loft high-arcing shots that swished through, often without touching the backboard. The Portland native was average sized for a regular man, but in a league with an average height of six foot seven, he seemed a child among grownups who played like a man amongst boys, earning himself the nickname "Mighty Mouse" after the lightning-quick 1950s cartoon character.

The same night as the Raptors entered the win column for the first time, the Grizzlies made their regular-season debut on the road, and an amazing day in Canadian basketball got even better when the Griz surprised the Portland Trailblazers 92–80, behind 29 points and 13 rebounds from centre Benoit Benjamin, a talented but underachieving malcontent trying to resuscitate his career north of the border. There was a cloud over Benjamin's performance that night, since he had firmly displaced Bryant Reeves in the rotation even though the rookie was expected to be the team's franchise player. "Big Country" was out of shape, overwhelmed, and feeling the criticism from fans and the Vancouver media. The shy giant's background didn't exactly prepare him for the early struggles. Reeves's Oklahoma hometown had just 250 residents and his father admitted that Gans was "a little place on the map that nobody would ever notice."

Reeves's emergence as a star at Oklahoma State took him to every corner of America, but he admitted that he was never really relaxed unless he was back home, casting lines from a fishing boat with his childhood friends.

His rural charm didn't translate during mandatory NBA media sessions in which his thick drawl and short answers only served to confound journalists. "He was not a great talker and you could barely understand what he was saying," said one Grizzlies staffer.

Coach Brian Winters was more interested in his centre's lack of production than his lack of erudition. He was just hoping for half of the production Reeves had managed in college, where his 21.5 points-per-game average earned him All-American honours. Instead, Reeves only managed two double-figure scoring games in the first month of the 1995–96 season, and didn't grab 10 rebounds in a game until January. Big Country earned a measure of redemption on December 17, when his 25-point, 17-rebound performance broke a 19-game losing streak in a game against the Blazers, their opening-night foil and the only team in the league that was having trouble beating the expansion team. The Grizzlies finished with a league-worst 15–67 record, the first of their six consecutive bottom-dwelling campaigns in Vancouver.

Back east, the Raptors weren't much better, though Stoudamire had become a fan darling with a series of spectacular performances including a stunning 21-point, 12-rebound, 11-assist performance in a win against the Seattle SuperSonics, the best team in the Western Conference.

One star rookie didn't translate to wins in the brutally tough Eastern Conference, however, and Toronto managed just 21 victories. But history had been made nonetheless, as the NBA's Canadian expansion was deemed a success and sponsors jumped on board, mainly to the Raptors.

Stoudamire garnered international attention with a 1996 Nike commercial that featured him doing ball-handling tricks to the Mighty Mouse theme song, while the pint-sized animated superhero darted around him.

NBA writers and broadcasters voted Stoudamire the 1996 Rookie of the Year, with his 19 points and 9.3 assists some of the best numbers ever posted by a first-year point guard. Some analysts expressed surprise that the diminutive player had taken the league by storm, and Thomas basked in his vindication. The feisty Chicagoan had faced similar naysayers in the 1980s as he and his Pistons had tried to knock Magic Johnson and Larry Bird off of their perches, and the emotion came pouring out at a news conference where he presented Stoudamire with his Rookie of the Year trophy. "I shouldn't do this, but I'm going to kiss you," said the smiling executive, leaning over to smooch and hug his protégé to laughter from journalists and the pop of flashbulbs.

Stoudamire, for one, was just as confident as his boss, saying he knew he belonged in the NBA from the start of the season when he dropped 26 points and 11 assists on the powerful Indiana Pacers in just the second regular-season game of his career. "I had a great game against them and that was when I knew that I could be something special," said the confident 22-year-old.

Stoudamire was even better in his second season, averaging 20.2 points per game and 8.8 assists, but the Raptors had their second of three consecutive last-place finishes. Off the court, the team was rocked by the stunning departures of Isiah Thomas and John Bitove within a few months of each other in 1997. Both men had a falling out with majority owner Allan Slaight, with Bitove wanting to move more quickly than Slaight on the arena project and Thomas wanting a bigger share of the team. Stoudamire was devastated. He and Thomas had grown extremely close as the young American adjusted to life in Canada and his unfamiliar position as franchise player. With Thomas now in the NBC broadcast booth, Stoudamire requested a trade, and just after the 1998 All-Star Game he was dealt to Portland for three players including fellow point guard Kenny Anderson, who would sing a refrain that would become all-too-familiar to Canadian NBA fans. The slender New Yorker refused to report to the Raptors, saying he didn't want to play in Canada, forcing new Toronto general manager Glen Grunwald to deal him to Boston for stocky sharpshooter Chauncey Billups. Adding to the carnage was the fact that Grunwald had fired the team's second head coach, Darrell Walker, the day before the Stoudamire trade, replacing him with yet another hard-nosed former team assistant, Butch Carter, who like Walker had had no previous NBA head-coaching experience. Toronto fans, with good reason, were in shock, and there was every reason to expect last place to be a familiar spot for the limping new franchise for years to come.

The post-Stoudamire Raptors sputtered to a league-worst 16–66 record in 1997–98 and had nine players who were either first- or second-year players. The most promising among them was oversized rookie shooting guard Tracy McGrady, but the six-foot-eight jack-of-all-trades had jumped to the NBA straight out of high school and made as many clueless plays as spectacular ones in his first season.

A deep 1998 draft gave Grunwald and his staff a chance to add another young piece to a team that already the youngest in the league. Finally allowed to have a top-five pick, the Raptors earned a high lottery spot by virtue of their dismal record, a mark that was three games worse than the basement-dwelling Grizzlies. When the Denver Nuggets selected Kansas All-American Raef LaFrentz, Toronto had a tantalizing choice between NCAA Player of the Year Antawn Jamison or his high-flying teammate, Floridian Vince Carter, who also happened to be Tracy McGrady's cousin. Many NBA types thought Jamison, a fundamentally sound post player at six foot nine, would be the better NBA performer than Carter, a dunking phenom who brought pyrotechnics mixed with sometimes indifferent defence. Golden State, which was picking fifth right after Toronto, struck a deal that saw the Raptors pick Jamison, the man the Warriors really wanted, while Golden State selected Carter and traded him to the Raptors along with $250,000 cash. With Michael Jordan not likely returning to the Bulls, some prognosticators pegged Carter as his heir apparent, noting they both attended North Carolina, preferred to go bald, and were both six-foot-six super-athletes. Carter, for one, tried to downplay expectations. "It's a great honour to be placed in Michael's company, but I want to put my name on the map with what I can do," the 21-year-old told Toronto reporters on draft day.

Grunwald's draft-day trade proved to be a steal for Toronto, as the rookie made an immediate impact with a team-leading 18.3 points per game, the franchise's second Rookie of the Year Award in four seasons, and an array of highlight-reel dunks that proved to be more of an inspiration than a distraction. Perhaps the best gravity-defying move of Carter's rookie season came against the Indiana Pacers, who had nearly knocked off Jordan's Bulls in the previous year's Eastern Conference finals. Carter went baseline against Indiana, losing his defender and throwing down a surprise double clutch reverse jam. It was voted the Play of the Year by *NBA.com* and served notice that the 21-year-old from Daytona Beach would be a big-ticket draw in the team's brand-new Air Canada Centre, a luxurious arena near the harbourfront that's wrapped with art-deco façades from the city's old postal delivery building.

The rookie immediately vaulted the Raptors to near the top of the league attendance charts, despite a 23–27 record in a lockout-shortened campaign that left them out of the playoffs for the fourth straight season.

But Carter made a bold playoff promise for 1999–2000 season, and by training camp it was obvious the team was starting to jell under new coach Butch Carter, a fiery, tough, and emotional boss. Grunwald had traded for veteran forwards Charles Oakley and Kevin Willis to teach Vince Carter and McGrady the ropes of the NBA.

Oakley became the team's emotional leader, 15 years after he served as Michael Jordan's power forward/enforcer. The sharply dressed Cleveland native took Carter under his wing, imparting his unique brand of street wisdom while serving as on-court bodyguard for the gentle Floridian, as Carter's cousin and teammate McGrady recalled years later on TSN. "The one thing that I really appreciate about Oak … is he always had our back," said McGrady. "If we got fouled hard in a game, you best believe somebody on that other team is going to get fouled hard. He just took care of us."[4]

Oakley didn't give an inch and always backed up his threats, refusing to tolerate even perceived injustices such as opposing teams that over-stayed their welcome at pre-game shootaround. "Oak" was known to fire basketballs at the heads of rivals who refused to clear the court, and no one dared retaliate. This, after all, was the same man who once collected a $54,000 gambling debt from opposing power forward Tyrone Hill by simply punching or slapping him every time they met, then charging Hill double for the privilege. "Everything in life is double," Oakley deadpanned to reporters seeking an explanation for the violent outbursts. "If he didn't pay me $108,000, he didn't pay me."

Oakley usually stuck to basketball matters on the court, anchoring a defensive unit that included long, athletic guard Doug Christie and clever young backcourt mate Alvin Williams for a core that was well placed for a run at the franchise's first playoff berth.

When a lockout wiped out nearly half of the 1998–99 NBA season, much was made of the fact that the billionaire owners could simply wait it out while the millionaire players grew increasingly desperate and des-titute. But the Vancouver Grizzlies weren't exactly sitting pretty as the NBA's first work stoppage dragged past Christmas and into the New Year. The Canucks, despite their ongoing woes, had won over the city decades earlier, while basketball still had to be sold to sports fans on the lower B.C. mainland. They certainly weren't endeared to the NBA amid lockout tales that included Nets guard Kenny Anderson joking about having to tighten his belt by selling his Mercedes, neglecting to mention that he had seven other vehicles. When league play resumed in February 1999, attendance at GM Place sagged. Fan support had been surprisingly strong for the first three Griz seasons as the novelty of the new team, the promise of future success, and yearly visit by Michael Jordan's Bulls boosted interest. But pedestrian performances by Big Country, coupled with the disastrous 1997 drafting of shoot-first guard Antonio Daniels, led to perennial last-place finishes. They had a star in the making with 1996 draftee Shareef Abdur-Rahim, but his 20-point scoring average wasn't enough to carry the team, and the Grizzlies managed just eight wins in the 50-game lockout season after recording 15, 14, and 19 wins in their first three years. What's more, the Griffiths family was completely out of the picture, having sold their interest in the team to the McCaw brothers in 1996. The new American owners were a reclusive bunch, rarely granting interviews and fuelling speculation about the Grizzlies' future. On the court, things were about to hit rock bottom by 1999 at a time that's supposed to represent promise for NBA teams — the draft.

Vancouver finally had a top-five pick, holding the second selection in a top-heavy talent pool. College Player of the Year Elton Brand of Duke was vying with Maryland All-American guard Steve Francis for the prestigious top spot. The Bulls went with Brand, and Vancouver fans figured they couldn't go wrong with Francis, obviously unaware of what was going on inside the former streetball player's head.

The draft was held in Washington, D.C., a stone's throw from Steve Francis's hometown of Silver Spring, Maryland, and his grandmother, brothers, and stepfather were gathered at the MCI Center to watch the life-changing event. But when Commissioner Stern announced that the Bulls had selected Brand with the first pick, Francis was devastated.

Francis' agent, Jeff Fried, says he had warned Grizzlies brass that picking his client would backfire. "Don't draft Steve, he does not want to play here," Fried insists he told GM Stu Jackson, who nonetheless believed he could persuade the emotional Maryland native to start his career 4,600 kilometres away in Vancouver.[5] When Commissioner Stern walked up to the podium and called Francis's name, the rookie's head was already in his hands. When he finally dragged himself out of his seat to hug his grandmother, his lower lip was quivering and he pouted all the way to the stage, a blank stare in his eyes. It was an expression rarely, if ever, seen by a young 'baller who had just hit the NBA jackpot.

Francis was like a lot of inner-city kids from the States whose world ends beyond their block. He had spent his entire life in Maryland, and another country might as well have been another planet for him. But he would never get Vancouver fans to sympathize, and he became perhaps the most hated athlete in the city's history when he publicly demanded a trade before he had played a single game. Jackson tried to negotiate with his disappointed young athlete, but finally admitted defeat and traded Francis to the Houston Rockets as part of a three-team, 11-player deal involving the Orlando Magic. Francis went on to win Rookie of the Year while the players Vancouver received in return became little more than rotation pieces during a miserable 22–60 campaign that saw the Grizzlies replace coach Brian Hill with Lionel Hollins, their fourth bench boss in five years.

Francis's reaction to Vancouver was typical of many American players; though the city was only minutes from the U.S. border, many NBA athletes were unable to see past the city's foreign locale and 250 rain days a year. Twelve months before Francis was drafted, veteran guard Doug West had a visceral reaction when the Minnesota Timberwolves announced they were trading him to the Grizzlies after nearly a decade in Minneapolis: "I stood at the bar and drank 17 Heinekens."[6]

The Francis debacle was a perfect storm of darkness for the Grizzlies. Vancouver's economy was slumping and business leaders were loath to sponsor the team; the exchange rate had plunged to 65 cents U.S. by January 1999 while the team had to pay players in American dollars; and the McCaws sold the team to Chicago construction entrepreneur Michael Heisley in late 1999. The fact that the Grizzlies were being batted about between American owners caused many to figure the team's days in Vancouver were numbered, despite Heisley's declaration in January 2000 that "I intend to do everything in my power to make this franchise a success in Vancouver." Heisley's stated commitment to "building a winning team here" rang hollow given that the McCaw brothers had tried to sell the Grizzles to St. Louis Blues owner Bill Laurie, a man who made it clear he wanted to move the team to his town. The NBA vetoed the Laurie deal, and Vancouverites were left to trust that the weak dollar, a weak team, and weak revenues wouldn't drive Heisley out of town.

Facing $40 million in annual losses, Heisley reneged on his pledge in the summer of 2001 and moved the Grizzlies to Memphis, an abject failure that elicited rare public regret from David Stern. "Maybe we should have only expanded into Toronto," the commissioner told the ESPN sports network, adding, "I wish we hadn't had the Vancouver experience."

Some of Vancouver's jilted basketball fans felt the same way while others were indifferent. "Who cares," season-ticket holder Garnett Pawliw said after the Memphis move was made official. "Basically I didn't go to see the Grizzlies. I went to see the teams coming in. The product was bad. The Grizzlies were just a bad team."[7]

The problem for the Grizzlies, says former team executive David Cobb, was that Vancouverites didn't live and die with the club's wins and losses. Making matters worse was the fact that the Canucks were scratching their way into perennial contender status just as the Grizzlies crawled out of town. "Every other sport, in my opinion, will always play second fiddle to hockey," said Cobb, who moved over to the hockey side of the operation prior to the move. "Hockey's in our DNA."

You knew that Toronto had arrived as an NBA city when Samuel L. Jackson started turning up at the Air Canada Centre. Jackson, comedian Chris Rock, and other Hollywood celebrities were flocking to Raptors games by 1999 to catch a glimpse of the league's rising star — Vincent Lamar Carter.

The forward had elevated dunking to an art form, combining finesse with power and a surprisingly deft outside touch to emerge as perhaps the league's top wing player. His high-wire act lifted the Raptors from obscurity to the nightly highlight reels on both sides of the border.

His popularity was soaring, and the franchise was reaping the benefits, but in a sign of the imposing shadow that hockey casts over everything in Canadian sport, the Maple Leafs had bought the Raptors and their still-uncompleted arena in 1998, altering the plans in order to make the building more NHL-friendly. Leafs brass knew a hot commodity when they saw one, and the Raptors, boosted by Carter's jersey sales, were quickly growing in value. Fans voted Carter to start in the 2000 NBA All-Star Game in Oakland, California, which would be the scene of the reborn Slam Dunk Contest.

The dunk-off had been put on hiatus for the previous two years after top stars stopped competing and the competition became downright lame. But when Carter, McGrady, and Vancouver's favourite son Steve Francis expressed interest, the league revived the event, providing Carter with a stage to launch himself to the top of the post-Jordan world.

As superstars such as Shaquille O'Neal, Kevin Garnett, and Chris Webber watched from the sidelines, Carter unleashed the most spectacular show the event had seen since Jordan and Dominique Wilkins's classic showdown in 1988. Carter started off with a reverse windmill 360-degree dunk that moved TV analyst Kenny Smith to declare "Let's go home!"

but the man dubbed "Air Canada" was just getting started.

For his third dunk, with McGrady as his passing partner, Carter caught a bounce pass in midair, put the ball between his legs, and slammed it through with authority, part of a mind-bending performance that captivated fans, stars, and media alike.

"It's over! It's over, ladies and gentlemen! Oh my goodness gracious, it is over!" an apoplectic Smith screamed as competition judge Isiah Thomas, old legs and all, jumped over his table to slap hands with the man who had just shut down the competition. "I really thought the top was going to come off of the building," Smith said afterward.

Commissioner Stern, normally subdued, said, "All I can remember is that he did something and ... you turn to someone sitting next to you and say, 'Did he really do that?'"

O'Neal said he wouldn't have believed the between-the-legs dunk happened unless he had recorded it himself. "I had the camera and I thought I saw it, and I did see it," he said. "That right there was probably the number one dunk ever."

O'Neal, the league's master of the one-liner, was the one who had earlier coined a new nickname for Air Canada: "Half-Man, Half-Amazing."

Dunking pioneer Julius "Dr. J" Erving was one of the first people to congratulate Carter after a performance that made him the king of the NBA, a position not held by a Canadian-based player in any U.S. sports league since Wayne Gretzky's days in Edmonton. The phenomenon dubbed "Vin-sanity" transformed the nascent Raptors into one of the NBA's hottest commodities, and their young thoroughbred had every intention of proving he could deliver in real games, as well. He wouldn't do it alone, as McGrady had emerged as one of the NBA's best young talents, matching some of Carter's devastating dunks and explosive scoring outbursts during the drive to the 2000 playoffs.

NBC had the good sense to put the Raptors on national TV for the first time ever when they hosted the Phoenix Suns on February 27, 2000. Carter didn't disappoint, pouring in a career-high 51 points in a thrilling 103–102 victory before a sold-out crowd, and millions more watching at home. "This is a lifetime high for me," said Carter, who had turned 23 a month earlier. "The most points I scored in a high school game was 47. And in college, my high was 26."

He made a game-winning shot to beat Boston in a tough road game a week later, prancing off the court with his teammates. Bill Cosby, guest hosting *The Late Show with David Letterman*, even invited Carter onto the show, an honour rarely bestowed upon a Canadian-based athlete.

Maple Leaf Sports and Entertainment (MLSE), the new name for the company that owned the Raptors, the Leafs, and their arena, were at the head of a runaway train that was gathering steam, and cash. Tom Anselmi, senior vice-president of MLSE, admitted taking a hands-off approach to marketing their new superstar. "You don't market him," Anselmi told the CBC. "You hand him the ball and let him do his thing, and the results will be there."[8]

With Carter and McGrady shouldering the offensive burden while Oakley, Davis, and Willis manned the paint, the Raptors ran off seven straight wins, and 11 of their next 12 after the Phoenix victory, to finish the regular season with a franchise-record 45 wins and a date with the New York Knicks in the team's first-ever playoff appearance.

Though all three games were decided by seven points or less, Knicks guard Latrell Sprewell harassed Carter into 30 percent shooting and the Knicks swept the Raptors in three games, leading to an off-season of uncertainty in which McGrady was traded to the Orlando Magic after signing a seven-year, $93-million contract.

Butch Carter had also worn out his welcome in Toronto. The fiery coach let his emotions get the best of him even as the team reached its zenith, and the veteran trio of Oakley, Davis, and Willis had had enough of his tirades. There was also an embarrassing $5-million lawsuit that the coach had filed against former Raptors centre Marcus Camby, who had accused the coach of lying to him about being the team's franchise cornerstone just before the skinny forward was traded. Though GM Glen Grunwald was friends and former classmates with Butch Carter, his decision to fire his outspoken employee and replace him with calm, cool Lenny Wilkens was seen as a good move, especially since the New York–born coach had steered the SuperSonics to an NBA title in 1979.

Wilkens was the antithesis of Butch Carter, never raising his voice and preferring to stay out of on-court or off-court disputes. His quiet, dignified style came off as aloof to some, but few were complaining publicly when the Raptors sailed into the 2001 playoffs with another team-record 47 wins and a first-round rematch with the Knicks.

This time Vince Carter wouldn't be denied. The teams split the first four games to set up a decisive Game 5 at Madison Square Garden in Manhattan and Carter was brilliant, netting 27 points to offset 29 by Sprewell as the Raptors advanced to the conference semifinals with a 93–89 victory.

The second-round matchup against Allen Iverson and the Philadelphia 76ers went down to the wire as well, with the decisive game again being played on the road. On the eve of the game, Carter raised some eyebrows by flying to Chapel Hill, North Carolina, hours before the game to pick up his long-sought-after university diploma at convocation, a controversy that perhaps said more about fan and media priorities than about Carter's dedication to the game.

He didn't have his usual scoring outburst that night, but turned in a great all-around game (20 points, nine assists, seven rebounds) and had the ball in his hands down by one with two seconds left and a chance to shoot his team into the conference finals and a shot at a championship berth. He caught the ball deep in the left corner, made a great pump-fake to lose his defender, and let a shot fly that bounced off the rim and went long as the buzzer sounded.

"It's something you live for," he told reporters after the game. "Maybe next year," he added with obvious disappointment that only fuelled some of Carter's critics who grew louder as the pressure mounted on the young superstar to lead his team to greater heights.

Though the Raptors made it back to the playoffs in 2002, they were the seventh seed and bowed out to conference powerhouse Detroit in five games.

While Carter was voted a starter in the All-Star Game for the fourth consecutive season, he missed 39 games with a knee injury and the team sputtered to a 24–58 record, including a 1–16 record from early December to early January.

Toronto had soured on Carter by 2003, and when he demanded a trade through his agent in July, the vitriol came pouring out in local newspapers. "Is there anyone willing to take a picture of me burning my Vince Carter jerseys?" one fan wrote in a letter to the *Toronto Sun*, while another evoked patriotic pessimism. "Winning starts with Vince Carter — he let this team, its fans, and a whole country down. Good riddance."[9]

As is often the case in sports, losing had brought out the worst in everyone. Carter feigned indifference to the town that he had previously owned and which gave him the platform to become a superstar, and fans feigned indifference toward the player who had put their city on the map south of the border.

When Grunwald traded Carter to New Jersey 20 games into the 2003–04 season, the team sunk back into mediocrity. The Raptors had lost their fourth franchise player in nine years, a typical trend in a league where the basement-dwelling clubs act as virtual farm teams for league powers. Though the Raptors would make two more playoff appearances under sweet-shooting power forward Chris Bosh, who took over the franchise tag from Carter in 2004, both post seasons ended in the first round, and Bosh, too, was gone after a seven-season stint.

The Raptors began the second decade of the 20th century searching for an identity and trying to recapture the glory days of the Vince Carter era, but without any players of nearly his stature. But while the on-court product dipped, the team finally gave a platform to some of the Canadian talent that was emerging on the world hoops scene. Most notably, Glen Grunwald's successor as GM, Brian Colangelo, made history by appointing long-time national team stalwart and former Simon Fraser player and coach Jay Triano of Niagara Falls, Ontario, as interim head coach to replace Sam Mitchell in December 2008 after the team was routed 132–93 by the Denver Nuggets. There were inevitable suggestions that the hiring of a Canadian basketball legend was aimed at appeasing local fans, but the Raptors had never made a token Canadian hire in any public position, and Colangelo insisted Triano got the job because he was the most qualified of the team's three assistants.

Though Triano was fired after his second full season with an 87–142 record and no playoff appearances, he was already part of the NBA's inner circle, landing back on his feet as an assistant coach in Portland.

The Raptors' legacy in Canada can't be measured only in wins and losses; by that measure four playoff appearances in the team's first 17 seasons ranks near the bottom of the league. But once the Grizzlies left town, the Raptors expanded their footprint across the country, holding training camps in Winnipeg and Halifax and staging successful exhibition games in other cities. Then there's the Raptors Foundation, which has spent millions renovating indoor and outdoor courts across Toronto.

Montreal, the largest North American market without an NBA team, played host to Raptors exhibitions against the Knicks in 2010 and 2012, selling out a Bell Centre building that usually only fills up for Canadiens games or Britney Spears concerts.

John Bitove Jr., the team founder who has now reverted back to his role as a fan, says he has no regrets despite the sour departure from his creation. "I would do it again in a heartbeat," he said. "It was awesome."

Despite the failure of the Grizzlies and dozens of semi-pro teams in Canada over the years, Bitove remains bullish on basketball. Frequent television footage of turban-wearing car dealer Nav Bhatia waving a towel in his usual spot at the Air Canada Centre is a reminder that basketball is an international sport that appeals to a different fan base than hockey. "NBA games are more about what the new Canada's all about," says Bitove, who is among those who dare to think a team will one day return to Vancouver. "There'll always be an ingrained level of hockey here, but I think actually the following of basketball will just continue to rise every year. And I'm not talking generations, I'm talking years."

CHAPTER 11

– CAPTAIN CANADA –

It was December of 1990, and the sun had just set behind the mountains overlooking picturesque Victoria, British Columbia, leaving only a single spotlight to illuminate a hoop in the schoolyard of Hillcrest Elementary School in the town of Saanich, a north end suburb of the B.C. capital. Large and medium-sized detached homes lay nestled among an eclectic array of trees and bushes in the Gordon Head neighbourhood, with well-kept gardens displayed year-round in Canada's only snow-free capital region. Less than a kilometre away, waterside mansions and rugged shoreline gave way to the sparkling blue waters of the Haro Strait, a great whale-watching area separating southern Vancouver Island from adjacent islands off the west coast of Washington State.

Despite the encroaching twilight on this winter evening, the solitary beam shining on the schoolyard asphalt was more than enough for the skinny teenager who lived just behind the property; young Stephen John Nash hopped his backyard fence and dribbled on a full run toward the basket, piercing blue eyes squinting to make out the silhouetted obstacles around him.

The rhythmic bouncing of the 11th grader's worn-out ball ricocheted off the school walls before dissipating into the evening sky as he planted his feet and launched a jump shot.

Swish.

It would be the first of many shots he would fire up that night, alone, while other local teens were microwaving popcorn and popping rented videos into their VCRs or phoning up buddies to plan an evening at the mall.

The 16-year-old's tireless devotion to hoops was an eyebrow raiser for his dad, John, a dyed-in-the-wool soccer aficionado whose British sensibilities couldn't quite make sense of this North American sport played with the hands. But he was nonetheless happy that his son had developed a passion for sports, a pursuit that was certainly dear to the father's heart.

John Nash and his Welsh wife Jean had arrived in Victoria back in 1976 with two-year-old Steve, not wanting to raise him in South Africa, where millions of blacks were being oppressed under the apartheid plan. John, a former pro soccer player in Johannesburg, got into marketing, while Jean, once a national team player in netball, worked with special-needs kids at a local elementary school. Two more children, Martin and Joann, soon followed, and the parents encouraged their youngsters to take up sports to stay out of trouble. "We felt it was a good way for them to meet people and develop their social skills as well as their sporting skills," John recalled. "Also it kept them off street corners. You know, kids' idle hands are the devil's playground."[1]

The Nash kids avoided idleness by playing an array of sports including but not limited to hockey, lacrosse, soccer, and baseball. One notable early exception was basketball, a traditional mainstay in Victoria for 100 years but which Steve's father and grandfather referred to as "a girl's game." John Nash insists he never pushed his kids into his treasured sport, though Steve received a soccer ball for his first birthday and Jean insists her son's first word as a toddler was "Goal!"

John, for one, was all about Tottenham Hotspur, the London-based club that's a mainstay of the British First Division. "My dad, my grandfather, and my uncle grew up watching [Tottenham]. That's tradition," said Steve, who had dribbled with his feet before he ever used his hands.[2]

Nash also developed an early passion for hockey ("My hero was Wayne Gretzky," he once said) and his mother noticed that her eldest son had a deep focus on whatever sport he took to. "When he was a young boy, if he was playing soccer or lacrosse, whatever the sport of the day, he'd come home and play it in the backyard," she told the CBC in 2005. "Say it was soccer. He'd set himself a goal for maybe 600 juggles with his feet. And he'd go out there and he'd do it."

By 1987, several friends had taken up basketball and they talked him into picking up the sport for the first time at Hillcrest Elementary, giving birth to a lifelong love affair. "Within a month at fundamental basketball practice, you just knew he was something special," says Mike Gallo, Hillcrest's vice-principal who ran Wednesday evening scrimmages for young teens.[3]

The 13-year-old's soccer roots were evident from the start, as he loved setting up others to score. Basketball quickly became everything to Steve and he put up shots every chance he could get and forced himself through incessant dribbling drills, eventually growing so comfortable with the ball that it seemed glued to his hand. Every one of Nash's amateur coaches says the same thing — he had an obsession with getting better that bordered on the pathological.

"If I had 15 minutes before school or a half-hour before school, let me see how many shots I can make," Nash said. "And if I had 15 minutes or a half-hour at lunchtime, let me see how many shots I can make. Before practice … I can get in the gym and make 100 shots before we start and after practice maybe I can make 100 more."[4] Nash marvelled at the exploits of Jordan, Magic, and Bird, and told his mother that he would one day follow them onto the 94-foot court reserved for the world's best. "I didn't doubt him," said Jean. "Whether he'd make it or not you don't know, but I knew he was going to give it a heck of a try, because he works hard for what he gets."[5]

His father remembers Nash putting his math skills to work, along with his wrist, in marathon shooting drills. "Steve came in from the court one day and he told me, 'I shot 69 percent from the free-throw line.' I said, 'How did you work that out?' And he said, 'Well, I took 100 shots and I made 69 of them.' That's the way he was. And if he thought he wasn't shooting well, he would triple the shots. Instead of 100 shots, he'd take 300."[6]

Nash had made the sport a part of his life, so much so that a friend's grandmother referred to the basketball he carried around as "Steve's girlfriend." Brother Martin Nash recalls that Steve would dribble to and from school, a common sight in inner-city America, but quite the novelty in rugby and hockey-focused Saanich.

The young man's love for hoops meant that the news he had received in December of 1990 was that much tougher to swallow. As a transfer student he wasn't allowed to play the second half of his grade 11 season for St. Michaels University School (SMUS), a private boarding institution where he was slated to begin studies in the New Year.

It was quite the downer from the semester that had just ended at his old school, Mount Douglas Secondary, as the buzz-cut athlete's staccato dribbling and behind-the-back and over-the-shoulder passes wowed fans and frustrated opponents for the first two months of the season. When he wasn't quarterbacking the Rams to early-season wins he was honouring his family's sporting roots, starring for the Mount Douglas soccer team, where he was named the province's Most Valuable Player. Between travel for soccer and basketball and the personal workouts, the hardworking athlete missed some exams and got no breaks from several teachers who refused to let him re-take the tests. That led to a nasty surprise when Steve brought home his first-term report card just before the Christmas break — his grades were sagging and his parents weren't having any of it. They pulled their eldest son out of Mount Douglas and enrolled him at St. Michaels in the hopes that the university-like campus environment, smaller class sizes, and intense focus on prep work would boost his marks.

Ian Hyde-Lay, teacher and juvenile boys' basketball coach at St. Michaels, knew Nash well from the young 'baller's days starring for Artubus Junior High School, a rival of St. Michaels at the top tier of middle-school basketball on Vancouver Island. Hyde-Lay knew more than a bit about the game himself, having played and coached for the UVic Vikes under Ken Shields, architect of seven straight CIAU championships from 1980–86. The 33-year-old Shields disciple looked forward to eventually adding Nash to an already-strong Blue Devils squad, but he would have to work with him to tone down a helter-skelter style that left teammates baffled.

"He was sort of unnecessarily flashy," the coach remembered from those early days. "Some of his turnovers were where he makes a pass that actually should be completed for a dunk but the guy doesn't even see it coming."

Hyde-Lay nonetheless saw something special in his raw young transfer, who had the kind of court vision that you can't teach with passing drills. Nash had the ability to see a play before it developed, a gift Hyde-Lay first noticed three years earlier when he coached against Nash's Artubus teams. The coach also saw a rare, contained intensity that he couldn't quantify, "just kind of a sparkle in his eyes that just tells you he's a little different than most guys." But everyone would have to wait 10 months to see how it would all pan out.

By April 1991, Nash's marks had shot up and he began to prepare for his big grade 12 hoops debut that would come in the fall. The 17-year-old began by practising against Canada's best during the summer prior to his graduating season as Shields, by then the Senior Men's National Team coach, had relocated the program from Toronto to the Victoria seat of his former UVic dynasty. It was an off year, but national team players were practising at various gyms around town in preparation for the 1992 Olympic qualifier and Shields asked Steve to join them. The matchups would have been daunting for any high school player; six-foot-five guard J.D. Jackson of Vernon, B.C., one of the great players in CIS history and a French pro; six-three Montreal native Stewart Granger, an All-Big East player at Villanova and former NBA first-round draft pick; and natural-ized Canadian Ronn McMahon, a Utah native who was the second-leading steals man in NCAA history and was fresh off a stint in the U.S.-based World Basketball League.

What's more, Nash was just six foot one and about 155 pounds, nowhere near big enough to handle professionals physically. But the teenager played like he belonged right from the start. He was chomping at the bit after missing the entire basketball season, and he left any jitters at the gym door. Coach Hyde-Lay made it to a few of the scrimmages and immediately realized Nash was more than just a talented local player. "He was holding his own, more than holding his own," said the coach, who started thinking about ways to get his young star a Division I scholarship. "Once I saw him play with the national team, he's torching guys that have been [college] stars."

Nash was only picked as an alternate for the Canadian under-19 team that summer despite a good showing during an exhibition game in California against Long Beach State, a Division I team that featured future NBA players Bryon Russell and Lucious Harris.

For the remainder of the summer, Nash made do with a spot on the B.C. provincial team that would be travelling to a big Amateur Athletic Union tournament in the States, where he would finally get a chance to be seen by big schools. Things were looking up when the B.C. boys were scheduled to take the court immediately after a highly anticipated game featuring the top guard in America, Oakland, California passing wizard Jason Kidd. Had a player of Nash's calibre been playing on an American team, coaches and national media would have flown in to catch the double-header. But while dozens of college scouts watched Kidd work his wonders that day, they fled the gym in droves as soon as his game ended, clearly not expecting to find any future Magic Johnsons on an anonymous outfit from Canada.

Reality began to sink in when Nash and the team returned home — he was a complete unknown, absent from recruiting lists, not exactly the best position for someone chasing a D-I scholarship. But he got right back to work, taking a summer job at a basketball camp run by UVic legend Eli Pasquale, a Europro and one of the best Canadian college guards in history.

Ilario Enrico "Eli" Pasquale was a cat-quick six-foot-one guard of Italian descent who had the rare ability to play at high speed while remaining under control. Shields had snatched the dark-haired, boyish-looking Sudbury native from under the nose of Laurentian University's coaching staff in 1979 to add to the Vikes' mountain of All-Canadian talent. Pasquale dominated the CIAU and led the team to its first five championships while making the smooth transition to starting point guard for Jack Donohue's world-class national teams. He was also the final cut by the NBA's Seattle SuperSonics in 1984 training camp, realizing too late that he had the talent to play in the NBA all along but hadn't set his sights early enough on the world's top league.

One day after his 1992 skills camp, Pasquale offered Nash a ride as well as some career advice the young counselor never forgot. "He said to me, 'You know, if you want to play in the NBA, you should decide right now,'" Nash recalled in 2009. "And [Pasquale] went on to explain that he decided he wanted to play in the NBA before his fifth year at UVic and he felt like it was too late … what he was trying to say was that it's important to declare your intentions. It's really important to say out loud, write down what your goals are, what your intentions are. I think once you admit to yourself … what you intend to do, it's the first step to holding yourself accountable and making a tangible path to realizing your goals and your dreams."[7]

Until that pivotal talk with Pasquale, the NBA had been little more than a Utopian vision for Nash. Now it was time to come up with a plan, and he counted on his coach to help him make it happen. But the plan wouldn't mean a thing unless he turned in a senior season for the ages.

As the 1991–92 school year began at St. Michaels, the basketball players were optimistic that they could restore Vancouver Island hoops to prominence on the provincial scene. It had been 13 years since a team from the island had won the juvenile provincials, but Nash served notice early on that he wouldn't be denied. Watching tapes from his senior season it was clear that he wasn't just another talented Canadian player. First, the ball-handling, it was extraordinary, with a dribble so low that the defender couldn't bend down low enough to steal it, and Nash also had the ability to spin-dribble to the left and drive with his off hand, effortlessly ambidextrous after countless hours bouncing balls everywhere he went.

Then there was Nash's sublime passing, which resembled the pinpoint accuracy and sleight-of-hand of his idol, Utah Jazz icon John Stockton. Nash could read the play as it was happening and deliver sharp passes through traffic, right into teammates' hands, at full speed and sometimes without even looking directly at the target. On one play, Nash wove around and through three defenders simultaneously in the open court, deking out two of them before losing the third on a behind-the-back dribble to the basket followed by a spinning drive into a crowd. He leapt into the air on the left side of the hoop, faking a layup that got two opponents in the air before he flipped the ball behind his back to an open teammate for the score on the right side.

And although his lunging shooting stroke was awkward, it was effective as a finishing move — when the pass-first point guard chose to use it. Coach Hyde-Lay grew annoyed that his team's cornerstone would often start games slowly, deferring to teammates instead of looking for his shots. A decade earlier Hyde-Lay had worked his way up from walk-on to starter at UVic and refers to himself as a "credible, functional CIS player," but he knew Nash could be far greater. The talented guard's occasional passivity prompted the bench boss to channel some blunt motivational techniques from his old mentor, Shields. "Maybe sometimes if I felt the team needed a bit of a kick start, I think on a couple occasions I said to him, 'You know, Steve, if I had your kind of talent … I'd be a little bit embarrassed by how you're playing right now.' And you could just see the emotion well up in him and he would just come out in the second half and just explode. As a coach you just sat back and ... enjoyed the show."[8]

Nash took well to instruction, always managing to glean something positive even amidst criticism. Hyde-Lay had managed to persuade Nash not to over-dribble, making sure to get rid of the ball as soon as a man was open; the coach also instructed his pupil to work on his mid-range game to keep defences honest. The results were immediate, as the Blue Devils steamrolled through the early part of the season. But while their run to the provincials was going smoothly, the same couldn't be said for the coach's attempts to get his guard onto the Division I radar. Hyde-Lay made copies of one of Nash's performances and sent tapes to dozens of schools, along with a letter imploring them to actually watch the footage and to contact Shields as a reference.

"Most of them didn't," Hyde-Lay recalled.

The rejection letters piled up nearly as quickly as Blue Devils wins that season; major programs including Duke, Arizona, and Maryland said thanks but no thanks to the increasingly dejected teen wonder. There was an exchange of letters with Virginia, a major program in the Atlantic Coast Conference, which said it would send a coach to the provincials in March. It never happened. Bob Knight's three-time national champion Indiana Hoosiers sent vague letters but made no firm offer. Florida State suggested it might give Nash a scholarship but ultimately refused.

Perhaps most painful was the lack of interest from his two favourites, Washington and Syracuse. After all, Syracuse teams from the '80s had featured the likes of Dwayne "Pearl" Washington and Sherman Douglas, two of the most exciting point guards in college basketball. Equally attractive were the Washington Huskies, located in Seattle, just a three-hour ferry and road trip from Victoria. Both programs rejected Nash outright, putting a damper on his triumphant swan song of a season. "The lack of response hurt me, because I thought I was good enough that people would come knocking on my door," he said a few years later. "It was like I was trapped in an elevator and I'm screaming, but nobody could hear me."

One west coast coach admitted that Nash had much more than anonymity working against him. The dominance of black athletes at the top levels of American basketball had become overwhelming over the previous three decades. Just one of the 15 Associated Press All-Americans in the 1961–62 season was black; by 1990–91 the script was reversed, with only one white among 15 players selected. No more than three Caucasians made the AP first, second, or third teams in any one season for the ensuing 20 years. Whether it was socio-economic factors, racial stereotypes, marketing preferences, or a combination of the three, top NCAA programs were increasingly less likely to give white basketball players the benefit of the doubt, especially if they came from unknown cities in a foreign country best known for producing sports stars on skates, not in sneakers.

"You get 300 letters a year [from players]," Pepperdine basketball head coach Tom Asbury told *Sports Illustrated* in 1995. "And for a white guard from Canada, you're probably not going to do a lot of follow-up."

Hyde-Lay was incredulous. He had played with, guarded, or coached the best Canadian players over the previous 20 years and knew his crown jewel might be better than all of them. "I'm just shaking my head and going, is it possible that a guy this good, nobody even offers him anything? And we just kept checking along and laughing at all the no letters and just said 'Hey, it only takes one.'"

As it turned out, the one fish that bit hadn't even been baited.

Nash's short stint on the junior national team in 1991 hadn't been fruitless after all, since one Long Beach State assistant liked what he saw during the exhibition game against the Canadians. The coach contacted Scott Gradin, a volunteer assistant at Santa Clara University near San Jose, California, to suggest he keep an eye on the talented kid from up north. Gradin called St. Michaels, somewhat ironic since Hyde-Lay had never contacted them and Nash hadn't heard of the small Jesuit college that had just three NCAA tournament appearances in the previous 23 seasons. Nash's coach sent off a grainy, hand-held camcorder video of an early-season game against one of the region's bottom-feeders. The tape showed a determined but skinny and nondescript young player in short shorts, mid-calf striped socks, and a buzz cut, sending hapless defenders wobbling to the ground with his ball fakes and hesitation dribbles.

"It made me laugh out loud," Gradin said of Nash's performance against less than stellar talent. "No one could keep up with him. Guys were falling all over the place." He screened the raw footage of the raw recruit to Dick Davey, a long-time Santa Clara assistant. Neither of them was exactly sure of what they had, but both were interested enough to ask for a better-quality video that showed Nash running roughshod over a well-drilled team. Davey made plans to head up to the B.C. provincials to see this recruit for himself. The original faded Steve Nash tape has since become a favourite around the Broncos office.

That St. Michaels would make some noise at B.C.'s final tournament was becoming a foregone conclusion by early 1992. Nash was nearly averaging a triple-double that season with 21 points, nine rebounds, and 11 assists per game and St. Michaels rolled into the provincials, a tournament the Blue Devils had never won. The event was held in the 5,000-seat Agrodome at Vancouver's Pacific National Exhibition, which annually draws some of the largest crowds for amateur basketball anywhere in Canada. Davey made the two-hour flight north to see if this unknown Canadian could duplicate in real life what he had shown on tape.

St. Michaels players were warming up for their first game, with Nash drilling one shot after another and blazing through the ball-handling drills like a professional. Remember that this is the same guy who earlier in the season had returned from an MVP performance at an in-season tournament so unsatisfied that he demanded his coach let him shoot in the school gym the next morning. That insane work ethic was so apparent to Davey in warm-ups at that opening provincials game that the Californian started looking around nervously to see if any of his coaching peers from down south were in the building. "I'm hoping — praying — there are no big boys there," he told an interviewer years later. "Because if there are, they're going to have some interest in the guy and I'm going to be out of luck."

He needn't have worried, as 1992 was one of the few years in history when a future NBA Most Valuable Player was completely unknown as late as his senior year of high school.

When the game ended in yet another Blue Devils win, Davey decided on the spot to offer Nash a scholarship, but first he would test the young star's toughness in a novel way. He met Hyde-Lay after the game with Nash standing nearby, and said in a loud voice "He might be one of the worst defenders I've ever seen." Instead of getting angry, Nash agreed to have coffee with the American, taking the opportunity to ask him what he could do to improve his game.

Davey knew then that he had found his future point man, but Nash decided to think about winning a championship before accepting the offer. He quarterbacked Saint Michaels all the way to the final, where they trounced Pitt Meadows Secondary 76–48 to take their historic first provincial crown, capping a 50–4 record. The tournament MVP award went to Nash, and as the team made its triumphant return to the island, he was ecstatic but still facing uncertainty about his future.

He didn't know what to make of the offer from Santa Clara. The small school in Silicon Valley had no national profile, and even though the team played in the same conference as Gonazga, John Stockton's alma mater, Nash couldn't dodge that nagging feeling that he could have done better. Even some of his teammates teased him, referring to the school as "Santa Claus State." But with no other D-I offers forthcoming, his prospects appeared limited.

As the spring of 1992 harkened the stretch run of his senior year, Nash still hadn't ruled out his local options, which included UVic down the street from his house and Simon Fraser across the straight in Vancouver, which was playing in the U.S.-based NAIA division for small schools. All the while he dreamt of much a bigger stage for his talents, presenting a dilemma for Simon Fraser head coach Jay Triano.

The former Team Canada star was building his alma mater into a consistent performer in America, and would have loved to sign a program-changer like Nash, but he was realistic when the young star came to the mainland to meet him for a visit.

Nash spent the day at the tree-lined campus atop Burnaby Mountain, and when it was over, Triano drove the teen down to the water to catch the ferry, but they missed the boat, leaving them with plenty of time to talk. The young guard's head was spinning with thoughts about the looming decision. He asked Triano whether he should choose Simon Fraser or Santa Clara. Triano's selfless answer would be decisive. "Go to Santa Clara," Triano said, aware that the school, while small and unheralded, still offered Nash a chance at getting on TV or into the NCAA tournament.

Nash was convinced. He contacted the Broncos to accept their offer and started preparing for his new life in California. Meanwhile, Davey had been tabbed to replace outgoing coach Carroll Williams, who had been promoted to athletic director, and the new coach wanted Nash to focus

Santa Clara University Athletics.

Victoria, B.C.'s Steve Nash parlayed his only college scholarship offer into an All-America career at Santa Clara University from 1992 to 1996. He went on to become one of the greatest point guards in NBA history, winning two MVP awards (2005, 2006). He's the first and only basketball player to win the Lionel Conacher Award as Canada's male athlete of the year, earning top honours three times (2002, 2005, 2006).

exclusively on basketball drills in the off-season. But the signee had made a promise to some of his teammates that he wasn't about to break. Several of the St. Mikes rugby players had suited up for the basketball team that season and Nash returned the favour by taking the field in organized rugby games for the first time in his life. He fit right in, excelling at placekicking, so much so that he recorded an incredible 10 of 10 kicks in his very first game — with both feet, no less. The squad, coached by Hyde-Lay, went on to win the provincial title and Nash had sent a message to everyone that he hadn't forgotten about the team even as he pursued individual success.

Nash arrived in Santa Clara, California, in the summer of 1992 as one of seven freshmen on a team that prognosticators had already written off. The Broncos had just completed their second losing season in three years and hadn't won a West Coast Conference regular season title since 1969. If Nash was hoping to be seen on TV, he seemed to be in the wrong place, since the Broncos hadn't been in the NCAA tournament since 1987. Former coach Carroll Williams ran tightly disciplined teams that competed despite a major talent deficit, but the squad was in dire need of a sparkplug. With just one starter returning, Dick Davey's squad seemed to be in a rebuilding mode and none of the preseason previews had Santa Clara any higher than seventh in the league.

None of that bothered Nash as he settled into an off-campus house with four teammates. His summers and winters were about to get a lot warmer, even compared to the temperate Victoria region with its year-round flower gardens. Professors and classmates took to the affable Canadian who was quick with a joke and whose ways were very similar to many of the Californians around him. Before, between, and after classes, the sound of a bouncing basketball could be heard long before onlookers recognized the smiling, laid-back Canadian dribbling his way to classes or ambling into Toso Pavilion, the on-campus arena where janitors would pretend not to see the unknown player sneaking in to get up shots at weird hours of the night.

Nash had little to smile about in his early Broncos practices, where he had trouble adjusting to the speed of the game and the challenges from defenders who could actually slow him down. On the other end, he made Dick Davey's earlier remark about his defensive skills look prophetic, getting burned time and time again by the other guards. Doubt set in, and the youngster called home to his parents and his old coach to share his frustrations. "I kept on reminding him that good players don't become bad players overnight," said Hyde-Lay.

Nash began the season on the bench as the Broncos sputtered out of the gate, losing seven of their first 11 games, capped by a heartbreaking 59–57 loss to San Diego in the conference opener. Nash wasn't getting the minutes, but he made up for it on the practice court, his manic work ethic rubbing off on teammates. He would haul bleary-eyed mates out of the dorms for late-night pickup games, and was even seen shooting hoops during a violent overnight downpour on Christmas Eve.

Davey took notice, and finally inserted him into the starting lineup for the stretch run of the season, with instant results. Buoyed by Nash's growing confidence, the Broncos sailed into the conference tournament, winning six of the last seven games, including a key 63–58 road victory over league-leading Pepperdine to finish with a 9–5 league record.

The Broncos travelled an hour up Route 101 to San Francisco for the West Coast Conference tournament. They easily handled St. Mary's in the opener before edging out Gonzaga in the days before the Bulldogs became a perennial WCC powerhouse. The underdogs from down the road were then set to face the three-time regular season champs, the Pepperdine Waves, and their conference Player of the Year, Dana Jones. The Waves jumped out to an early 23–10 lead before Nash began to dominate like he was back in the Vancouver Island league. When the Waves played Nash tight, he would pass or drive around them. When they played off of him, he would knock down shots with aplomb, including seven three-pointers. The Broncos blew Pepperdine away 41–28 in the second half, making all nine of their threes in the game, and the Broncos won only their second WCC championship in school history.

Nash, with 23 points in the final, became the first freshman to be named tournament MVP, and the team was his to keep, as the *San Francisco Examiner* noted: "Everyone knew that Steve Nash, point guard, militantly self-effacing freshman and the non-hockey-playing pride of Victoria, British Columbia, had put the Broncos in the NCAA Tournament for the first time in six years. Defiant three-point jump shots, [fist]-punching at the audience to keep them engaged in the spectacle below, that give-me-the ball-if-you-know-what's-good-for-all-of-us look in his eye … it was, in a field of hundreds of images, the most noticeable part of the Broncos 73–63 win over the presumptive favorite Waves."

Santa Clara had every reason to consider their automatic berth in the NCAA tournament to be a victory in itself, but history shows that mid-major schools facing heavily hyped first-round opponents always play with house money. Santa Clara's first-round opponent, Arizona, certainly knew all about the burden of great expectations. Arizona, though a perennial Pacific-10 power, had a habit of losing in big games, including an embarrassing defeat the previous year to East Tennessee State in the first round of the tournament. But in 1993 the Wildcats were a Number 2 seed, and the Broncos were seeded 15th, seemingly lambs for the slaughter for Arizona's future NBA players Chris Mills, Khalid Reeves, Ed Stokes, and Damon Stoudamire. All seemed to be going according to plan when Santa Clara fell behind by 13 points in the second half before storming back to take a late three-point lead. With time running out and Nash handling the ball, the Wildcats were forced to foul the Canadian time and time again, and he converted six straight free throws to seal at 64–61 stunner that one sportswriter said "stretched the limits of credulity." It was only the second time in history that a 15 seed had beaten a 2, and though Temple knocked the Broncos out of the tournament in the second round, it was clear that the team had new life, and a new star.

In the summer of 1993, Nash made the first of what would be several appearances in major tournaments for Team Canada, quarterbacking the World University Games team to a matchup in the final against the always-powerful United States, with Nash once again squaring off against Damon Stoudamire. For the first time in the tournament, the Americans faced a stiff challenge, barely fighting off the Canadians 95–90. The silver medal fulfilled Nash's belief that Canada needn't bow down to anyone, including their bigger cousins to the south. "Some people in this country have a complex that we're inferior to the U.S. in basketball," Nash had told reporters that summer. "I think the individuals on this team feel we can play with them."[9]

Nash headed into his sophomore year swelled with confidence. He was in command of his skills and the game was starting to become easy for him. He was so dominant for stretches of his second year that NBA scouts started taking notice. The Broncos, having lost several starters, counted on Nash to lead them in scoring, and he reluctantly obliged, pacing the team with 14.6 points per game to go along with a school record 67 three-pointers. But as talented as Nash was, and as much as he scored, he could have scored even more, but was hard-wired to get his teammates involved. "He over-passed," recalls Randy Winn, a roommate of Nash's who went on to become a Major League Baseball All-Star. "You could see it. He wouldn't even shoot 10-footers."

The players didn't mind being on the receiving end of Nash's generosity and league coaches rewarded him with a spot on the all-conference team. Nash was by then considered one of the best guards in the nation, but he wasn't satisfied, challenging himself during ball-handling drills by trading in his basketball for a tennis ball. He could be seen bouncing the fuzzy green sphere around campus, sharpening his already dazzling dribbling talents to a sublime level.

Davey said he had never seen anything like it in his 25 years in the coaching business. "Every sprint that we run, he wins. Every drill he tries to be first. He has such deep, deep competitive desire. Steve is really deranged. He's addicted to basketball, and fortunately he's helped derange the whole team."[10]

Nash was hitting his stride just in time for his home country's rare role as host of the basketball world. Toronto businessman John Bitove Jr. had realized a long-time dream by landing the FIBA World Championship, which would be making its first appearance on Canadian soil. It was a perfect lead-in to the NBA's return to the Queen City, which had been awarded an expansion franchise for the 1995–96 season along with Vancouver.

Ken Shields had persuaded Toronto-born, Indiana-raised Boston Celtics starter Rick Fox to be the feature attraction for his team, which had an automatic berth as the host country, and Nash had had no trouble making his mark in early exhibitions despite his amateur status. Two and a half weeks before the tournament, the 20-year-old dropped 28 points and 11 assists on Spain, making all 12 of his foul shots in an eye-popping performance that was the clearest indication to his coaches that this sensational young talent had a real shot at the world's top league. Canada went on to finish seventh at the Worlds, and Nash led the team in assists.

Team adviser and former NBA coach Del Harris told him that the NBA was definitely in his future.

After his star turn in the summer, Nash's junior year was a breeze, as he averaged 20.9 points per game to win West Coast Conference Player of the Year, the first Canadian ever to be named the top player in a Division I conference. He had led the Broncos to their first regular season title since 1970 and the team received an at-large tourney bid, rare for a WCC team in those days.

By the end of the 1994–95 season, NBA scouts were saying Nash could be a first-round pick if he skipped his senior season. The fact that the Toronto Raptors and Vancouver Grizzlies were slated to begin play that year, with the draft happening in Toronto, was extra incentive for Nash to become the first Canadian ever to leave school early for the NBA. But Nash loved Santa Clara campus life, and his teammates, and decided to stay for one more year, giving the program another chance to play giant killer in the NCAA tournament.

Santa Clara was the trendiest mid-major school in America by the fall of 1995, and Nash was so popular that his team got an invite to the Maui Invitational, the top preseason tournament in the nation. Santa Clara's 78–69 opening-round win over UCLA was all the more of a stunner given that the storied Bruins were the defending national champions. That year the Broncos also upended high-major mainstays Oregon State, Georgia Tech, Michigan State, and Illinois. Nash repeated as conference player of the year and some experts said he was best guard in the country. He would get a chance to prove it in the first round of the NCAA tournament against the Maryland Terrapins, a team that had won 12 consecutive opening games in March Madness. Nash dominated in a 91–79 victory, breaking traps all by himself and dishing to open teammates to the tune of 12 assists to go with 28 points and a marvellous 17 of 18 free throws. Nash closed out his college career on the losing end of a 76–51 rout at the hands of Kansas in which fellow draft prospect Jacque Vaughn held him to just seven points.

The tearful exit couldn't mask his brilliance, as Nash had gone from unwanted high-schooler to the best player in Santa Clara history in just four years. He graduated as the Broncos' all-time leader in assists, free throw percentage, and three-pointers made and attempted. He was third on the school's career scoring list and was named an Honorable Mention All-America as a senior by the Associated Press and the U.S. Basketball Writers Association.

Then there was that little matter of the NBA draft.

All-American prospects such as Allen Iverson, Stephon Marbury, and Tony Delk were part of the deepest draft pool in more than a decade, but some scouts felt that Nash was the best pure point guard prospect of the bunch. Rick Majerus, then head coach at Utah, called him a "poor man's John Stockton" and he seemed a perfect fit for the Grizzlies and a surefire draw to fill the team's new arena. "It's clear that, marketingwise, having a B.C. player is a no-brainer," said Vancouver GM Stu Jackson, whose team would be picking third. Nash, who had previously expressed interest in the Raptors, was now pining for Vancouver. "The Grizzlies would be my number one choice if I had to pick a team," he told *Sports Illustrated* prior to the draft, "but if there were an NBA team in Moose Jaw, I'd be glad to play for it."

In the end, the Grizzlies went with Shareef Abdur-Rahim, a high-scoring six-foot-nine power forward from the University of California, while the Raptors, picking second, opted for University of Massachusetts All-American centre Marcus Camby. Nash, who some had projected as a top-14 pick, fell to 15th, where the Phoenix Suns snatched him up. When NBA commissioner David Stern announced his name the draftee pumped both of his fists, hugged his parents, brother, and sister, and made the walk up to the stage that millions of young players can imagine but never experience. When he shook Stern's hand, it was noteworthy that he didn't tower over the commissioner like most of the other athletes.

An everyman in every sense of the word, but as he would soon find out, the cut-throat business of basketball can be uncharitable to nice guys.

Thousands of fans had packed America West Arena on Wednesday, June 26, 1996, to watch one of the deepest drafts in years on the building's big screens. The Suns were a proud franchise that had slumped the previous season, limping into the playoffs before making an early exit. They were having trouble recovering from the departure of Charles Barkley, the bullish force of nature who had led the team to an NBA Finals berth just three years earlier.

In need of excitement, and holding a decent draft position by virtue of their .500 record, there were hopes a star player might still be available at the 15th spot, even though surefire talents such as Iverson, Marbury, and Antoine Walker had been snagged early.

When Sacramento, picking right before Phoenix, selected Croatian sharpshooting giant Predrag Stojakovic, Suns fans immediately turned their attention to All-American guard Tony Delk, who had just led the University of Kentucky to an NCAA championship in dominating fashion.

But instead, NBA commissioner David Stern announced Steve Nash's name and the boyish-looking guard's high-fives and hugs, beamed across the country to Phoenix, elicited a hail of boos and catcalls from bewildered fans who still hadn't heard of the Canadian despite his college exploits. Nash addressed the critics head-on. "I don't look like I'm going to be a tremendous basketball player on appearance," the rookie told reporters with a smile. "I probably would've booed myself too, but I'm going to be a really good player and I'm going to help the team a lot. I have a lot of faith in myself and hopefully they'll enjoy watching me play."[11]

But he wouldn't get that chance right away, since he would be playing behind three-time NBA All-Star Kevin Johnson as well as Sam Cassell, a crafty scorer who had won two championships with the Houston Rockets. Despite showing promise in limited court time, Nash remained parked on the bench for most of the early season as the Suns lost their first seven games and veteran coach Cotton Fitzsimmons started contemplating retirement. His final game in front of the bench would be on November 14, when the Suns flew up to Vancouver for Nash's big homecoming. The highly anticipated game even knocked the Canucks off the front of the sports pages and Fitzsimmons obliged by giving Nash his first start of the young season. The 22-year-old scored a team-high 17 points, with a game-high 12 assists, but the Suns couldn't beat the lowly Grizzlies before 15,158 fans with clearly split allegiances. Nash bought more than 50 tickets for family and friends in B.C., including his proud parents and his brother Martin, who had become a promising professional soccer player. The rookie made sure to accommodate the endless media requests and demands for personal appearances, admitting to reporters that the whirlwind posed a challenge. "This being a rookie has been difficult but enjoyable at the same time," said Nash, aware that he had realized a near-impossible dream. "This is a lesson that dreams can come true. It's just a matter of perseverance, having faith in yourself, never giving up."

His young career was about to face another challenge after Johnson returned to action in December, relegating the rookie to the bench once again. Fitzsimmons resigned following the Vancouver game to make way for recently retired guard and former NBA champion Danny Ainge. Nash's minutes briefly picked up but the Canadian's prospects for playing time looked even dimmer on December 26 when the team traded starting forward Michael Finley and Cassell to Dallas for Jason Kidd, the star who had stolen Nash's thunder at that AAU tournament back in 1991 and who would have a chance to do it again as the Suns' hyped franchise player. Ainge initially floated a plan that involved playing Kidd, Nash, and Johnson together to create matchup problems for opposing backcourts, but in fact the veterans got the better of the bargain as Nash watched most games from the bench for the last three months of the season.

While most rookies might have sulked and waved their rally towels half-heartedly, Nash's enthusiasm didn't wane and he was the first to jump up off the bench during timeouts, encouraging his teammates through the difficult season. Team Canada head coach Steve Konchalski, who had taken over for Ken Shields two years earlier, remembers calling Nash in February of his rookie year to talk basketball and the upcoming World Championship qualifier. He remembers marvelling at the young man's relentless optimism in the face of dwindling court time. "As I picked up the phone I expected to encounter a perhaps discouraged Steve Nash," Konchalski said in 2006. "I was wrong. When I asked him how he was doing, he responded 'great' and explained that playing behind the Suns' Jason Kidd and Kevin 'KJ' Johnson — two of the best guards in the NBA — was a great opportunity to improve."[12]

It turns out that Nash employed the same attitude to basketball excellence as the league's best player at the time, Michael Jordan. Practice for such workaholics wasn't just a necessary evil, it was a chance to get better, to gain an edge on other multimillionaires who were content to pace themselves for the playoff run.

Nash's legendary work ethic started to play off in his second season as he showed an accurate touch from the three-point line (41.5 percent) and the free throw line (86 percent), emerging as one of the best backup point guards in the league as Phoenix improved to 56 wins. He had a style all his own, growing out his hair into an unkempt mop and displaying some decidedly bizarre on-court mannerisms. He would constantly lick his hands and slick back his hair, even when dribbling, often allowing the ball to lay out in front of him, untouched, while he passed his hands through his mop. While other, more explosive guards would use raw power to blast by defenders, Nash would actually slow down, throwing off his opponent by coming to a complete stop mid-drive before continuing on his way to the basket.

Ainge boosted his minutes in early December and he responded, averaging 12 points and 5 assists off the bench. Ainge recognized that Nash was a top-flight guard in just his second season. "He's better than half the starting point guards in the league right now," said the bench boss. "I love the guy."[13]

But with Kidd firmly entrenched at the point, Suns general manager Jerry Colangelo shipped Nash to the Dallas Mavericks, a perennial doormat that just a few years earlier had won 11 of 82 games, flirting with the worst record in league history. Nash would be teamed up with oversized German forward Dirk Nowitzki, an unheralded 18-year-old who Mavs coach and GM Don Nelson insisted was a future superstar. Critics, including many Mavericks fans, scoffed at the idea that Nelson would hand over his franchise to a steady but unspectacular Canadian backup point guard and an untested German giant who detested rough play near the basket.

Their inaugural news conference in Dallas was awkward, with the hulking Nelson sitting between the two fresh-faced newcomers, and Nash the only one whose smile looked genuine. Nelson asked the tall German if he wanted to make a statement. Nowitzki, clearly not ready to improvise, said "no" three times, ramping up the level of awkwardness. Nash, trying his best to lighten the mood, interjected "pass me the ball," eliciting a nervous laugh from his new teammate, who admitted he wasn't sure what to make of the Canadian wisecracker.

The two fish out of water quickly bonded, however, leaning on each other as the foreigners on a team of Americans. A lockout wiped out 32 games of the 1998–99 season, delaying the start until January of 1999, and when things finally got underway, the Mavericks played like they were still on vacation. Their 19–31 record, including a miserable 4–21 road mark, left them out of the playoffs as Nash struggled with nagging injuries and saw his statistics drop in most categories. The 1999–2000 season wasn't much better as the Mavs once again missed the playoffs and Nash actually found himself coming off the bench. If his ego took a hit, he wasn't showing it, telling reporters that coach Nelson's move gave him a chance to reprise the reserve role that made him so effective on the Suns.

But the long-suffering Dallas fans cut their franchise cornerstones no slack whatsoever, showering them with boos after particularly poor plays. Nash kept his chin up and took responsibility. "They brought in a new point guard, gave him a nice contract, and he wasn't producing," Nash told a 2007 segment on NBA TV. Nowitzki had his own struggles those first two years against the league's physical inside behemoths, and remembers the catcalls. "They booed him in our own gym every time he touched it and I remember sitting on the floor like 'wow, this is pretty messed up.'"

Nash's tendency to pass up shots in favour of dishing to teammates caused fits for Coach Nelson, who preferred a high-octane offence where guards put up lots of shots. "He wants to pass first," Nelson told *Sports Illustrated*. "I guess it's okay to be that way on a certain kind of team, but I needed him to get 15 points every night." Nash barely averaged half that amount and although Dallas had the league's third-best offence in 1999–2000, they finished 40–42 and out of the playoffs for the 10th straight season.

Nash responded in the only way he knew — by hitting the gym with Nowitzki, recalled Mavericks assistant coach Donnie Nelson, son of Don. "It was trial by fire, both these guys were thrown into this element, lots of expectations, and a lot of patience, they spent lots of time in a dark gym back there, late night hours."[14]

They went through intense drills, but Nash also lightened the mood in those long, solitary sessions by challenging his talented teammate to trick-shot games of H-O-R-S-E or one-on-one challenges, building a close friendship that served them well once tech billionaire Mark Cuban bought a controlling stake in the franchise in 2000 with promises to spend freely and pilot the team to Western Conference supremacy.

Nash and Nowitzki didn't take long to get on the wrong side of their new boss for decisions both had made years earlier. The two stars were the centrepieces of their respective national teams, both of which were vying for a spot in the 2000 Olympics in Sydney. Cuban was perhaps the most vocal critic, among owners, of NBA players competing in the Olympics, reasoning that his human assets were too valuable to loan to national sides where injuries could throw a wrench into his rebuilding plans. But he also didn't want to be the first owner to order a player not to suit up in their nation's colours, which was all the better for Team Canada, which stood to benefit from Nash's emergence as a budding star on the world stage. The program had made an unlikely run in the 1999 Olympic qualifier, finishing in second place to easily earn an Olympic berth for the first time since Jack Donohue's final season in 1988.

Nash, a multimillionaire, could have lived like many Olympic stars and checked himself into a five-star hotel while his teammates made do with accommodations at the athletes' village. But he insisted on bunking with teammates in Sydney, secretly funnelling $300,000 to Team Canada head coach Jay Triano to divide between his 10 non-NBA teammates. Prior to the Games, Nash had even agreed to ride the team bus to and from Montreal for an exhibition game organized by the perennially cash-strapped national team. He admitted the experience was "very different from the NBA" but that the more modest arrangements kept him in touch with the average athlete. "This is much closer to the game I played as a kid," he told reporters in Sydney. "I love it; it's just like college to me. You're in the dorms. You're hanging out together. You're going around meeting people in the Village. I pretty much fit right in.'"

Triano gushed about Nash's off-court performance as much as his on-court exploits, calling him "a consummate professional" and mentioning that he's "so caring of his teammates."[15]

"Nash Embodied Olympics Ideals" was the headline in the *Toronto Sun* following the tournament, with writer Steve Simmons saying Nash was a breath of fresh air among the "gymnasts who took the wrong cough medicines and the weightlifting cheaters."

"[The] skinny, wealthy, long-armed, fuzzy-haired, smiling Canadian … doesn't just symbolize all that can be still right about the Olympics, but is living it here every day," Simmons wrote. "Meet Steve Nash and instantly you'll feel better about yourself, about Canada, about the Olympic experience."

On the court, Nash led the Olympic tournament in assists as Canada upset Spain and Yugoslavia before falling to France, and a news photographer caught the Canadian captain sobbing as he walked off the court following the elimination game, a show of emotion that helped to vault his popularity to new levels on both sides of the Canada-U.S. border. His self-deprecating comments after the gutwrencher only increased his status in his homeland. "It hurts," Nash told reporters in the post-game interview. "It hurts a lot. I feel like I let everybody down. We could have been in the championship game. We were good enough."

The remarks said everything fans needed to know about how much this 26-year-old athlete cared about the game in an era of jackpot salaries and passion-killing fame. The *Winnipeg Free Press* suggested the gritty display by Nash and his team would pay dividends far beyond the Olympics. "Nash has done what not even Vince Carter or the mighty NBA could do — namely, make a country care about the game," said the newspaper. "He has given the game in Canada, which has never established more than a beachhead in Toronto, a lease on the future that never existed before."[16]

By the fall of 2000, Nash was more than just the face of Canadian basketball, he was approaching iconic status, and it was around that time that sportswriters and fans alike began referring to him as Captain Canada.

Nash shook off the disappointment of Sydney and returned to his day job in Dallas, determined to keep pressing forward. Things finally clicked in 2000–01 when he emerged as one of the best point guards in the NBA, with averages of 15.6 points and 7.3 assists per game that were by far the best statistics of any Canadian to have played in the league. He had rediscovered the pinpoint shooting touch that had made him such a hot prospect in the first place, and showed off a gift for delivering precise passes through jumbles of limbs that was almost Gretzky-like.

Through a decade-plus of maniacal workouts, Nash displayed a level of ball control rarely seen in the history of basketball. He kept up a frenetic pace of herky-jerky movements, shifting eyes constantly surveying the floor and the chin always up to better spot an opening in the writhing mass of arms and legs between him and the basket. "Going 100 miles per hour all the time — that's his game," said Nowitzki, while another teammate, forward Loy Vaught, noted that the Canadian somehow always seemed to know where he was going despite the breakneck pace. "You just can't startle him. When you see Steve Nash, the first thing that pops into your head is 'cool.'"

Nash almost never picked up his dribble, and contrary to convention wisdom, he preferred to pass off the bounce in mid-stride, allowing the defence little time to react. His vision was so advanced that he could make the off-the-dribble passes between a defender's legs at full speed, adding a dose of humiliation to the opponent that the humble Canadian would never rub in with preening or trash talk.

Though laid back and friendly off the court, Nash was all business on it, displaying an intense, fiery personality with his teammates. He wasn't afraid to raise his voice at guys who weren't getting it done and the Mavericks responded in 2000–01, making a 13-game improvement and appearing in the post-season for the first time since 1990. The Mavs edged out Utah in the first round before falling to the San Antonio Spurs as Nash recorded career highs in assists and free throw percentage. Meanwhile, Nowitzki had emerged as one of the league's best players and Mark Cuban opened his bank account to buy supporting talent. It seemed the Mavericks were in line to make a run at a championship.

Nash's scoring and assist numbers increased over the next three seasons and 2003 became a landmark year. That season he was the first Canadian ever to appear in the NBA All-Star Game, but the antiwar T-shirt he wore at media day drew more attention than his two-point, three-assist, four-turnover performance in the showcase match. His shirt was emblazoned with the slogan NO TO WAR. SHOOT FOR PEACE, as President George W. Bush formulated a plan to invade Iraq, a military move Nash said was "a very dangerous mistake to make at this time in history." The athlete's comments drew ire from conservatives, including veteran Spurs centre and ex-naval officer David Robinson, who retorted "If [the war is] an embarrassment to them, maybe they should be in a different country."

Nash didn't back down from Robinson's suggestion to deport dissenters, explaining that his T-shirt wasn't an indictment of America but of war as whole. "I'm not embarrassed by America," Nash said. "I'm embarrassed by humanity. More than embarrassed, I think it's really unfortunate in the year 2003 that we're still using violence as a means of conflict resolution."

Nash's willingness to take a stand and stick to it in the face of controversy gave the public a glimpse into a social consciousness that would become apparent as his career marched on. Back in 2001 he had created the Steve Nash Foundation, a charity that helps children in Canada, the

United States, Paraguay, and Uganda. Paraguayan children have benefited from free clinics while in Uganda, which suffered terribly under dictator Idi Amin, the foundation promotes reconciliation projects that have been successful in South Africa and Rwanda. Nash's childhood friend Jenny Miller was put in charge of the foundation along with his mother, Jean, and his sister Joann.

Also in 2001, when the money-losing Grizzlies and their new American owner bolted town, Nash jumped in to rescue the team's youth basketball program, rechristening it Steve Nash Youth Basketball. He singlehandedly bankrolled the program at first, and 8,000 British Columbians between grades four and seven had him to thank for the life preserver. Under Nash's watch the program has since expanded across Canada, providing a comprehensive framework of drills, training methods, and coaching strategies, along with a list of fair-play principles that even involve a code of conduct for parents on the sidelines.

Nash was a two-time All-Star by 2004, but when his contract came up for renegotiation that year, Cuban wasn't willing to give him a long-term deal, even going so far as to tell reporters that the 30-year-old was on the downside of his career. When Nash's old Suns team came calling with a six-year, $63-million contract offer, Nash could have dropped the Mavericks right away, but he actually went back to Cuban to ask the billionaire if he would match the deal. Cuban's refusal set the stage for Nash to join a powerhouse offensive unit in Phoenix that included six-eight scoring guard Joe Johnson, super-quick six-foot-ten power forward Amar'e Stoudemire, and jumping-jack six-seven wing Shawn Marion under the direction of offensive-minded coach Mike D'Antoni.

Nash managed to make a statement about where he planned to take his new team before he had even met them for training camp. Suns owner Jerry Colangelo walked into the team's practice facility at 7:00 a.m., a full month before veterans were required to report, only to see the long-haired Canadian drilling one shot after another, alone, just like he had done back at Hillcrest Elementary in Saanich.

The team had already jumped from 29 wins to 62 the year before Nash arrived, and the team was even better with Nash in charge, equalling their win total as Nash recorded the highest assists per game average (11.5) since his idol John Stockton a decade earlier. Nash was also one of the few

NBA players who regularly appeared on highlight reels for his passing, not his dunking.

It was clear from the season-long glowing reviews in the U.S. media that Nash was going to get plenty of MVP votes, but larger-than-life Hall of Fame–bound Shaquille O'Neal was having yet another dominant season for his new team, the Miami Heat.

When the votes came in during the 2005 playoffs, Nash had edged out O'Neal in one of the closest-ever MVP votes, going where only Oscar Robertson and Magic Johnson had gone before — winning the Most Valuable Player award from the point guard position. Nash beat out Shaq by 34 votes, and although critics, including Shaq himself, derided Nash's selection over a host of stars including LeBron James and Kobe Bryant, the statistics showed a massive improvement in the Suns offensive output after the arrival of Captain Canada.

The Suns led the NBA with 110.4 points per game in 2004–05, the 16.2-point jump representing the largest single-season increase in NBA history. In typical Nash fashion, he insisted on accepting the NBA's Maurice Podoloff Trophy with his teammates surrounding him.

Accolades poured in from around the league and for a few days basketball actually supplanted hockey as the top sports story in Canada. Ian Hyde-Lay, the high school coach who a dozen years earlier was screaming to the basketball world that his starting point guard was the real deal, still found himself in shock at the MVP news. "In one sense, you can't get your mind around it … it's incredible," said the coach, who in 2005 was still working at St. Michaels and who Nash had called shortly before the news broke. "Nobody could have anticipated this back then … from high school when I first coached him on the court … and now to NBA MVP is too big a jump to even comprehend."

Even Nash himself, who had resolved to be an NBA player back in grade 11, seemed to have finally reached a goal that he didn't plan for. "I don't think I ever dreamed about this reward," he told Paul Coro of the *Arizona Republic*. "I don't know what to say, I just kept trying."

Nash's rise was almost too unlikely to pass muster as a Hollywood script. This former junior national team alternate had not only leap-frogged every Canadian prospect who ever donned sneakers, he had even eclipsed the three Hall of Fame–worthy point guards who had beaten him out for playing time in Phoenix. Jason Kidd, Kevin Johnson, and Sam Cassell had all shone much brighter than their quiet, reserved Canadian teammate in the mid-to-late 1990s, but Nash ended up arguably a better pure point guard than all of them.

No Canadian basketball player had ever moved the meter to such a degree in world hoops, and sportswriters took notice of Nash's stunning rise to notoriety when they handed out their year-end awards in December of 2005. Nash became the first basketball player to win The Canadian Press's Lionel Conacher Award. He also snagged the Lou Marsh Trophy awarded by Canadian sports editors. In a country where basketball is seemingly forever in the shadow of winter sports, voters picked Nash over NHL rookie sensation Sidney Crosby, triple world champion speed skater Cindy Klassen, and world champion curler Randy Ferbey.

"It's cool, amazing," said the winner. "Anytime you can share an award like this with athletes like The Great One and all the other great athletes who've won it, it's a really great feeling. Part of me wants to share this with all the other nominees because I'm sure they had great years, too."

Nash repeated his MVP feat in 2006, becoming only the eighth man in NBA history up to that point to win back-to-back MVPs. The awards began pouring in north of the border after that — the Order of Canada in 2007, Olympic torch-bearer in 2010, and a host of honorary degrees. Nash's championing of environmental causes led to his being named one of *Time* magazine's 100 Most Influential People in the World.

Canada had taken notice by then, as Nash's face graced magazine covers, cereal boxes, and TV commercials. Young Canadian 'ballers had a living, homegrown hero to follow as they tried to make it big in the sport they loved. Steve Nash Youth Basketball continued to expand, helping grow the game on the ground through the creation of new leagues or the remaking of existing ones across Canada.

Captain Canada had almost single-handedly steered his sport a little closer to the Canadian mainstream, and he had done it without sacrificing the same humility that endeared him to teammates at St. Michaels University School back in Victoria. Canada's Sports Hall of Fame noted as much in its entry on Nash: "Though he was born in South Africa and now lives in the United States, Nash is undeniably Canadian: Unfailingly polite, self-deprecating and with a dry sense of humour, he's not your typical NBA star."

As for Nash's impact on the Canadian game, the proof can be seen in any gym where kids wear Steve Nash Youth Basketball jerseys as they zig-zag across courts from Victoria to Halifax, or in seminars where coaches study Steve Nash training manuals as they prepare to teach kids the game while exhorting them to have fun as well.

Toronto native and former NBA forward Leo Rautins, Nash's spiritual predecessor as the anointed one of Canadian basketball in the 1980s, makes sure to mention Nash's normalcy while touting his extraordinary accomplishments. "Here's a guy who's no different than these kids sitting in the gyms, 14- and 15-year-olds that I talk to," said Rautins, who might have enjoyed NBA stardom of his own if not for 15 knee surgeries. "Steve didn't have any more talent, jumping ability, quickness, size, anything than a lot of these kids, but he just worked his tail off to get where he is, to now get MVP."

Up-and-coming point guards took the message to heart, and by the second decade of the 21st century, a new crop of world-class young set-up men popped up on the radar. Among these were Cory Joseph, Myck Kabongo, and Kevin Pangos, who spoke confidently of leading Team Canada to an elusive Olympic medal — one of the few honours missing from Nash's trophy case.

But one former Victoria-area high school student wasn't about to start gloating about his legacy. "If my career has somehow inspired or gained interest in kids across the country, that would be unbelievable to have that sort of impact," said Nash.

Consider it done, Steve.

EPILOGUE

– ON THE CUSP –

It was a surreal atmosphere for Canadian basketball fans. For five days in late August of 2012 at Toronto's Air Canada Centre, 30 players from three generations of Canadian hoops buried their collective hatchets and rejoined a national team program that had struggled for years amid chilly relations with its own talent. Canada was the only country that continued to enter major world tournaments without many of its top players, for reasons that ranged from frustration over shoestring budgets and personnel decisions (Steve Nash) to outright indifference (Jamaal Magloire). The effects were predictable, as the Senior Men's National Team had failed to qualify for three consecutive Olympics for the first time in its history despite the fact that at the same time a record number of Canadians graced NBA rosters.

But whatever had kept players away in the past, all appeared be forgotten as they went through their paces inside the cavernous Toronto sports palace. There were no important tournaments to be played that summer, not a single game on the schedule and no guarantees that even half of the young athletes would be picked to play in an Olympics or a World Championship in the foreseeable future.

Anyone who had followed Canada Basketball's trials and tribulations over the previous quarter-century understood why the star-studded get-together was so important. The event had even drawn interest from the national media corps, a group that normally gave only a passing glance to any hoops news not related to the Raptors.

The prodigal sons who had returned to the Team Canada fold represented a who's who of players and coaches, spurring talk of a return to the Olympics and a medal run that hadn't been a realistic prospect for more than a decade.

Overseeing the reunion was Nash, the two-time NBA MVP who had just been named general manager of the program after a nine-year estrangement from the team he had nearly led to the Olympic medal round in 2000. Canada Basketball president and CEO Wayne Parrish called the hiring "one of the most important moments in the history of the sport in Canada since the day Dr. Naismith invented the game," and, given Captain Canada's stature as a world sportsman, entrepreneur, and social activist, Parrish might not have been exaggerating.

Nash was just one of several big names in attendance. Donning a red-and-white jersey — finally — was Magloire, the long-armed centre from Toronto who had previously refused to play a single game for his country during a 12-year NBA career that included an All-Star appearance.

Holding a clipboard was Carleton University coach Dave Smart, author of a record nine CIS championships, his usual fiery intensity softened by the jovial mood.

And the pivotal event wouldn't have been complete without Jack Donohue's eight-time captain Jay Triano, the only man to lead a Canadian national team to a gold medal, who was making his triumphant return as head coach after the old regime unceremoniously dumped him nearly a decade earlier.

Former Team Canada CEO Fred Nykamp's decision to fire Triano in 2005 caused head-scratching that morphed into outrage when USA Basketball scooped Triano up and made him the first foreigner ever to work as an assistant coach for their near-unstoppable men's national team. The Niagara Falls native spent five years giving pep talks and leading drills with the likes of Kobe Bryant, LeBron James, and Dwyane Wade as the U.S. returned to the top of the podium with gold medals at the 2008 and 2012 Summer Games. Triano was also on the bench as the United States rolled to a 2010 World Championship while Canada sputtered to an 0–5 record, tied for dead last with Tunisia and Jordan.

It was the country's worst-ever showing at an international tournament, a stinging slap in the face to incredulous Canadian fans and a smear on a national program that had seen nothing but bad news since Triano and Nash quarterbacked the surprise run to the Olympic quarterfinals in 2000.

But the instability, underachievement, and bad blood all dissipated when Nash welcomed his old buddy and mentor back to the bench with a snazzy news conference on the eve of the reunion camp. The rehiring closed a circle and reversed roles as the superstar point guard was now the boss of his former coach, a man who two decades earlier had advised the flop-haired teen to chase his only Division I scholarship offer.

There were smiles all around to start Triano's introductory news conference at Air Canada Centre, but the joviality soon gave way to the blunt acknowledgement that Team Canada would have to build bridges with an alienated talent pool. A camp with personalized training sessions was the first step. "We wanted to make sure that we gave to our players," said the new coach. "I think in the past one of the complaints [was] 'Canada Basketball always asks us for something, [but] what do they do for us?'"[1]

With that in mind, the practices were focused not only on individual skills but on forging relationships, and the smiles and good-natured ribbing was contagious.

Nash, still an active NBA player at 37, led the drills by displaying his dazzling dribbling skills. At one point he grabbed two basketballs and did a full-speed side-to-side shuffle from baseline to baseline, hammering balls into the floor with blinding speed and typewriter precision.

At the other end of the court, seasoned 34-year-old Magloire joined 16-year-old Trey Lyles, an Indiana big man born in Saskatchewan to a Canadian mother and an American father who was a player for a long-since-forgotten minor-pro team.

Triano and Nash masterminded the unprecedented turnout by cleverly appealing to players' personal goals of NBA success while building toward Team Canada's objective of returning to the Olympic podium for the first time since 1936.

"If we're successful in converting as much of this talent to the NBA and Olympic quality basketball players, we can inspire the next generation," said Nash. "We can change the game for the better."

There had likely never been as much Canadian talent assembled on one floor, and European and American media noted the potential for a hoops renaissance, though the best prospect of all wasn't even there.

Andrew Christian Wiggins started his life no differently than any other sports-minded kid in Vaughan, a bedroom community north of

Toronto. He loved basketball but was routinely beaten up on the court by older brothers Nick and Mitch Jr., both of whom went on to college careers in the States.

There were hints, however, that the shy little brother might eventually have his own day in the sun. For starters, his father was Mitchell Wiggins, former star guard at Florida State University who went on to a six-year career with three NBA teams. Florida State was where Mitchell met his future wife, Toronto-born Marita Payne. A long, lean track star, Marita won two silver track-and-field medals in the 100-metre and 400-metre relays at the 1984 Olympics. The genetic possibilities were tantalizing, and it wasn't surprising when Mitchell and Marita's first two boys became basketball stars by the mid 2000s. It was about that time that Wiggins, then just 13, sprouted up to six foot four and started dunking when most other eighth graders were just happy to touch the bottom of the net. Wayne Dawkins, a local basketball trainer and founder of the long-running All-Canada Classic all-star game, came to Wiggins's elementary school to run a camp and quickly realized he wasn't training an ordinary sixth grader. "He was already dunking. He's … dunking consistently. When you saw him he was this lanky [kid], and he doesn't look like he's explosive, but when he gets off the ground, it's so effortless."

Other Toronto-based talent evaluators immediately took notice of the teen's fluid drives and high-rising dunks. Rowan Barrett, a former high school phenom and one of the greatest leapers in the history of the Canadian game, had an idea of what was to come. "Here was a 13-year-old — six foot three with length and size — slam-dunking the ball in a way that even pros have difficulty doing," he said. "It was very clear to anyone who knows basketball that we had a phenom on our hands."[2]

Though he had been beating up on his Canadian peers for some time, Wiggins's profile really blossomed when he shone at a camp in North Carolina in the summer of 2009, dribbling around and through defenders and taking the ball far above the rim where shorter competitors couldn't touch it. His AAU coach at Grassroots Elite, Ro Russell, told CBS Sports that his young charge "will eventually be the best player I've ever had,"[19] a major statement given that Grassroots stars Denham Brown, Cory Joseph, and Tristan Thompson went on to become NBA draft picks.

Vaughan, Ontario, native Andrew Wiggins, nicknamed "Maple Jordan," is seen as the future of Canadian basketball because of his athleticism, explosive scoring ability, and peerless accolades against top competition on both sides of the border and overseas.

But Russell's prediction proved prophetic by the summer of 2010 when Wiggins soared on the international stage as the youngest player at the FIBA U-17 World Championship. In his first tournament wearing the Team Canada jersey, the 15-year-old poured in 20 points against a U.S. squad packed with future NBA players and found himself on the pro radar for the first time. Even at the tender age of 15, Wiggins was already the rarest of talents, combining solid ball-handling, an accurate jump shot, and blazing speed with a six-foot-seven frame and 44-inch vertical leap.

His package was too much for Toronto-area opponents to handle, as Wiggins dominated in his only year of Canadian high school ball at Vaughan Secondary School in 2010–11. He led his Vaughan squad to an Ontario provincial championship, catching the attention of prep schools south of the border. In an unprecedented move, the U.S. scouting services unanimously anointed the Canadian as the number one player in the class of 2014 despite the fact he had played the previous season in Canada.

When Wiggins did eventually head south in the summer of 2011, enrolling at Huntington Prep in West Virginia, he only confirmed the hype by grabbing two consecutive state Player of the Year awards and an avalanche of spectacular highlights in regular-season play as well as for his new AAU team, CIA Bounce. Wiggins even wowed NBA superstars, with seven-time NBA All-Star Alonzo Mourning saying "the sky is the limit for his potential" while comparing the soft-spoken Canadian to "a LeBron James, a Carmelo Anthony."[3]

Wiggins, meanwhile, remained typically Canadian despite his budding superstar status, preferring quiet time with teammates and friends while eschewing interviews and refusing to boast about his talents. While the long, lanky teen remained strangely impervious to the attention, he retained a low-key confidence and didn't seem at all surprised that he had become the first Canadian ever to reach the top of the American amateur basketball totem pole. "It doesn't matter where you are from or where you live," he told reporters as he accepted a national player of the year award following his final season at Huntington. "If you have talent and you can do well in school, the sky is the limit."

By 2013, Wiggins was considered the best amateur player on the planet and some scouts pegged him as a future franchise cornerstone at the pro level. His rise had a trickle-down effect on the global perception of Canadian basketball. No longer was the country considered simply a hockey factory, and with Nash elevating Canada Basketball's profile, long-dormant sponsorship and media interest began to pick up.

In the second decade of the 21st century, Canada was projected to put more players into the NBA and WNBA than in all previous eras combined, a confidence-booster for young Canadians who now expect to make the pros as opposed to merely entertaining vague dreams about playing at the highest level.

Equally crucial is the fact that basketball has finally begun to force its way into the Canadian consciousness. While a passion for hockey continues to course through veins in the Great White North, there's clearly room for more than one love interest among sports fans, and Canada's other game has a chance to emerge from the shadows of anonymity, corporate indifference, and seemingly perennial stepchild status.

Canada is gradually learning to love its long-neglected gift to the world, a gift nurtured by cousins and even strangers but one which could finally thrive in the birthplace of its inventor.

NOTES

CHAPTER 1: Y THE GAME WAS CREATED

1. James Naismith, *Basketball: Its Origins and Development* (New York: Association Press, 1941), 18–19.
2. Ibid.
3. Rob Rains and Hellen Carpenter, *James Naismith: The Man Who Invented Basketball* (Philadelphia, PA: Temple University Press, 2009), 1–3.
4. Ibid., 4.
5. R. Tait McKenzie, "Reminiscences of James Naismith," New York University School of Education, Department of Physical Education and Health, June 1, 1932. Courtesy of Springfield College Digital Collection.
6. James Naismith, *Basketball: Its Origins and Development* (New York: Association Press, 1941), 21.
7. Ibid.
8. James Naismith, *Basketball: Its Origins and Development* (New York: Association Press, 1941), 22.
9. Rob Rains and Hellen Carpenter, *James Naismith: The Man Who Invented Basketball* (Philadelphia, PA: Temple University Press, 2009), 22.
10. Ibid., 27.
11. Michael Kilmartin, "Springfield College Campus," Springfield College Archives and Special Collections.
12. James Naismith, *Basketball: Its Origins and Development* (New York: Association Press, 1941), 24–25.

13. Rob Rains and Hellen Carpenter, *James Naismith: The Man Who Invented Basketball* (Philadelphia, PA: Temple University Press: 2009), 35.
14. Ibid., 37.
15. 1930s James Naismith Typed Manuscript with Handwritten notes re: Evolution of Basketball.
16. "Basketball Was Born Here," Springfield College: 11.
17. "Basket Ball," *The Triangle*, Vol. 1, No. 10, January 15, 1892.
18. James Naismith, "Basket Ball Rules for 1893," *The Triangle*, 9.
19. James Naismith, *Basketball: Its Origins and Development* (New York: Association Press, 1941), 63.
20. "Basketball Was Born Here," Springfield College, 20.

CHAPTER 2: TAKING ROOT

1. James Naismith, *Basketball: Its Origins and Development* (New York: Association Press, 1941), 145.
2. Barry Edward Mitchelson, "The Evolution of Men's Basketball in Canada, 1892–1936," Thesis (M.A.) University of Alberta (1968): 39.
3. Ibid., 40.
4. Ibid., 82.
5. Bruce Kidd, *The Struggle for Canadian Sport* (University of Toronto Press, 1996), 18.
6. Brian Flood, *Saint John: A Sporting Tradition, 1785–1985* (Saint John, NB: Neptune Publishing, 1985), 152.
7. Ibid.
8. "Three Cheers for Mount A! Sports at Mount Allison, 1843–1919," Mount Allison University Archives, 2008.
9. *Old McGill Yearbook*, 1905.
10. *Queen's University Journal* (vol. 31, no. 7).
11. *Manitoba Free Press*, November 9, 1921.
12. Barry Edward Mitchelson, "The Evolution of Men's Basketball in Canada, 1892–1936," Thesis (M.A.) University of Alberta (1968): 113.
13. Ibid.
14. Curtis J. Phillips, "Norm Baker: Canada's Player of the Half Century," *frozenhoops.com*.
15. James Naismith, *Basketball: Its Origins and Development* (New York: Association Press, 1941), 146.

CHAPTER 3: GRADS SCHOOL THE WORLD

1. James Naismith, *Basketball: Its Origins and Development* (New York: Association Press, 1941), 162.

2. Ibid.

3. Margaret Ann Hall, *The Girl and the Game: A History of Women's Sport in Canada* (Toronto: University of Toronto Press, 2002), 34–37.

4. *Edmonton Grads: 25 Years of Basketball Champions* (1975). Booklet sponsored by the RBC.

5. Joan Dixon, "James Naismith and the Edmonton Grads: Canada's Wonder Team," in *Trailblazing Sports Heroes: Exceptional Personalities and Outstanding Achievements in Canadian Sport* (Canmore, AB: Altitude Publishing, 2003).

6. Ibid.

7. *Edmonton Grads: 25 Years of Basketball Champions* (1975). Booklet sponsored by the RBC.

8. Frank Cosentino, *Not Bad, Eh? Great Moments in Canadian Sports History* (Burnstown, ON: General Store Publishing House, 1990), 78–80

9. *Edmonton Grads: 25 Years of Basketball Champions* (1975). Booklet sponsored by the RBC.

10. Frank Cosentino, *Not Bad, Eh? Great Moments in Canadian Sports History* (Burnstown, ON: General Store Publishing House, 1990), 82.

11. Brian Bergman, "When Girls Ruled: 'The Greatest Team That Ever Stepped' on a Court," *Maclean's* July 9, 2001.

12. Frank Cosentino, *Not Bad, Eh? Great Moments in Canadian Sports History* (Burnstown, ON: General Store Publishing House, 1990), 82.

13. *Edmonton Grads: 25 Years of Basketball Champions* (1975). Booklet sponsored by the RBC.

14. Ibid.

15. Walter Hugh Johns, *A History of the University of Alberta, 1908–1969* (University of Alberta, 1981), 102.

16. Terry Jones, "Still Toast of the Town," *Edmonton Sun*, April 11, 2010.

17. James Naismith, *Basketball: Its Origins and Development* (New York: Association Press, 1941), 145.

18. *Edmonton Grads: 25 Years of Basketball Champions* (1975). Booklet sponsored by the RBC.

19. Margaret Ann Hall, *The Girl and the Game: A History of Women's Sport in Canada* (Toronto: University of Toronto Press, 2002), 55.

20. Linda Goyette and Carolina Jakeway Roemmich, *Edmonton in Our Own Words* (University of Alberta, 2005).

21. Brian Bergman, "When Girls Ruled: 'The Greatest Team That Ever Stepped' on a Court," *Maclean's*, July 9, 2001.

CHAPTER 4: OPENING NIGHT

1. John McGourty, "NHL celebrates 90th anniversary today," *NHL.com*, November 26, 2007.

2. Naismith Typed Manuscript with Handwritten Notes re: Professional Basketball.

3. Charley Rosen, *The First Tip-Off: The Incredible Story of the Birth of the NBA* (McGraw-Hill Professional, 2008), 21–23.

4. Ibid.

5. Jamie Bradburn, "Huskies and Hoops," *Historicist*, November 13, 2010.

6. Doug Smith, "League Finally Pays Homage to Its Past," The Canadian Press, November 2, 1996.

7. Charley Rosen, *The First Tip-Off: The Incredible Story of the Birth of the NBA* (McGraw-Hill Professional, 2008), 9.

8. *Toronto Telegram*, November 2, 1946.

9. Jamie Bradburn, *Historicist: Huskies and Hoops*, November 13, 2010.

10. Ibid.

CHAPTER 5: OLYMPIAN EFFORT

1. Remembering V8's Olympic glory: *Windsor Star*, July 30, 2011.

2. History of Victoria Basketball (Greater Victoria Sports Hall of Fame).

3. Ibid.

4. Ibid.

5. James Naismith typed manuscript with handwritten notes re: "The Future of Basketball."

6. Adolph H. Grundman, *The Golden Age of Amateur Basketball: The AAU Tournament, 1921–1968* (University of Nebraska Press, 2004), 42.

7. Tony Techko and Carl Morgan, *The Olympians Among Us: Celebrating a Century of Excellence* (Tecumseh, ON: TraveLife Pub. Enterprises, 1995), 9.

8. Ibid., 10.

9. Brad Herzog, "The Dream Team of 1936," *Sports Illustrated*, July 22, 1996.

10. Chris Broussard, "Pro Basketball; A Game Played Above the Rim, Above All Else," *New York Times*, February 15, 2004.

11. *Toronto Daily Star*, 1936.

12. Private letter from Julius Goldman to *Sports Illustrated*, July 30, 1996.

13. *www.duchessofbedford.com*.

14. United Press Release, July 15, 1936.

15. Rob Rains and Hellen Carpenter, *James Naismith: The Man Who Invented Basketball* (Philadelphia, PA: Temple University Press: 2009), 153.

16. Tony Techko and Carl Morgan, *The Olympians Among Us: Celebrating A Century of Excellence* (Tecumseh, ON: TraveLife Pub. Enterprises, 1995), 12.

17. Ibid.

18. Brad Herzog, "The Dream Team of 1936," *Sports Illustrated*, July 22, 1996.

19. "Canada & the 1936 Olympics," Vancouver Holocaust Education Centre.

20. Rich Hughes, *Netting Out Basketball 1936: The Remarkable Story of the McPherson Refiners, the First Team to Dunk, Zone Press, and Win the Olympic Gold Medal* (Victoria, BC: FriesenPress, 2011), 328.

21. "Canada & the 1936 Olympics," Vancouver Holocaust Education Centre.

22. "Remembering V8's Olympic glory," *Windsor Star*, July 30, 2011.

23. Tony Techko and Carl Morgan, *The Olympians Among Us: Celebrating a Century of Excellence* (Tecumseh, ON: TraveLife Pub. Enterprises, 1995), 11.

24. James Naismith, *Basketball: Its Origins and Development* (New York: Association Press, 1941), 160.

25. Jonathan V. Plaut, *The Jews of Windsor, 1790–1990: A Historical Chronicle* (Toronto: Dundurn, 2007), 252.

26. Curtis Phillips, "Hoop dreams: The Windsor Ford V-8s and the Edmonton Grads," *Frozenhoops.com*.

27. Brad Herzog, "The Dream Team of 1936," *Sports Illustrated*, July 22, 1996.

28. *Toronto Daily Star*, August 15, 1936.

29. Letter from Julius Goldman to *Sports Illustrated* dated July 30, 1996.

30. Private letter by Gino Sovran, March 2012.

31. Rob Rains and Hellen Carpenter, *James Naismith: The Man Who Invented Basketball* (Philadelphia, PA: Temple University Press: 2009), 166.

32. Ibid.

33. Letter from Julius Goldman to *Sports Illustrated* dated July 30, 1996.

CHAPTER 6: JACK'S BIG DREAM

1. Etobicoke Sports Hall of Fame.

2. UBC Sports Hall of Fame.

3. Mike Hickey, *Dream Big Dreams: The Jack Donohue Story* (Montreal: Maya Publishing, 2006), 143.

4. "Godfather of Canadian Court Remembered," CanWest News Service, December 14, 2006.

5. Mike Hickey, *Dream Big Dreams: The Jack Donohue Story* (Montreal: Maya Publishing, 2006), 144.

6. Ibid., 145.

7. Ibid., 149.

8. Ibid., 154.

9. "Time Out with Alex Devlin." Excerpted from *Coaches Clipboard*, a publication of Basketball B.C., September 2009.

10. Mike Hickey, *Dream Big Dreams: The Jack Donohue Story* (Montreal: Maya Publishing, 2006), 149.

11. Steve Simmons, "Donohue Touched Many in His 70 Years," *Toronto Sun*, April 21, 2003.

CHAPTER 7: MINOR PRO

1. Paul Patton, "Tornados Lose Home Debut Before Supportive Crowd," *Globe and Mail*, December 5, 1983, S6.

2. Jennifer Hunter, "The Storm Around Stepien Tornado Owner 'Easy Target for Criticism,'" *The Globe and Mail*, March 16, 1985: S1.

3. Randy Sportak, "88s A Slam Dunk Success," *Calgary Sun*, January 30, 2005.

4. "Mickey's Secret Life," *Newsweek*, August 30, 1992.

5. Brian Daly, "Fledgling Basketball League Eyes Canadian Expansion Amid Obstacles," The Canadian Press, November 15, 2004.

6. Stephanie Myles, "Matrix Joins ABA Turmoil," *The Gazette*, December 23, 2005.

7. *Halifax Chronicle-Herald*, Chad Lucas, December 20, 2006.

CHAPTER 8: HOMEGROWN

1. University of Windsor Athletics.

2. Christine Rivet, "Tragedy to Triumph: 1974–75 Waterloo Warriors Overcame Adversity to Win National Championship," *Kitchener-Waterloo Record*, October 14, 2010.

3. Ibid.

4. "The Mind of Smart," *Ottawa Citizen*, March 9, 2008.

5. "5-peat for Dave Smart and Carleton U," *CBC News at Six*, March 20, 2007.

6. Cam Garbutt, "Missing the Boat: Leo Rautins Discusses the State of Canadian Basketball," *The Charlatan*, March 6, 2012.

7. UBC Vancouver Campus and NCAA Division II Membership: A Review of the Issues: 4.

8. *The Ubyssey*, March 27, 2011.

9. *The Ubyssey*, May 9, 2011.

CHAPTER 9: LOOSE BALLS

1. CBC Radio interview, Monday, June 27, 2011.

2. Ibid.

3. Ibid.

4. Nathan Dinsdale, "Wiggins: Is Next Great Baller from Canada?" *RivalsHigh*, August 17, 2010.

5. Royson James, "Ro Russell, Toronto's Coaching Pipeline to the NBA," *Toronto Star*, June 11, 2011.

6. *Findlay College Prep: SEASON 3, Episode 24 — "The Ontarians."*

7. Ibid.

8. Ibid.

9. Ibid.

10. Ibid.

CHAPTER 10: THINKING BIG

1. Mark Sclabach, "Philadelphia School Questioned." *Washington Post*, February 12, 2006.

2. Umar Ali, "Canada's Basketball Brain Drain?" *CBC Sports*, June 7, 2011.

3. George Gross, "Bitove Jr. Pulls Strings for Toronto," *Toronto Sun*, November 13, 1992.

4. Ibid.

5. Grant Robertson, "Meet John Bitove," *Globe and Mail*, March 28, 2008.

6. TSN's *Off the Record*, November 2011.

7. ESPN's *Beyond the Glory*, November 2008.

8. Gary Kingston, "Hunting Down Grizzlies, 10 Years Later," *Vancouver Sun*, February 18, 2011.

9. Jim Morris, "Grizzlies Gone and Mostly Forgotten by Vancouver Fans," The Canadian Press, October 30, 2001.

10. "Vince Carter: Half Man, Half Amazing," *CBC Evening News*, March 3, 2000.

11. "Fans' Fury," *Toronto Sun*, September 18, 2004.

CHAPTER 11: CAPTAIN CANADA

1. Jeramie McPeek, "The Canadian Kid," in *Fastbreak* magazine, September/October 1996.

2. Ryan Basen, *Steve Nash: Leader On and Off the Court* (Berkeley Heights, NJ: Enslow Publishers, Inc., 2007), 12.

3. Paul Arseneault and Peter Assaff, *Steve Nash* (Victoria, BC: Heritage House Publishing Co., 2006), 12.

4. Steve Nash Returns to SMUS. Video by St. Michaels University School.

5. Ryan Basen, *Steve Nash: Leader On and Off the Court* (Berkeley Heights, NJ: Enslow Publishers, Inc., 2007), 12.

6. Jim Caple, "Nash-ville, British Columbia," *ESPN Page 2*, May 27, 2005.

7. Steve Nash Returns to SMUS. Video by St. Michaels University School.

8. Ian Hyde-Lay on Steve Nash. Video by St. Michaels University School.

9. Mark Keast, "Canada Hangs In," *Toronto Sun*, July 5, 1993.

10. Ryan Basen, *Steve Nash: Leader On and Off the Court* (Berkeley Heights, NJ: Enslow Publishers, Inc., 2007), 25.

11. Jeramie McPeek, "The Canadian Kid," in *Fastbreak* magazine, September/October 1996.

12. Paul Arseneault and Peter Assaff, *Steve Nash* (Victoria, BC: Heritage House Publishing Co, 2006), 67.

13. Steve Ryan Basen, *Steve Nash: Leader On and Off the Court* (Berkeley Heights, NJ: Enslow Publishers, Inc., 2007), 35.

14. NBA TV documentary, 2007.

15. "Hoopla Helps Raise Nash's Profile," The Canadian Press, October 1, 2000.

16. Craig Daniels, "Nash Sparks Life into Canada's Hoops Future," *Winnipeg Free Press*, September 29, 2000.

17. "Jay Triano Sit Down." Video by Toronto Raptors, 2012.

EPILOGUE: ON THE CUSP

1. Dave Zarum, "The Rise of Andrew Wiggins: The Best High School Baller on Earth," *Sportsnet Magazine*, December 13, 2012.

2. Gary Parrish, "Canada's Elite Team Steamrolling American Competition," CBSSports.com, July 24, 2009.

3. Grant Taylor, "Wiggins Wins Player of Year," *Herald-Dispatch*, March 28, 2013.

INDEX

Page numbers in italics refer to photographs.

OF RELATED INTEREST

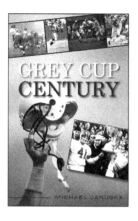

Grey Cup Century
Michael Januska
978-1-459704480
$14.99

The Terrible Tripper of 1957, the 1962 Fog Bowl, Vic Washington's Fabulous Fumble in 1968, Tony Gabriel's Classic Catch in 1976, Henry "Gizmo" Williams's Wild Run in 1987, and Dave Ridgway's Magnificent Kick in 1989 are some of the legendary moments that led up to the 100th Grey Cup game in November 2012 in Toronto. You'll find all of them in *Grey Cup Century* and much more.

Canadian football has had a long and storied history dating back to the 1860s. In 1909, Earl Grey, the governor general of Canada, donated a trophy to honour the best amateur rugby football club in the country. The first team to win a Grey Cup was the University of Toronto Varsity Blues.

In 1954 the Canadian Football League, a professional organization, took over sole control of the Cup. Since then, gridiron giants such as Sam Etcheverry, Norm Kwong, Jackie Parker, Russ Jackson, Ron Lancaster, Lui Passaglia, Doug Flutie, and Michael "Pinball" Clemons have dazzled fans in an annual championship that now attracts as many as six million television viewers.

Hope and Heartbreak in Toronto
Life as a Maple Leafs Fan
Peter Robinson
978-1-459706835
$19.99

False hope, hollow promises, and a mind-numbing lack of success — these words describe the Toronto Maple Leafs and the hockey club's inexplicable mediocrity over much of the past decade.

Author Peter Robinson has attended some 100 games over the past six seasons and has little to show for it except an unquenched thirst that keeps him coming back. Why does a team that hasn't won a Stanley Cup since 1967, long before many of its followers were even born, have such a hold on its fans? Robinson tries to answer that question and more while detailing what it's like to love one of the most unlovable teams in all of professional sports.

Being a Leafs fan requires a leap of faith every year, girding against inevitable disappointment. This book tells what that's like, how it got to be that way, and what the future holds for all who worship the Blue and White.

Now You Know Big Book of Sports
Doug Lennox
978-1-554884544
$29.99

Ever wonder where the figure skating terms axel, salchow, and lutz came from? Or why a curling tournament is called a "brier"? And how about a "haymaker" in boxing or a "high five" in any sport? Well, Doug Lennox, the world champion of trivia, is back to score touchdowns, hit homers, and knock in holes-in-one every time with a colossal compendium of Q&A athletics that has all anyone could possibly want to know from archery and cycling to skiing and wrestling and everything in between. What's more, Doug goes for gold with a wealth of Winter and Summer Olympics lore and legend that will amaze and captivate armchair fans and fervent competitors alike.

- What do the five Olympic rings and their colours represent?
- Why does the winner of the Indianapolis 500 drink milk in victory lane?
- Who was the first player ever to perform a slam dunk in a basketball game?
- Why are golfers' shortened pants called "plus-fours"?
- When was the Stanley Cup not awarded?
- Why does the letter *k* signify a strikeout on a baseball score sheet?
- Where is the world's oldest tennis court?

Available at your favourite bookseller

 DUNDURN

VISIT US AT

Dundurn.com
@dundurnpress
Facebook.com/dundurnpress
Pinterest.com/dundurnpress